HARMONIC ASTROLOGY

IN

PRACTICE

David Hamblin

The Wessex Astrologer

Published in 2019 by
The Wessex Astrologer Ltd
PO Box 9307
Swanage
BH19 9BF

For a full list of our titles go to www.wessexastrologer.com

Cover Design by Jonathan Taylor

A catalogue record for this book is available at The British Library

ISBN 9781910531327

To my beloved wife Helen

and

to the departed spirit of Alicia, my wonderful Muse

Also by David Hamblin

Harmonic Charts Aquarian Press 1983

The Spirit of Numbers: A New Exploration of Harmonic Astrology
The Wessex Astrologer 2011

Contents

Preface

In the Preface to my book *The Spirit of Numbers* I wrote: "I am now in the autumn of my life, and I do not intend to do any more writing after I have finished this book".[1] Yet here I am, seven years later, writing another book. So this is a warning to all astrologers: Do not make rash and unnecessary predictions.

I am writing this book because I feel that in *The Spirit of Numbers*, although I described harmonic astrology to the best of my ability, I did not give sufficient practical guidance to astrologers on how to integrate harmonics into their work. So I will now attempt to offer this guidance. I presume that my readers will mainly be working astrologers, familiar with conventional astrological techniques, who would like to add harmonics to their "repertoire", and I will do my best to help them to do this.

The practical advantage of harmonic astrology is that it offers a far richer and more complete insight into the interrelationship of planetary forces. In conventional astrology we are limited to the traditional aspects – opposition, trine, square, etc. – all of which are based on divisions of the circle by Two, Three, or multiples of Two and Three. But in harmonic astrology we can also study aspects that are based on Five, Seven, or any other number. These aspects, which are ignored in conventional astrology, can hugely increase our understanding of the ways in which the planets interact with one another. For some charts that are weak in traditional aspects (Amy Winehouse's natal chart, which I present in Chapter 6, is a good example), the identification of these harmonic (non-traditional) aspects is, in my opinion, absolutely essential. But for every chart (whether natal or mundane), the harmonic aspects can yield additional insights which are very valuable for interpretation.

The concept of "harmonics" was introduced into Western astrology by John Addey (born June 15, 1920, 08.15 a.m., Barnsley, England, RR:A), who was the co-founder and the second President of the Astrological Association of Great Britain. (I say "Western astrology" because harmonics also have a place in traditional vedic astrology, and I will say more about this in Chapter 11). And in his books (*Astrology Reborn*[2] and *Harmonics in Astrology*[3]) Addey makes it clear that, in his view, the concept of harmonics is a concept which underlies, and makes sense of, the whole of astrology. He says:

> "What is needed is a vision of the underlying realities of our science in the light of which astrological concepts can be **coordinated, simplified and unified.** Now at last we appear to be in sight of such a vision … The picture that has so emerged is one of the *harmonics,* that is the rhythms and sub-rhythms of cosmic periods, which can be demonstrated to provide the basis of all astrological doctrine both ancient and modern".[4]

So Addey is saying that, in doing astrology, we are dealing with harmonics, whether we realize it or not. But he is also saying that, if we *consciously* use the concept of harmonics, we can obtain many insights into astrological reality which might otherwise have remained hidden. This is the basis of harmonic astrology, as it has been developed by Addey and by others since his time.

I first came into astrology in the 1960s, and from the start I was a dedicated follower of John Addey and of his theories. He was a great man and a great astrologer, and I revere his memory. But I think that my enthusiasm for harmonics was due to the fact that my passion has always been to separate the *reality* of what is happening in the heavens from the *stories* that Man has told. (By "Man" I do of course mean the whole human race, including women as well as men.) The system of twelve signs and twelve houses is a man-made system, which Man has imposed upon the heavens. Thus, if we say that the Sun is in Gemini in the 5th house, this is a statement about its position within this man-made system. But, if we say that the angular distance from the Sun to the Moon is one-fifth of the circle, forming a quintile aspect, this is not dependent on Man's stories. It is not dependent on whether we use the Tropical or the Sidereal zodiac, or on whether we use Placidus or Koch houses. It is, quite simply, a fact.

It is a fact because the numbers have always been there. They were not created by Man. "All things are number," said Pythagoras. The universe is composed out of the interaction between numbers, and, the more we can discover about the *qualities* and the *properties* of these numbers, the better we shall understand the nature of the universe and of our place in it, and the better we shall understand astrology,

Sadly, John Addey died in 1982 (March 27, 1982, 5.17 p.m., London), at the age of only 61, when his work on harmonics was far from complete. Nevertheless, I published my book *Harmonic Charts*[5] (to which John Addey had hoped to write a Preface) in 1983, and for a few years during the 1980s I edited the *Harmonic Astrology Newsletter* which was a forum in which astrologers could share their views about harmonics. But at the end of the 1980s I turned away from astrology, for the reasons which I explained in Garry Phillipson's book *Astrology in the Year Zero.*[6] During most of my time away from astrology I was practising psychotherapy (having been trained in Psychosynthesis), and I believe that this has helped me to understand natal charts more deeply. When I came back to astrology in around 2005, I was filled with a renewed enthusiasm for harmonics. This led to my research project, in which I investigated more than a thousand charts, studying the harmonics of all the prime numbers up to 31 (whereas previously I had not been concerned with prime numbers beyond Seven). And then it led to my book *The Spirit of Numbers,* and then to this present book.

My own view is that the study of harmonics – or, more specifically, the harmonics of interplanetary aspects – gives us a far clearer picture of the dynamics of a chart. By looking at the signs in which the planets are placed, we obtain a picture of the qualities of the planets. By studying their house placements of the planets, we obtain a picture of their orientation. But this is essentially a *static* picture. It is the harmonic aspects which tell us most about the ways in which the person is likely to combine these planetary forces in order to build up a pattern of behaviour. Thus (to take an infamous example), if we are studying the birth chart of Adolf Hitler, we need to know that he was exceptionally strong in the 2nd, 5th and 7th harmonics, and exceptionally weak in the 3rd harmonic. Without this knowledge, we would not know how Hitler was able to behave as he did.

Of course, this book can only be an introduction. The study of harmonics is essentially a study of the meaning of numbers, and this is something about which we are only beginning to obtain clarity. Thus, many of the interpretations which I will offer in this book (based, as they are, on my own beliefs about the meanings of particular numbers) are of a tentative and exploratory nature, rather than statements of definite facts. My greatest hope is that this book will inspire astrologers to continue this exploration, and to share their findings with one another, so that eventually there will be a consensus about the meaning of harmonics throughout the worldwide astrological community. In my view this is the greatest challenge, and the greatest opportunity, facing astrology at the present time.

I would like to express my heartfelt thanks to my wife Helen, who once again has given me loving support throughout the writing of the book, and has willingly tolerated the fact that it has occupied so much of my time.

Also I would like to give my sincere thanks to David Cochrane, who created the "Table of Harmonics 1-32" software program (which is specifically designed to help with the techniques described in this book) and has helped me with the presentation of the charts in the book; also he has created a video promoting my work.

My thanks also go to Margaret Cahill of The Wessex Astrologer for her meticulous yet sensitive editing of the book. It is a joy to work with her.

Above all, I wish to express my gratitude to Alicia Gaydos, who acted as my Muse throughout the writing of the book. I sent her the chapters as I wrote them, and she responded with very valuable suggestions, many of which have been incorporated into the book; also, she helped me through some difficult periods of "writer's block", and raised my spirits when they were low. Without Alicia's help and support, the book could not have been written.

Tragically, Alicia died in a road accident on 13 February 2018. I have written a tribute to her in Appendix III of this book.

List of Figures

Chapter 1
Introduction to Harmonic Astrology

This book is intended as a companion volume to my earlier book *The Spirit of Numbers: A New Exploration of Harmonic Astrology.*[1] Its purpose is to help the working astrologer to use harmonic astrology in his or her work, and to integrate it into the other techniques that he or she may be using.

First, we need to define the word "harmonic". A harmonic has been defined as "a signal or wave whose frequency is an integral (whole-number) multiple of the frequency of some reference signal or wave". Thus, "for a signal whose fundamental frequency is f, the second harmonic has a frequency of $2f$, the third harmonic has a frequency of $3f$, and so on ... A signal can, in theory, have infinitely many harmonics".[2]

In physics and in music (which are the fields in which the term "harmonic" was first used), the "reference signal or wave" (the first harmonic) can be of any length. But *in astrology we are always talking about the harmonics of a circle.* Therefore, in astrology, the first harmonic always has a length of 360 degrees (the whole circle), the second harmonic has a length of $360 \div 2 = 180$ degrees, and so on. So this means that the second harmonic refers to a signal that occurs (or a wave that peaks) at *two* points around the circle.

John Addey makes it clear that the concept of harmonics can be applied to all of the circles that are used in astrology: the circle of the Zodiac; the diurnal circle (the circle of the houses); and the aspectual circle (i.e. the circle of interplanetary aspects, starting from the conjunction and moving round to the opposition and back to the conjunction again).[3] However, the advances that have been made in the interpretation of harmonics have been almost entirely in relation to the aspectual circle, and it is with this circle that this book will be concerned. (In Chapter 11 I will briefly discuss the harmonics of the zodiacal and diurnal circles.)

Thus, we shall be talking about the *harmonics of interplanetary aspects*. And we can see at once that the concept of harmonics does in fact underlie the traditional aspects that are used in conventional astrology, as shown in the following table:

Traditional Aspects used in Conventional Astrology

Aspect	Length of Arc	Harmonic Number	Quality of Number
Conjunction	0°	1st	Oneness
Semi-Sextile	30°	12th = 2 x 2 x 3	Twoness, Threeness
Semi-Square	45°	8th = 2 x 2 x 2	Twoness
Sextile	60°	6th = 2 x 3	Twoness, Threeness
Square	90°	4th = 2 x 2	Twoness
Trine	120°	3rd	Threeness
Sesquiquadrate	135° = 45° x 3	8th = 2 x 2 x 2	Twoness
Quincunx	150° = 30° x 5	12th = 2 x 2 x 3	Twoness, Threeness
Opposition	180°	2nd	Twoness

Thus, for instance, if we look at the aspects between the Sun and the Moon:

- When the Sun is *conjunct* the Moon, a signal occurs which has the quality of the number One. This is the aspect of the first harmonic: it occurs just once in the 360° circle.

- When the Sun is *opposite* the Moon (i.e. at a distance of 180° from the conjunction), a signal occurs which has the quality of the number Two. This is the aspect of the second harmonic.

Similarly, the trine has the quality of the number Three, and is the aspect of the third harmonic. The square is the 4th harmonic; the sextile is the 6th harmonic; the semi-square and sesquiquadrate are the 8th harmonic; and the semi-sextile and quincunx are the 12th harmonic.

The first principle of harmonic astrology is that each prime number introduces a new quality. Thus, Two is a prime number (divisible only by itself and One), so in the opposition (the 2nd harmonic) a new quality is introduced that was not present in the conjunction. We can call this quality Twoness (the quality of being Two, just as Oneness is the quality of being One). Again, Three is a prime number, so in the trine (the 3rd harmonic) a new quality is introduced, which we can call Threeness.

But Four and Eight are not prime numbers, because they are 2 x 2 and 2 x 2 x 2. Therefore the quality of the square and the semi-square (the 4th and 8th harmonics) is the quality of Twoness, raised to a higher power. (We will discuss later what this means in practice.)

Again, Six and Twelve are not prime numbers, because they are 2 x 3 and 2 x 2 x 3. Thus the sextile and the semi-sextile (the 6th and 12th harmonics) combine the qualities of Twoness and Threeness.

Another way of putting this is that the 6th harmonic is a *sub-harmonic* of the 2nd and 3rd harmonics. The 6th harmonic implies a signal that occurs at six equidistant points around the circle: but in fact, only two of these six points are sextiles: there are also two trines (Threeness), one opposition (Twoness), and one conjunction (Oneness). Thus, we can see that Sixness (the quality of the 6th harmonic) is the quality in which Twoness and Threeness come together.

Also, we can see that *all* of the higher harmonics are sub-harmonics of the first harmonic (because all numbers are divisible by One). Thus, for instance, the 3rd harmonic implies a signal that occurs at three equidistant points around the circle; but only two of these points are trines; the third is the conjunction. The implication of this is that *all the harmonics partake of the nature of Oneness,* which is union, or coming together. If there is a Sun-Moon trine, the Sun and the Moon are brought together; but, in this case, the quality that unites them is the quality of Threeness.

So we can see that all the traditional aspects that are used in astrology can be viewed as harmonic aspects. And, if we see them this way, this will have important effects on the way in which we identify and interpret these aspects. This brings me to the second and third principles of harmonic astrology (we have already mentioned the first). I will print these principles in bold type, because they are central to the whole argument of the book, and must be constantly remembered when practising harmonic astrology.

The second principle of harmonic astrology is that, the closer an aspect is to exactitude, the stronger it will be. In conventional astrology we may allow an orb of 8 degrees for a square or a trine, and we may not pay much attention to how close the aspect is to exactitude. But in harmonic astrology we are saying that a signal occurs at the point at which the aspect becomes exact. The closer the aspect is to this point, the more powerful will be its effect.

In applying this principle, I have chosen to distinguish between "very close" aspects (very strong), "close" aspects (less strong), and "wide" aspects (relatively weak). For the conjunction, the orbs that I have chosen are:

- 2 degrees for "very close" conjunctions
- 6 degrees for "close" conjunctions
- 12 degrees for "wide" conjunctions.

The third principle of harmonic astrology is that the orb allowed for any harmonic is the orb for the conjunction, divided by the number of the harmonic. In conventional astrology we usually allow the same orb for all of the major aspects (the conjunction, the opposition, the square and the trine). But in harmonic astrology we are saying that the opposition (2nd harmonic) and the trine (3rd harmonic) are *sub-harmonics* of the conjunction: the signal is therefore less strong, and should have a smaller orb. Also we are saying that the square (4th harmonic) is a sub-harmonic of both the conjunction and the opposition, and so should have a still smaller orb. We achieve this by dividing the conjunction orb by the number of the harmonic: that is, by 2 for the opposition, by 3 for the trine, and so on.

If we apply this principle to the conjunction orbs listed above, we see that the orbs allowed for the traditional aspects are as follows (where *n* is the conjunction orb):

Harmonic Orbs for Traditional Aspects

	Very close aspects	Close aspects	Wide aspects
Conjunction (*n*)	2°	6°	12°
Opposition (*n* ÷ 2)	1°	3°	6°
Trine (*n* ÷ 3)	0°40'	2°	4°
Square (*n* ÷ 4)	0°30'	1°30'	3°
Sextile (*n* ÷ 6)	0°20'	1°	2°
Semi-square (*n* ÷ 8)	0°15'	0°45'	1°30'
Semi-sextile (*n* ÷ 12)	0°10'	0°30'	1°

Thus, we are saying that a square aspect with an orb of less than 0°30' is very powerful; but, if the orb is more than 3 degrees, we are no longer counting it as being a square aspect at all.

* * * * *

So, now we have looked at how harmonic theory affects our understanding of the traditional aspects, and we can go on to examine the introduction of other harmonic aspects that are not used in conventional astrology.

At the start of this chapter we said: "A signal can have infinitely many harmonics". So why should we confine ourselves to the traditional aspects, which involve no prime numbers beyond Three? Why should we not also investigate non-traditional aspects involving higher prime numbers such as Five, Seven, Eleven and Thirteen? Can we not expect that these numbers too will have astrological significance, and will introduce new qualities that have hitherto remained hidden?

This is the reasoning that has caused some astrologers to investigate the non-traditional harmonic aspects between planets. But clearly, we cannot investigate *all* the harmonics, since their number is infinite. And we can surely expect that, as the number of the harmonic increases and we are dividing the circle into smaller and smaller segments, the astrological significance of the aspect will gradually become less and less. So we have to stop somewhere. In my own work I have chosen to stop at 32: that is to say, I have investigated only the first 32 harmonics. There is nothing magical about 32, but it is 2 x 2 x 2 x 2 x 2, and so seems to be a good round number at which to stop.

The first 32 numbers comprise:

- Twelve prime numbers: 1, 2, 3, 5, 7, 11, 13, 17, 19, 23, 29 and 31. We can expect that each of these numbers will introduce a new quality.

- Seven numbers which are higher powers of prime numbers: 4, 8, 16, 32, 9, 27 and 25. We can expect that 4, 8, 16 and 32 will exhibit the quality of Twoness, but maybe in a purer or more concentrated form; 9 and 27 will do the same for Threeness, and 25 for Fiveness.

- Thirteen numbers which are composite numbers, composed of more than one prime number: 6, 10, 12, 14, 15, 18, 20, 21, 22, 24, 26, 28 and 30. Just as 6 combines the qualities of Twoness and Threeness, so we can expect that 15 will combine Threeness with Fiveness, and 26 will combine Twoness with Thirteenness.

Following the principle that "the orb allowed for any harmonic is the orb for the conjunction, divided by the number of the harmonic", we can now set out the orbs allowed for the non-traditional aspects. (This can be done for each of the harmonics up to 32, but in this table I will include only the prime-number harmonics.)

Harmonic Orbs for Non-Traditional Aspects
(Prime Numbers Only)

	Very close aspects	Close aspects	Wide aspects
Conjunction (*n*)	2°	6°	12°
Quintile (*n* ÷ 5)	0°24'	1°12'	2°24'
Septile (*n* ÷ 7)	0°17'	0°51'	1°42'
11th harmonic (*n* ÷ 11)	0°10'	0°32'	1°05'
13th harmonic (*n* ÷ 13)	0°09'	0°27'	0°55'
17th harmonic (*n* ÷ 17)	0°07'	0°21'	0°42'
19th harmonic (*n* ÷ 19)	0°06'	0°18'	0°37'
23rd harmonic (*n* ÷ 23)	0°05'	0°15'	0°31'
29th harmonic (*n* ÷ 29)	0°04'	0°12'	0°24'
31st harmonic (*n* ÷ 31)	0°03'	0°11'	0°23'

Before I go any further, I will describe here the *notation* that I use in this book to describe harmonic aspects.

Firstly, the planets. SO = Sun, MO = Moon. ME = Mercury, VE = Venus, and so on. I have also sometimes used the four principal asteroids: CE = Ceres, PA = Pallas, JN = Juno, and VT = Vesta.

When two planets are connected by a harmonic aspect, I have placed the harmonic number between these planetary letters. Thus, SO-7-MO indicates that Sun has a 7th harmonic link to Moon (i.e. that the Sun-Moon angle is one-seventh, or a higher number of sevenths, of the circle.)

If the harmonic number is printed in ordinary type (SO-7-MO), the aspect is "wide".

If it is in ordinary type but <u>underlined</u> (SO-<u>7</u>-MO), the aspect is "close".

If it is in ***<u>bold underlined italics</u>*** (SO-***<u>7</u>***-MO), the aspect is "very close".

(Note that, for the 7th harmonic as for every other harmonic, the orbs used are *the conjunction orb divided by the number of the harmonic*.)

Very often, three or more aspects will come together in a "cluster" of interrelated aspects. For instance, if we have SO-*7*-MO, it might be the case that both Sun and Moon were linked to Mars in the 21st harmonic (because 21 is 7 x 3, and so the 21st harmonic is a sub-harmonic of the 7th harmonic). If all three of these aspects were "very close", we would write this as (SO-*7*-MO)-**21**-MA. If the Sun-Mars link was "very close" but the Moon-Mars link was only "close", we would write it as (SO-*7*-MO)-**21**/21-MA.

There are two questions that need to be answered. Firstly, how do we identify the harmonic aspects? And secondly, how do we interpret them? I will deal with each of these questions in turn.

Firstly, the identification of non-traditional harmonic aspects. The problem, of course, is that, unlike the traditional aspects, most of these aspects are not immediately visible from looking at the chart. When we look at a chart, we can easily see any oppositions, trines, squares and sextiles that are present. But we cannot see septiles (7th-harmonic links) because one-seventh of the circle is 51°26', rather than a whole number. And the same is true of nearly every other non-traditional harmonic aspect. So we have to find a method of identifying these aspects, other than by simple observation.

The majority of astrologers who have worked with harmonics have done so by the use of *harmonic charts*. This was the method that I used myself in my first book, which indeed had the title *Harmonic Charts*.[4] A harmonic chart is a chart in which the zodiac is divided by the number of the harmonic. Thus, for example, in the 7th-harmonic chart, septiles (7th-harmonic links) appear as conjunctions, 14th-harmonic links appear as oppositions, 21st-harmonic link appear as trines, and 28th-harmonic links appear as squares. Thus, the harmonic links for the number Seven and its multiples are very clearly visible in the 7th-harmonic chart. In *Harmonic Charts* I recommended that harmonic charts should be cast for the 4th, 5th, 7th and 9th harmonics, thus giving insight into Fiveness and Sevenness and into the higher powers of Twoness and Threeness.

There is no doubt that harmonic charts are an easy and convenient way of studying harmonic aspects, and any astrologer who wishes to use this method has my full support. Every astrological software package now contains an icon which you can click to immediately obtain a harmonic chart for any number. However, harmonic charts do give rise to a number of problems.

The first problem is the sheer number of charts involved. At the time that I wrote *Harmonic Charts* I was not interested in the prime numbers beyond Seven. But if (as in this present book) we are investigating all the harmonics up to 32, including all the prime numbers up to 31, we have to create a large number of harmonic charts in order to obtain insight into all these numbers. We would have to cast harmonic charts for the prime numbers 5, 7, 11, 13, 17, 19, 23, 29 and 31; also we would have to cast the 8th, 9th and 25th harmonic charts, in order to visualize aspects at the higher levels of Twoness, Threeness and Fiveness. That makes 12 harmonic charts in all. If we were to print all these charts, this would use up a large quantity of paper; and, when we were trying to interpret the chart, we would be constantly cross-referencing between all these papers, which (in my view) would be a laborious, time-consuming and confusing task.

The other problem is that each harmonic chart can give the appearance of being an entity in itself, when really it is just a convenient way of presenting certain features of the radical chart. Thus, each harmonic chart will have its own Ascendant and Midheaven, and will have the planets placed in signs and houses which are different from those in the radical chart. It is very easy to be misled by these signs, houses and Angles, and to start trying to interpret them. But really, these signs, houses and Angles are entirely meaningless; the planets shown in the harmonic chart belong in the signs and houses which they occupied in the radical chart.

Because of these difficulties I have now abandoned the use of harmonic charts, and have developed a method of identifying all the harmonic links up to the 32nd harmonic and studying them *as they occur on the radical chart* rather than on the harmonic charts. This is the method which I described in *The Spirit of Numbers,* and which I am using again in the present book. In the next chapter I will explain how to calculate harmonic aspects in accordance with this method.

So now we come to our second question: When we have calculated the harmonic aspects, how do we interpret them?

Really the essence of this question is: *What are the qualities associated with each prime number?* As astrologers, we think we already know a great deal about the qualities associated with Two and Three. We regard Twoness aspects as "hard" aspects and Threeness aspects as "soft" aspects. We believe that Twoness is associated with *effort* and Threeness with *pleasure.* All of our interpretations of the traditional aspects are built around this core belief about the nature of Twoness and Threeness. But the qualities of the higher prime numbers are unknown to us. We have to investigate them.

For me, it is essential that this identification of the qualities of prime numbers should be based on empirical research. We may have all kinds of ideas about the significance of particular numbers (for instance, we may believe that Seven is a magical number, and Thirteen is an unlucky number), but we should not reach any conclusions about the astrological significance of these numbers until we have investigated their incidence in actual charts. And here I need to say something about my own research.

In preparation for writing *The Spirit of Numbers,* I investigated more than a thousand charts. The great majority of these were the birth charts of famous (or fairly famous) people, but there were also some birth charts of people known to me personally, and also some mundane charts (charts of dramatic events). Within these charts, my aim was to identify those charts which were strongest in each of the prime numbers, and to try to identify the *qualities* that these charts (or rather, the owners of these charts) had in common. By "strongest", I mean the charts which contained the greatest number of interplanetary aspects in the relevant harmonics, and also in which a high proportion of these aspects were "very close" (rather than "close" or "wide").

As an example, let us suppose that we are investigating the qualities of Sevenness. The harmonics which partake of Sevenness are the 7th harmonic (pure Sevenness), the 14th and 28th harmonics (Sevenness combined with Twoness), and the 21th harmonic (Sevenness combined with Threeness). On page 8 I mentioned the possibility that a chart might contain a cluster of (SO-*7*-MO)-*21*-MA. If this cluster occurred in a chart, I would regard it as a very strong Sevenness cluster, causing the qualities of Sevenness to manifest strongly in the person's behaviour. If the same chart also contained another very strong Sevenness cluster – such as, for instance, (ME-*7*-JU)-*14*-UR – then I would regard this chart as being unusually strong in Sevenness, and I would examine this person's life in an attempt to identify the qualities which this person shared with other people who were also strong in Sevenness, in order to obtain insight into the core meaning of the number Seven.

Occasionally one finds clusters of four, five or even six planets. For instance, there might be a Sevenness cluster of ((SO-*7*-MO)-*14*-(MA-*7*-JU))-*28*-SA. This cluster on its own would qualify the person as being unusually strong in Sevenness.

So by studying the charts that were strongest in each of the prime numbers, amd making judgments about the qualities which the owners of these charts had in common, I have reached conclusions about the meaning of each of these numbers in the context of harmonics. In Chapters 4 and 5 I will discuss these conclusions for each prime number in turn, and in Chapter 6 I will present a brief summary (in the form of keywords) of the meaning of each number from 1 to 32.

Thus, my hope is that these conclusions will enable astrologers to interpret harmonic aspects as part of their overall analysis of a radical chart. Thus, an aspect of ME-*13*-SA would mean that Mercury and Saturn are linked together by the quality of Thirteenness. But the precise meaning of this will be affected by the signs and houses in which Mercury and Saturn are placed in the radical chart, and by the other aspects affecting them.

In the case of the prime numbers One, Two and Three, I have of course been influenced by the conventional astrological beliefs about the meaning of these numbers (and I have found that these beliefs are largely correct). In the case of the prime numbers Five and Seven, I have been influenced by the findings of previous astrologers who have worked with harmonics, and especially by Michael Harding and Charles Harvey in *Working with Astrology*.[5] But for the prime numbers from Eleven to Thirty-one, the conclusions are entirely my own and I take full responsibility for any defects and limitations in the analysis.

I have of course not *proved* anything, and any scientist would dismiss my findings as being anecdotal rather than scientific. Nevertheless, I believe that the anecdotal evidence is very strong. If one goes into a garden and finds that the flowers are all red, and then into another garden where they are all blue, and then into a third where they are all yellow, it is hard to believe that this is the result of chance, and that really the flowers are randomly distributed. In the same way, if I go into the land of Elevenness and find that all the cases have one quality, and then into the land of Thirteenness where they all have a different quality, I have to believe that this is not accidental. It is this that has convinced me, despite my initial agnosticism, that harmonic astrology *does* work and *is* valuable.

But my findings, and my definitions of the qualities of each number, are of course provisional, and I am sure that they will be improved and refined when they are worked on by other astrologers with different perspectives from mine and with access to a greater variety of cases. In the meantime, I hope that the guidelines and case studies offered in this book will be sufficient to allow astrologers to work with harmonics and to begin to unearth some of the riches that they offer.

Chapter 2
Calculation of Harmonic Aspects

If we wish to use harmonic aspects in the interpretation of a chart, we first need to compile a list of the harmonic aspects that we want to use. My suggestion is that this is best done in two stages. First, we have to construct a table of *all* the harmonic aspects between all the planets. I will call this the Table of Harmonic Aspects (THA for short). And secondly, we have to extract from this table a list of the aspects that we actually want to use in interpretation. I will call this the List of Significant Harmonic Aspects (LSHA for short).

As an example, we can take Iris Murdoch, who is the subject of the first of the case studies that we will present in Chapter 7. Iris Murdoch was born on July 15, 1919, at 8.00 a.m. in Dublin, Ireland, and her birth chart is shown in Figure 7.1. Her Table of Harmonic Aspects (THA) is as follows:

Table of Harmonic Aspects (THA) for Iris Murdoch

	1	2	3	5	7	11	13	17	19	23	29	31
SO/MO				30	7							
SO/ME			_27_		14							
SO/VE		_8_										
SO/MA					_21_							
SO/JU	_1_											
SO/SA				10								_**31**_
SO/UR			18							23		
SO/NE					21	22						
SO/PL			_24_							23		
SO/CH			_24_									31

	1	2	3	5	7	11	13	17	19	23	29	31
MO/ME		2										
MO/VE			9									
MO/MA							13					
MO/JU			9									
MO/SA								17				
MO/UR			24									
MO/NE										23		
MO/PL			18							23		
MO/CH					7							
ME/VE				20					19			
ME/MA		8										
ME/JU		16										
ME/SA	1											
ME/UR					28							
ME/NE	1											
ME/PL							26	17				
ME/CH						11						
VE/MA										23	29	
VE/JU			9									
VE/SA	1											
VE/UR		2										31
VE/NE				25			13					
VE/PL			6									
VE/CH			12									
MA/JU								17				
MA/SA					7							
MA/UR			3									
MA/NE		32			21							
MA/PL	1											
MA/CH		4										
JU/SA			12									
JU/UR				5								
JU/NE											29	
JU/PL			18						19			
JU/CH				10								
SA/UR		2										
SA/NE				20								
SA/PL					7						29	
SA/CH			18									31
UR/NE		16										
UR/PL				20						23		
UR/CH				10								
NE/PL						11						
NE/CH			3									
PL/CH		4										

The Table shows harmonic aspects between all the planets including Chiron. It is possible to expand the Table to include the four major asteroids (Ceres, Pallas, Juno, Vesta), but it should be noted that this increases the number of planetary pairs from 55 to 105.

In this Table (as in the rest of the book), "very close" aspects are shown in **_<u>bold underlined italics</u>_**, "close" aspects are shown <u>underlined</u>, and "wide" aspects are shown in ordinary type.

The harmonic aspects are placed in columns according to the *highest prime number that is a factor of the harmonic number.* Thus, the harmonics that are included in each column are as follows:

Column # in T.H.A.	Harmonic Number
1:	1
2:	2, 4, 8, 16, 32
3:	3, 6, 9, 12, 18, 24, 27
5:	5, 10, 15, 20, 25, 30
7:	7, 14, 21, 28
11:	11, 22
13:	13, 26
17:	17
19:	19
23:	23
29:	29
31:	31

Harmonic aspects between the planets and the Angles (Ascendant, Descendant, Midheaven, Imum Coeli) are not included. There are two reasons for this. Firstly, the Angles are not planets, but are points of intersection between two Great Circles, and it is far from clear that harmonic "signals" occur between the planets and the Angles in the way that they do between pairs of planets. And secondly, the Angles move so rapidly (approximately 1°00' every four minutes) that an error of even five minutes in the birth time would lead to major errors in the harmonic aspects.

Also, the Moon's Nodes are not included, and again there are two reasons for this. Firstly, the Nodes again are not planets but are points of intersection between the Sun's orbital path and the Moon's orbital path. And secondly, there is controversy about whether the True Node or the Mean Node should be used: the True Node and the Mean Node occupy different positions in the radical chart, and this would significally affect the harmonic aspects. (I have included the Nodes in the charts shown later in the book, but I have not used them in the harmonic analysis.)

In *The Spirit of Numbers* (Appendix I) I described a method of creating the Table of Harmonic Aspects without the use of computers. However, I accept that this method is unnecessarily laborious and error-prone, and I will here describe three methods by which astrological software can now be used to create the Table of Harmonic Aspects.

Method 1

This is the easiest method, but at the time of writing it is only available to astrologers who have the Sirius or Kepler software package available from www.AstroSoftware.com. Having cast the chart, click on "List", then click on "Harmonic Patterns Listings", then click on "Table of Harmonics 1-32", and the Table of Harmonic Aspects will be created for you. This Table includes the four major asteroids, as well as the major planets and Chiron. Note that in this presentation of the Table, "very close" aspects are shown in red, "close" aspects in green, and "wide" aspects in black.

Because, in this presentation, the Table spreads over several pages and cannot be viewed as a whole either on the computer screen or (if you print it) on paper, you may wish to copy the information onto a form on which the Table is presented on a single page. This will make it much easier to use the Table to create the List of Significant Harmonic Aspects. An example of such a form is given on my website, www.davidhamblin.net, and you are welcome to print it from this source.

Method 2

If you do not have the Sirius or Kepler software, I would advise you (within the astrological software package that you are using) to look for a listing of the *angular arc distances* (or *angular separations*) between all the pairs of planets (preferably including Chiron). For instance, in the case of Iris Murdoch, this listing would give the following as the angular distances between Sun and Moon, Sun and Mercury, Sun and Venus:

SO/MO   155°37'
SO/ME   26°30'
SO/VE   45°04'

For each of these distances, consult the Harmonic Aspect Conversion Table which is in Appendix II of this book. There you will see that:

- 155°37' is within the range 155°36'-155°47', indicating a "wide" aspect in the 7th and 30th harmonics.

- 26°30' is within the range 26°27'-26°34', indicating a "close" aspect in the 27th harmonic and a "wide" aspect in the 14th harmonic.

- 45°04' is within the range 44°45'-45°15', indicating a "very close" aspect in the 8th harmonic.

By doing this for all the pairs of planets, you can construct a Table of Harmonic Aspects which is identical to the one shown at the start of this chapter.

Method 3

If you are using an astrological software package that does not enable Method 1 or Method 2, then there is a third method (admittedly more laborious) that you can use to create the Table of Harmonic Aspects. This method involves the use of harmonic charts.

Every astrological software package now includes an icon for creating a harmonic chart for any number. In order to identify the harmonic aspects for all the harmonics from 1 to 32, we would have to cast the following harmonic charts:

1st harmonic chart (i.e. the radical chart); 5th harmonic chart; 6th; 7th; 8th; 9th; 11th; 13th; 17th; 19th; 23rd; 25th; 29th; 31th.

There is no need to print these charts; all you need to do is to visualize them on the screen, in order to identify the harmonic aspects that they reveal.

The harmonic aspects that are shown in these charts are as follows:

	Conjunction	Opposition	Trine	Square	Sextile
1st H.C.	1	2	3	4	
5th	5	10	15	20	30
6th	6	12			
7th	7	14	21	28	
8th	8	16	24	32	
9th	9	18	27		
11th	11	22			
13th	13	26			
17th	17				
19th	19				
23rd	23				
25th	25				
29th	29				
31st	31				

Thus, for example, 10th harmonic aspects appear as oppositions in the 5th harmonic chart; 21st harmonic aspects appear as trines in the 7th harmonic chart. The orbs that are allowed for these aspects are:

	Conjunction	Opposition	Trine	Square	Sextile
Very close	2°	1°	0°40'	0°30'	0°20'
Close	6°	3°	2°	1°30'	1°
Wide	12°	6°	4°	3°	2°

Thus, if we look at Iris Murdoch's radical chart (which is shown in Figure 7.1), we can see that she has:

- a SO/JU conjunction, orb 4°15': this counts as "close".
- a ME/SA conjunction, orb 8°22': "wide".
- a ME/NE conjunction, orb 9°52': "wide".
- a VE/SA conjunction, orb 10°11': "wide".
- a MA/PL conjunction, orb 2°08': "close".
- a MO/ME opposition, orb 2°07': "close".
- a SA/UR opposition, orb 4°31': "wide".
- a MA/UR trine, orb 3°17': "wide".
- a MA/CH square, orb 2°34': "wide".
- a PL/CH square, orb 0°26': "very close".

We can enter these aspects into the Table of Harmonic Aspects. Then we can look at her 5th harmonic chart, and identify the aspects in the same way; and the same with her other harmonic charts. In this way, we will end up with a Table of Harmonic Aspects which is identical with that arrived at by Method 1 or Method 2.

* * * * *

So now, using one of these three methods, you have created the Table of Harmonic Aspects (THA). This Table contains *all* the interplanetary harmonic aspects for the first 32 harmonics. But clearly, we do not want to use *all* these aspects in interpreting the chart. So we need to extract from the table a List of Significant Harmonic Aspects (LSHA): that is to say, a list of the aspects that we actually want to use. There are no firm rules about how this should be done, but I will describe here the method that I have found useful, and will offer the following guidelines:

a) The aspects should be listed under twelve headings, which are the twelve prime numbers shown at the top of the THA.

b) When three or more aspects are interlinked, they should be shown as "clusters" (as in the examples we have already given, e.g. (SO-7-MO)-*21*-MA).

c) "Wide" aspects should be omitted, unless they form part of a cluster which also contains "close" or "very close" aspects. Also, "close" aspects may be omitted if they involve only the outer planets (JU, SA, UR, NE, PL, CH) and if they are not part of a cluster.

d) If a planet is within 8 degrees of one of the Angles (Ascendant, Descendant, Midheaven, Imum Coeli) it should be marked with an asterisk, e.g. SO*. This is because proximity to the Angles makes a planet especially prominent in the personality. (For Iris Murdoch, the "angular" planets are MO*, ME* and SA*.)

Based on these guidelines, let us now construct a List of Significant Harmonic Aspects (LSHA) for Iris Murdoch, based on the information in her Table of Harmonic Aspects.

1. In the "1" column Iris has SO-1-JU and MA-1-PL. ME*-1-SA*, ME*-1-NE, and VE-1-SA* are "wide" and so can be omitted. Therefore, we start the LSHA as follows:

    1:   SO-1-JU

          MA-1-PL

2. In the "2" column she has SO-8-VE, MO*-2-ME* and ME*-16-JU. Also she has UR-16-NE, but this can perhaps be omitted (see guideline (c) above).

    Also she has MA-4-CH and PL-4-CH, and these aspects form a cluster with MA-1-PL which we have already listed. So the cluster can be written as (MA-1-PL)-4/4-CH.

    ME*-8-MA, VE-2-UR and SA*-2-UR can be omitted because they are "wide" and are not part of a cluster. (It could be argued that VE-2-UR and SA*-2-UR form a cluster with VE-1-SA*, but, since these aspects are all "wide", I have chosen to omit them from the list.)

    Thus, we can write:

    2:   SO-8-VE

          MO*-2-ME*

          ME*-16-JU

          (MA-1-PL)-4/4-CH

3. In the "3" column Iris has SO-27-ME*, MO*-9-JU, and MO*-24-UR.

Also she has a four-planet cluster which spreads across two columns: (SO-8-VE)-24/24/6/12-(PL-4-CH). This kind of cluster can be difficult to spot, but it is important to do so, because it may have great significance for interpretation. This particular cluster shows that SO-8-VE and PL-4-CH, which are the two closest Twoness aspects in Iris's chart, are linked together by aspects that contain an element of Threeness.

Thus, we can enter:

3: SO-27-ME*
MO*-9-JU
MO*-24-UR
(SO-8-VE)-24/24/6/12-(PL-4-CH)

5. In the "5" column, we see that Iris Murdoch has a cluster of (JU-5-UR)-10/10-CH. Also, we can note that (because of PL-4-CH in the "2" column) UR-10-CH also forms a cluster of (PL-4-CH)-20/10-UR. SA*-20-NE can be omitted in accordance with guideline (c) above. Thus:

5: (JU-5-UR)-10/10-CH
(PL-4-CH)-20/10-UR

7. In the "7" column, she has a cluster of (SO-21-MA)-21-NE, and also a cluster (involving MA-1-PL from the "1" column) of (MA-1-PL)-7/7-SA*. Also there are ME*-28-UR and MO*-7-CH. Thus:

7: (SO-21-MA)-21-NE
(MA-1-PL)-7/7-SA*
ME*-28-UR
MO*-7-CH

11. In the "11" column, the only "close" or "very close" aspect is ME*-11-CH.

11: ME*-11-CH

13. Here, the only "close" or "very close" aspects are MO*-13-MA and ME*-26-PL.

> **13:** MO*-13-MA
> ME*-26-PL

17. The only "close" or "very close" aspect in the "17" column is MO*-17-SA*.

> **17:** MO-17-SA*

19. There are no "close" or "very close" aspects in the "19" column, so we can write:

> **19:** none

23. Here there is a cluster of (UR-23-PL)-23-SO, and also MO*-23-PL and VE-23-JU.

> **23:** (UR-23-PL)-23-SO
> MO*-23-PL
> VE-23-JU

29. In the "29" column the only "close" or "very close" aspect is JU-29-NE.

> **29:** JU-29-NE

31. Here we have a cluster of (SO-31-SA*)-31-CH, and also VE-31-UR.

> **31:** (SO-31-SA*)-31-CH
> VE-31-UR

Thus, Iris Murdoch's List of Significant Harmonic Aspects is as follows:

1:	SO-1-JU	**11:**	ME*-11-CH
	MA-1-PL		
		13:	MO*-13-MA
2:	SO-8-VE		ME*-26-PL
	MO*-2-ME*		

ME*-<u>16</u>-JU
(MA-<u>1</u>-PL)-4/<u>***4***</u>-CH

17:   MO-<u>***17***</u>-SA*

19:   none

3:   SO-<u>27</u>-ME*
MO*-<u>9</u>-JU
MO*-<u>***24***</u>-UR
(SO-<u>***8***</u>-VE)-<u>24</u>/<u>24</u>/<u>6</u>/<u>***4***</u>-(PL-<u>***4***</u>-CH)

23:   (UR-<u>23</u>-PL)-23-SO
MO*-<u>***23***</u>-PL
VE-<u>23</u>-JU

5:   (JU-<u>5</u>-UR)-10/<u>***10***</u>-CH
(PL-<u>***4***</u>-CH)-20/<u>***10***</u>-UR

29:   JU-<u>***29***</u>-NE

31:   (SO-<u>***31***</u>-SA*)-31-CH
VE-<u>31</u>-UR

7:   (SO-<u>21</u>-MA)-21-NE
(MA-<u>1</u>-PL)-<u>7</u>/7-SA*
ME*-<u>***28***</u>-UR
MO*-<u>7</u>-CH

Armed with this list, we can proceed to interpretation. We will interpret Iris Murdoch's harmonic aspects in the first case study in Chapter 7, but first we need to explore the meaning of the prime numbers.

Chapter 3
What does the Chart Show?

In Chapters 4 and 5, I will discuss the meaning of each of the prime numbers within harmonic astrology. However, before I do this, I would like first to address a question which I believe to be important, not only in harmonic astrology but in astrology in general. The answer to this question will affect the way in which I interpret harmonic aspects, and the way in which I use these aspects to interpret the chart as a whole.

The question is: What does the chart show, and what does it not show?

My belief is that *the chart shows only potential.* This statement can be elaborated as follows: The chart only shows that there is a *potential* for certain kinds of behaviours or events. It never shows that a particular event, or a particular type of behaviour, will definitely happen. It only shows what *may* happen (or, if we are talking about the past, what *may* have happened).

To illustrate this, I would like to tell a story from my own experience. Two women whom I know are fraternal (i.e. non-identical) twins. They shared the same womb, but they developed from two eggs and so have different genes. But they have the same parents, and were brought up in the same environment. They were born half an hour apart, but, in spite of this time difference, they have virtually the same natal chart. They have the same signs on the Ascendant and the Midheaven, and all the planets are in the same signs and the same houses in both charts. Even the harmonic aspects are virtually the same for both twins, although some aspects are slightly stronger (i.e. closer to exactitude) for one twin than for the other.

And yet, these two twins have very different personalities, and very different life experiences. One of the twins is markedly more extrovert than the other. One of them has excelled in various sports, while the other has no interest in sports. One of them is deeply involved in a spiritual quest, while the other has no interest in spirituality. One of them is a mother of two children, while the other has no children. One of them became a nurse, while the other became a teacher and a therapist. These are just some of the more obvious differences, but at a deeper level there are profound differences between the twins in the whole way in which they see the world and in their patterns of behaviour. One of the twins wrote to a well-known astrologer asking for an analysis of her natal chart, and received in return a reading which was a very accurate description, not of herself, but of her sister.

When I first met these twins, as an astrologer I found these differences very troubling. How could two people with virtually the same natal chart (and also with the same parents and the same childhood environment) be so different from each other? Did this not cast doubt on the veracity of astrology? In fact, this was one of the main reasons why in the late 1980s I stopped practising as an astrologer, and for many years had no connection with astrology.

However, since I came back to astrology in about 2005, I have come to see that the natal chart does in fact make sense for both of the twins, but in different ways. I will not go into details about this, as I do not have the twins' permission to discuss their charts or to reveal their identities. So I will just say that the twins have been using their natal charts in different ways. One of them has displayed the solar qualities more strongly, while in the other the lunar qualities are more evident. Some interplanetary aspects which are very strongly evident in one twin's personality are less evident in the other. And some aspects are in evidence for both of the twins, but they have manifested in different kinds of behaviour. So we can say that these two charts, although they are nearly identical, contain the *potential* for both of these types of personality.

We must remember also that, while the natal chart remains the same throughout a lifetime, the personality may change. A criminal may become a law-abiding campaigner for justice. An atheist with no spiritual interests may find a spiritual awakening, and so develop a radically different personality. A person may be deeply traumatized by his experience in war, or by the death of a loved one, and so start to behave in different ways. In all kinds of ways, a person may develop personality traits in the second half of life that were not at all evident in the first. Of course, we can say that the natal chart is affected by transits and progressions; but the transits and progressions are brief, they pass quickly, whereas the personality changes may be long-lasting. So again, we can say that the person is learning to develop the *potential* of their natal chart in new ways as he or she grows older.

In *The Spirit of Numbers* I discussed this issue in relation to the serial killer Jürgen Bartsch, who as a teenager brutally murdered four young boys.[1] An astrologer would say that Bartsch's murderous behaviour was caused by certain patterns of stress and tension that are very evident in his natal chart. But in *For Your Own Good: The Roots of Violence in Child-Rearing*, Alice Miller claims that Bartsch's violence was caused by the violence to which he had himself been subjected as a young child.[2] As I said in *The Spirit of Numbers*:

> Many children must have been born around the same time as Bartsch who did not become serial killers, and also, many children must have suffered childhoods as deprived as Bartsch's and yet did not become serial killers. What turned Bartsch into a murderer was the combination of, on the one hand, an extremely repressed childhood, and, on the other hand, a chart that contained the *potential* for murder. If Bartsch had had a different upbringing, these same planetary patterns would have worked themselves out in different ways.

So, on this basis, we can say that the personality is the result both of the natal chart and of environmental factors. But, if we go back to the case of the non-identical twins, we see that, even when both the natal chart and the environmental factors are the same, the personality may still be different. These twins were both born to the same parents and brought up in the same environment, and yet they still developed markedly different personalities.

What could be the cause of this? The obvious answer is genetic factors. Although they shared the same womb, the twins developed from two different eggs and so had inherited different genes from their parents.

But I believe there are other possible contributory causes. We should not forget that the natal chart applies to the moment of birth (the moment when the baby emerges from the womb into the outer world), but that the birth is not the starting-point of the individual's development. Several researchers, including Stanislav Grof, have showed that the embryo, while in the womb, undergoes various experiences which sometimes are of a traumatic nature and can affect the person's behaviour after birth.[3] Thus, if two non-identical twins share the same womb, it is likely that their *in utero* experience will be affected by their relationship with each other. One twin may behave as the aggressor, trying to occupy as much space as possible, while the other twin sees itself as the victim, struggling to maintain some space for itself. Then, when the twins emerge from the womb and are both imprinted with nearly the same birth chart, it is likely that, because of their different experiences in the womb, they will be motivated to develop the potential of the chart in radically different ways.

And also (more controversially) we can suggest that a person's behaviour may be influenced by his or her experience of past lives. Believers in reincarnation suppose that a person comes into the world carrying a burden of *karma* which he or she has inherited from past lives, and which will affect the issues which dominate his or her behaviour in the present life. Because this karma is present before the birth, it is not caused by the natal chart; rather, it will affect the way in which the person *responds* to the natal chart, and the way in which he or she makes choices about how to develop its potential. Again, if we take the case of the non-identical twins, the twins may possibly feel that they have known each other in a previous life, but in a different relationship (for instance, as mother and daughter, or as boss and subordinate), and this again will cause them to utilize the natal chart in different ways.

So, for all these reasons, we can say that the natal chart does *not* describe the totality of who the person is. The ultimate source of the person's identity lies far deeper; it precedes birth, and perhaps it will also survive death. We can, if we wish, call it the Soul, or we can call it the true Self; but, whatever we call it, we can never fully *know* it. It is that which knows, rather than that which is known. It is that which sees, not that which is seen. It is that which *uses* the natal chart, not that which is used by it. It is who we *are,* not how we behave. Pierre Teilhard de Chardin expresses this well when he says:

> "We must try to penetrate our most secret self, and examine our be-ing from all sides ... And so, for the first time in my life (although I am supposed to meditate every day!), I took the lamp and, leav-ing the zone of everyday occupations and relationships where eve-rything seems clear, I went down into my inmost self, to the deep abyss whence I feel that my power of action emanates. But as I moved further and further away from the conventional certainties by which social life is superficially illuminated, I became aware that I was los-ing contact with myself. At each step of the descent a new person was disclosed within me of whose name I was no longer sure, and who no longer obeyed me. And when I had to stop my exploration because the path faded from beneath my steps, I found a bottomless abyss at my feet, and out of it came – arising I know not from where – the current which I dare to call my life![4]

"The deep abyss whence I feel that my power of action emanates". We do not all have to descend into the abyss as Teilhard did, but it is important for us to know that the abyss is there, and that our "power of action" originates not from our thinking mind, not from our natal chart, not from our genes, but from something far deeper and more unknowable. The natal chart is just one of the tools which we can use in choosing how to act in the world.

So what are the implications of this for astrological counselling?

It feels important to say that astrological counselling (like any kind of counselling or therapy) is an art, not a science. It is a *creative* process. Any act of counselling is a work of art; and, as a work of art, it can be inadequate, or adequate, or excellent, although the judgement of its quality depends, not on scientific measurement, but on subjective and intuitive criteria, in the same way as one judges works of art in an art gallery. We do not ask whether Leonardo found the right (as opposed to the wrong) way of painting the Mona Lisa; rather, we say that the painting is excellent because he created something beautiful, that could not have been anticipated, and that could have been created by nobody else. He brought something new into the world. In the same way, a counselling encounter is excellent if it brings something new and worthwhile into the world: new insights, new understanding, new behaviours, new freedom from suffering, new potential for self-fulfilment.

And, an act of astrological counselling is a work of art with two creators, the astrologer and the client. Together they can discuss the ways in which the client has been using the natal chart, and can look for ways in which he or she might be able to use it in the future. The aim is to bring into consciousness what, for the client, was until now unconscious, and to give the client more control over his or her life. By gaining greater understanding of the *potential* of the chart, the client may learn to use it in more positive ways: ways that are less stressful, more harmonious, and more conducive to happiness and self-fulfilment.

It is important to realize that in astrology *no feature of the chart is, in itself, either good or bad.* Its "goodness" or "badness" depends on whether it is used well, or badly. We may tend to think of Jupiter as "good", and Saturn as "bad", or to see the "soft" aspects as good and the "hard" aspects as bad. But Saturn and the hard aspects contain great potential for good if they are used wisely, and Jupiter and the soft aspects contain negative potential if they are used unthinkingly or recklessly. If the client has a good understanding of the chart, he or she can choose to use it in ways that he or she sees as good. In psychotherapy an important aim is to help the client to *love themselves.* Similarly, we can say that in astrological counselling the aim is to help the client to *love their natal chart:* to see it as a friend, not as a limitation; to see it as a valuable part of their own make-up.

All this applies to any kind of astrology, not just to harmonic astrology. But perhaps it is particularly relevant to harmonic astrology, because many of the harmonic aspects are essentially about *creativity.* We can learn from them about the ways in which we have been creative, and we can also learn from them about how we might be able to use our creative talents more wisely and productively.

So my advice to an astrologer who is embarking, for the first time, on a study of harmonic astrology would be to *apply it first to your own chart.* Study your own harmonic aspects, and see how they help you to understand your own behaviour and to make better choices in your life. Only when you have done this will you be able to help others to understand themselves through the use of harmonic aspects.

* * * * *

So far in this chapter I have been talking entirely about natal charts. But the same principle applies to mundane charts: the chart shows only *potential.*

I have, for example, studied the mundane charts for a number of air crashes. When the crash is caused by pilot error (rather than by a technical malfunctioning), I have usually found that the chart contains a clear indication of the pilot's state of mind at the time of the crash. On one occasion I had booked a flight, and I found that the chart for the take-off time looked risky: it looked as though the pilot might be in a distracted state of mind and might be disposed to take risks. I wondered whether to cancel the booking, but decided to go ahead and hope for the best. My flight arrived safely, but another aircraft, which took off at around the same time from a different airport, did crash. So we can say that, of all the planes that were taking off at that time around the world, only one was adversely affected by the chart.

In one respect, air crashes are a poor example, because if we are looking at the chart for a take-off time, our only concern is safety, and it is perhaps true that some charts are "safer" than others, and so contain less *potential* for a crash. But in other cases we are looking for other things besides safety. If we are looking, for instance, at the chart for a wedding, or a business deal, we want to know what *opportunities* the chart offers for developments in the future. In such cases, if the chart contains an element of risk, this could be seen as potentially positive, since it would show that the people involved would be less likely to become "stuck", and more likely to be adventurous in moving into a new stage of development. Thus, in these cases, we can say again that no mundane chart is in itself either good or bad; its goodness or badness will depend on how it is *used*.

So I will end this chapter as I began. The chart contains only *potential*. And this will have implications for the way in which we interpret harmonic aspects in this book.

Chapter 4
From One to Seven

As I said in Chapter 1, the first principle of harmonic astrology is that *each prime number introduces a new quality.* In this chapter and the next chapter I will take each of the prime numbers from 1 to 31, and I will examine, and attempt to define, the qualities that are attached to each prime number, as they are manifested in the harmonics of interplanetary aspects. I will do this mainly by examining those charts which are exceptionally strong in each of the numbers, but I will also offer guidance on how these numbers should be interpreted in "ordinary" charts – that is to say, charts which do not contain a predominance of any one number.

I should point out here that my previous book *The Spirit of Numbers* contains longer sections on the meaning of each of the prime numbers. Therefore, readers who refer to that book will find additional examples of charts that are strong in each number, and additional insights into the meaning of each number. In the present book I will summarize the findings presented in *The Spirit of Numbers,* and I will also add some new insights that I have developed since I wrote that book.

Before we start on this journey through the prime numbers, I think it is important for me to clarify my particular stance on the meaning of numbers, since it differs from that of most of the people (mathematicians, philosophers, astrologers, numerologists) who have studied this subject. The difference is that *I am not operating within the decimal system.* Rather, I am attempting to identify the cosmic significance of the numbers, *as they existed before men and women imposed the decimal system upon them.*

We have five fingers on each hand, and so have always chosen to count in fives and tens. We therefore created the decimal system, in which there are ten digits from 0 to 9, which reach completion at the number 10, where the digits start to repeat themselves. As a result, ever since Pythagoras in the 6th century BCE, ten has been seen as the number of completion. *But ten is the number of completion only because we have made it so.* There is nothing inevitable about the decimal system. If we had six fingers on each hand, we would doubtless have created a duodecimal system, with twelve digits rather than ten. (In fact there are many indications - twelve inches in a foot, twenty-four hours in a day, and so on - that we have often preferred to count in twelves rather than tens. I commented on this in detail in *TSON* pp.81-82.) Also, in computing, we have abandoned the decimal system and created instead a binary system, with only two digits, 0 and 1.

In nature, there are no digits; there are simply numbers, which go on increasing from 0 to infinity. The need for digits arises simply because of our need to *count* the numbers; but nature does not count, it simply is. Thus, in harmonic astrology, we are looking at the numerical relationships between the planets. The planets have been circling in the sky, and forming these numerical relationships, since before Man was there to observe them. They are not in any way dependent on Man or on his systems of counting. Thus, harmonic astrology offers a window through which we can free ourselves from the limitations of the decimal system and observe the pure essence of Number.

At the same time, however, I acknowledge that the decimal system has had an enormous influence on how we *think* about numbers, and on our *perception* of the meaning of particular numbers. Thus, I think that there is also value in the work of people who, operating within the decimal system, have studied the cultural history of our perception of numbers. Among these people is Joe Landwehr, who has studied "the spiritual psychology of numbers as implied in the teachings of Pythagoras", and has applied his findings to the study of individual birth charts.[1] Landwehr's conclusions about the meaning of particular numbers are different from mine, but I believe that his work can be seen as complimentary to my work (rather than in opposition to it), and that, in the long run, some kind of integration between the two approaches can be developed.

The other respect in which my approach differs from that of other researchers is that (as I explained in Chapter 1) is that I see each *prime* number as having a particular quality, which is present also in the multiples of that number. Thus (for instance) Landwehr looks at each of the numbers from one to ten *separately*, and reaches conclusions about Four and Eight which are different from his conclusions about Two. But I see Four and Eight as higher manifestations of Twoness, and therefore in the following discussion I will not treat Four and Eight separately, but will include them in my discussion of the meaning of Twoness.

We will now look at the qualities of each of the prime numbers from 1 to 31. In discussing each number, I will give several examples of birth charts, many of which are discussed in more detail in *The Spirit of Numbers (TSON)*.

The data (date, time, place) for all the charts mentioned in this chapter (and in the rest of the book) can be found in Appendix I.

Oneness

Oneness means union. When two or more planets are conjunct in the chart, they merge together and become One. In relation to each other, these planets are now at peace. Their complex interactions have come to an end.

If all the planets in a birth chart were conjunct, the person would be in a state of total peace and stillness. But of course, in practice this does not happen. Even if there are four or five planets in the conjunction, these planets still have complex relationships with the other planets in the chart; and, in relation to these other planets, the conjunction becomes a very powerful force, since the planets in the conjunction are combining their energies and acting together in unison. Since all the planets in the conjunction are in the same sign and the same house, the qualities of that sign and that house will be very strongly emphasized in the personality. (Sometimes, however, the conjunction straddles the boundary between two signs or two houses. In these cases, both of the signs or houses will be emphasized.)

We can illustrate this by looking at some of the examples which I gave in *TSON* of people with very strong multiple conjunctions. For example, I presented the case of the "decadent" poet Charles Baudelaire (*TSON*, pp.26-27). Baudelaire has ME, PL, MA, CH, VE and JU all conjunct in Pisces/Aries across the boundary between the 7th and 8th houses, with VE and JU also widely conjunct with SA and SO which are further on into Aries in the 8th house. As a result, Baudelaire was single-mindedly and obsessively concerned with 7th and 8th house matters (sex, love, death), portraying them in a dynamic and fiery Aries manner, arising out of a deep Piscean emotionality. This case of a multiple conjunction in Pisces/Aries contrasts with (for instance) the Christian mystic Pierre Teilhard de Chardin (*TSON*, pp.19-22), whose conjunction of SA, JU, SO, NE, VE and CH (with VE-*1*-NE almost exact) is in Taurus in the 11th house, enabling Teilhard to experience a very deep sense of groundedness, coupled with a passionate desire to serve humanity. (For other cases of people with very strong multiple conjunctions, see *TSON*, Chapter 3.)

The common factor linking all these people with strong multiple conjunctions seems to be their *single-mindedness*. They were all people who pursued their own highly individual and original paths with unwavering enthusiasm and commitment throughout their lives, and who paid little or no attention to the expectations of other people or of society as a whole. For each of them, the multiple conjunction created a very strong force, propelling them consistently in a particular direction indicated by the sign and house in which the conjunction occurred. Because the planets within the conjunction were at peace with one another, these people were less subject than most people are to all the self-doubts, uncertainties and confusions that arise from being pulled in different directions by different planets in the chart.

Such cases of conjunctions involving four or five planets are rare; but almost every chart contains at least one conjunction of two planets, and these "ordinary" conjunctions are of course familiar to all astrologers. We do not need harmonic astrology in order to understand them.

However, harmonic astrology can help by drawing attention to the harmonic links which the conjunction (if it is very close) can have with other planets. The closer the conjunction is to exactitude, the more complete will be the merging of the two planets into a single united force; and also, the more likely it is that the conjunction will have close harmonic links with other planets. These links can be in *any* harmonic number (because every number is divisible by One).

An example of this is the singer, songwriter, poet and novelist Leonard Cohen, who has a Venus-Neptune conjunction (in Virgo in

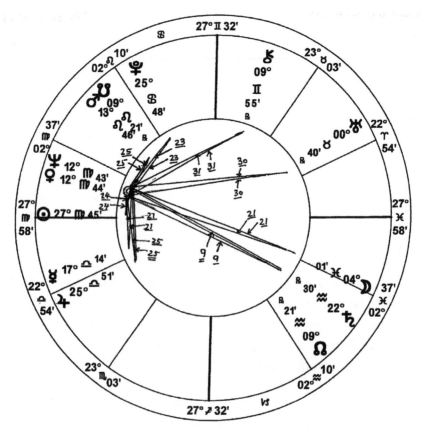

4.1 Leonard Cohen: Harmonic Links to VE-1-NE

the 12th house) with an orb of only 0°01'. In Chapter 1 I said that the second principle of harmonic astrology is: *The closer an aspect is to exactitude, the stronger it will be.* This conjunction is almost exact, and so is extremely powerful; and it has harmonic links with all the other planets, as follows: (VE-*1*-NE)-*24*-SO, -21-MO, 21-ME, -25-MA, 25/*25*-JU, 9/*9*-SA, -*30*-UR, -*23*-PL, and -31-CH. This is illustrated in Figure 4.1.

Note that in Figure 4.1, as in all the other charts in this book, "very close" aspects are shown with double lines, and the harmonic numbers are twice underlined; "close" aspects are shown with single lines, and the numbers are underlined; and "wide" aspects are shown with broken lines, and the numbers have no underlining.

Sue Tompkins gives the following as keywords for Venus-Neptune aspects:

Romantic love. Love of dreaming. Beautiful music. Clandestine relationships. Fairy-tale romance. Idealized beauty. [2]

While these qualities may be present for everyone with a close Venus-Neptune aspect, in Cohen's case they are much more dominant because of the extreme closeness of the VE-NE conjunction and its harmonic links with all the other planets. Cohen's whole life can be seen as an expression of the "idealized beauty" of VE-*1*-NE, and the harmonic links show the various ways in which he was able to bring this into realization.

So we can see that Oneness, which is the starting-point of our journey through the numbers, can also be a force that binds all the numbers together into a single united whole.

Twoness

Twoness, otherwise known as Duality, is the principle of separation. I am I, and you are you. We may fight each other, or we may co-operate with each other, or we may even move towards each other and try, as far as possible, to merge into Oneness; but, right now, we are separate beings, with boundaries separating ourselves from each other and from the outside world.

Twoness is also the principle of polarity. There is right, and there is wrong; there is good, and there is bad; there is love, and there is hatred; there is success, and there is failure. Within Twoness, we are always *striving:* striving to get things right, striving to be good, striving to be successful, striving to *achieve.*

Gareth S. Hill has written a book *Masculine and Feminine: the Natural Flow of Opposites in the Psyche,* in which he distinguishes between "four basic patterns that underlie all human activity".[3] These four patterns are the *static feminine,* the *dynamic masculine,* the *static masculine,* and the *dynamic feminine.* Within this typology, Twoness represents the *dynamic masculine.* Hill describes this as "the tendency towards differentiation expressed in the images of cleaving and penetrating. It is expressed in initiative and action directed toward a goal".

The geometrical figure representing Twoness is simply a line connecting two points. Similarly, Hill says that the symbol for the dynamic masculine is an arrow. Within Twoness, we are always striving to reach out beyond our boundaries, to connect from Self to Other, to get from A to B.

The harmonic aspects involving pure Twoness are harmonics 2, 4, 8, 16 and 32. The first three of these are familiar to all astrologers as the opposition, the square, and the semi-square or sesquiquadrate. However, we should note that in harmonic astrology the orbs used for these aspects are much narrower than in conventional astrology. This is especially true in the case of the square (4th harmonic). Astrologers have traditionally allowed an orb of 8 degrees for the square: but in harmonic astrology the orb used for the square is one quarter (1/4) of the conjunction orb, i.e. 30 minutes for "very close" aspects, 1½ degrees for "close" aspects, and 3 degrees for "wide" aspects. Therefore, in harmonic astrology squares (and also clusters such as T-squares and Grand Crosses) are far less common than they are in conventional astrology.

Astrologers have always understood that the different levels of Twoness require somewhat different interpretations. In the opposition (2nd harmonic) the two planets are facing each other directly across the chart. Each planet has a strong *awareness* of the other planet, and sees it as the "Other" with which it has to relate. There may be attraction between them, or there may be enmity, but, either way, there is a felt need to reach out towards the other planet, and to strive to enter into a relationship. Very often, the person will identify with one of the two planets and project the other planet out onto other people in their environment (so that, for instance, if Mercury is opposite Mars, the person may identify with Mercury and see Mars as "other people behaving towards me in a Martian way"). In *TSON*

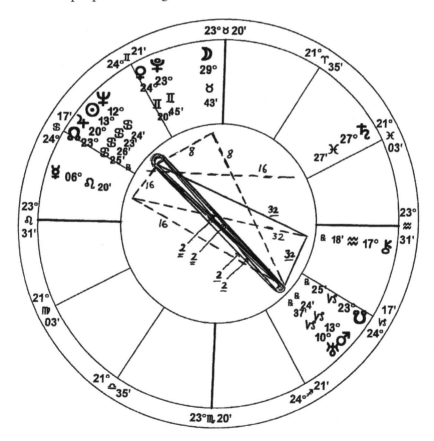

4.2 Frida Kahlo: Pure Twoness Aspects

(pp.40-41) I gave an outstanding example of this in the Mexican painter Frida Kahlo, who has SO-**2**-MA with an orb of only 0°01': Kahlo identified with Sun, and saw Mars, partly as her body (which was racked with pain), but also as her frequently unfaithful husband Diego Rivera. Her continuing struggle was to find a way of relating both to her body and to her husband. (Figure 4.2 shows the pure Twoness aspects in Kahlo's chart.)

When we come to the square (4th harmonic) the situation is different. Now we can say that each planet has a path towards its goal (the opposite point in the chart), but that one planet's path is at right angles to the other planet's path. So we can say that the two planets are at *cross purposes* with each other. The goal which one planet is

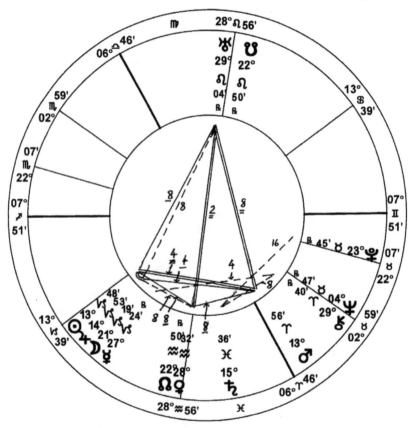

4.3 Augustus John: Pure Twoness Aspects

pursuing conflicts with the goal that the other planet is pursuing. So the person's task is to strive to reconcile these conflicting goals. An example of this (from *TSON* pp.43-44) is the painter Augustus John (whose pure Twoness aspects are shown in Figure 4.3), who had SO-*4*-MA with an orb of 0°08'. We can see how John's SO-*4*-MA differs from Kahlo's SO-*2*-MA. With John, there is no projecting out, but rather a struggle between the goal of Sun in Capricorn 2nd house (to find self-fulfilment through money and possessions) and the goal of Mars in Aries 5th house (to express energy in dynamic creativity).

However, to describe the square aspect simply as "a struggle between conflicting goals" is perhaps to present it in too negative a light. The square aspect can be a very constructive force, through which one strives to bring the energies of the two planets into One. In my own chart I have (SO-*1*-ME)-*4*-JU, and I feel that, if it were not for the tension induced by these aspects, I would not be writing this book.

Coming back to the cases of Frida Kahlo and Augustus John, we can see from their charts that their Sun-Mars aspects are part of a complex pattern of Twoness, and, if we were analysing their charts in detail, we would need to look at the whole of this pattern. But in both cases the Sun-Mars aspects are the most central and the most important, because they are so close to exactitude. This question of *closeness to exactitude* is always important in harmonic astrology.

Beyond the square, we come to the higher levels of Twoness: harmonic 8 (the semi-square and sesquiquadrate), and harmonics 16 and 32, which are not studied in conventional astrology. I have not been able to find words to express the precise meaning of each of these levels of Twoness, and so I can only say that, like the square (but perhaps at a deeper and more subconscious level), they represent conflicts and struggles between different aspects of the personality. It seems likely that single aspects in harmonics 16 and 32 can usually be ignored (unless they are extremely close, and/or they are highlighted by the closeness of one of the planets to the Angles). But, if these aspects form part of a cluster of Twoness aspects, they can be very important.

An example of this is Mohandas (Mahatma) Gandhi (*TSON*, p.49), whose Twoness aspects are shown in Figure 4.4. In addition to other Twoness aspects, Gandhi has (MO-*4*-JU)-*16*/16-SA. MO-*4*-JU (with Moon in Leo 10th house and Jupiter in Leo 7th) is in itself an optimistic aspect, showing Gandhi's efforts to bring peace and freedom to other people and to the world. But the close "16" aspects to Saturn (in Sagittarius 2nd house) show how Gandhi felt that, in order to achieve the goals of MO-*4*-JU, there were deeper Saturnian obstacles that had to be overcome. We can note also that Gandhi's Twoness links are centred on his Moon, whereas his Sun has no Twoness aspects at all: this suggests that, despite his struggles to

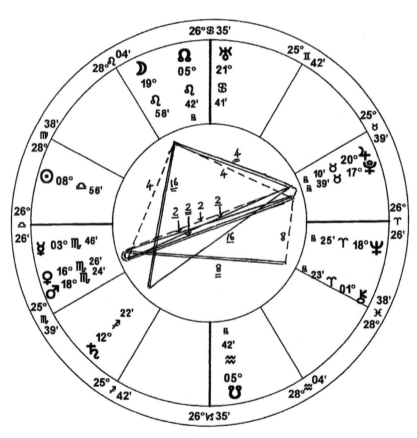

4.4 Mohandas Gandhi: Pure Twoness Aspects

achieve his goals in the world, Gandhi had no need to struggle to *find himself:* his sense of his own identity was free from Twoness striving.

Occasionally one finds a chart in which there is a very complex cluster of planets spanning all the levels of Twoness. An example of this is the psychiatrist R.D. Laing (*TSON,* pp.37-40), who has (((MO-*2*-NE)-8/*8*-SO)-16/*16*/*16*-ME)-32/*32*/32/32-VE (see Figure 4.5). In *TSON* I showed how this cluster can be analysed, layer by layer, in order to obtain a very detailed picture of the internal struggles with which Laing contended.

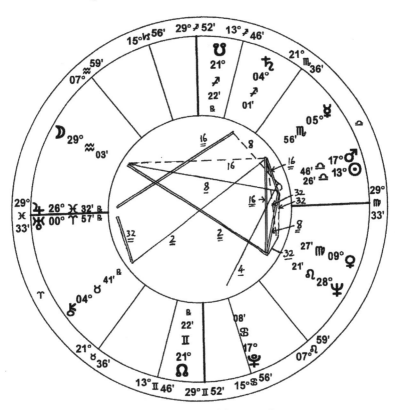

4.5 R.D. Laing: Pure Twoness Aspects

Another example is the adventurer Steve Fossett (*TSON,* pp.44-45), who has a very complex cluster of Twoness. As I said in *TSON,* Fossett was "an outstanding example of the characteristics of Twoness: restless activity, and constant striving to overcome obstacles, reach

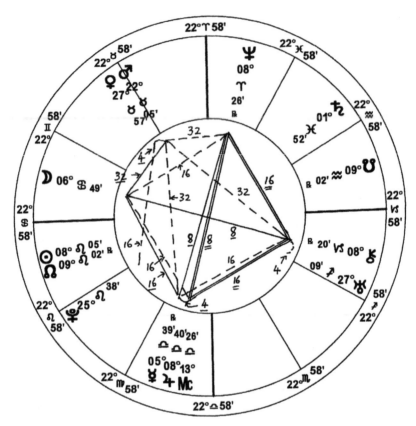

4.6 Steve Fossett: 4th Harmonic Chart

objectives, and notch up achievements". Because Fossett's Twoness aspects are mostly at the higher levels of Twoness (8, 16 and 32), they can be seen more clearly in his 4th harmonic chart (shown in Figure 4.6) than in the radical chart. However, we would need to look at the radical chart to find the signs and houses in which the planets are placed.

In Chapter 7 we will look at the chart of the murderess Patricia Columbo, in which the higher levels of Twoness (16 and 32) are very strong, and these aspects seem to have been the spur which enabled her to actually put into practice her fantasy of killing her father, her mother and her brother. The important thing to remember is that Twoness aspects, at all levels, are always *spurs to action*. The person is motivated to find *actions* which will help to resolve the differences between the planets.

However, we should not forget that Two is also the closest number to One. When two planets are linked by a Twoness aspect, they are reaching out towards each other; they are acutely aware of their separateness, but they may also be striving to overcome this separateness and to merge into One, and, very occasionally, this objective may be achieved. Thus, in *TSON* (pp.51-52) I gave the example of Saint Thérèse of Lisieux, who had a very strong pattern of Twoness (Figure 4.7), causing her as a child to display very neurotic patterns of behaviour, but succeeded in overcoming this and reaching a state of serenity and peace which has caused her to be an inspiration to very many Christian believers.

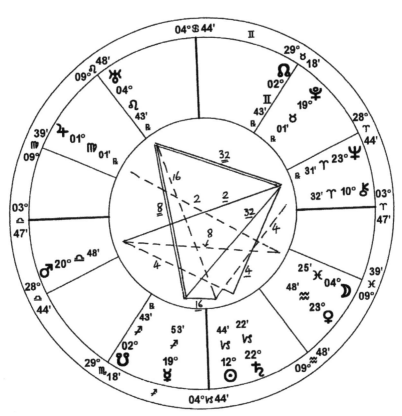

4.7 Saint Thérèse de Lisieux: Pure Twoness Aspects

In the majority of charts (but not in every chart), Twoness is stronger than any other prime number. We all have an element of Twoness in our makeup. Traditionally Twoness aspects (the opposition, square and semi-square) have been seen as "hard", "stressful", and (on the whole) negative. But we need Twoness in order to cope with life in this complex world. Twoness is the force which enables us to deal with the challenges of life and to overcome the difficulties as best we can.

Threeness

Three is the number within which we find our place in the world. In Twoness there is only Self and Other. But in Threeness there is Self, there is Other, and there is also the *environment* in which both Self and Other find themselves. The figure representing Twoness is simply a line; but the figure representing Threeness is a triangle, which is the simplest possible solid figure. In Threeness the solid world becomes real. You and I are relating to each other, not in a vacuum, but in an environment which we both share.

In Gareth Hill's typology, Threeness corresponds to the *static feminine*. Hill says of the static feminine: "Its essence is the impersonal, rhythmic cycle of nature, which gives all life and takes all life. It is *being*: organic, undifferentiated, all components interdependent, and no one component more important than any other. Events just happen, for no reason but that they happen".[3]

In other words, the essence of Threeness is *acceptance*. It is the opposite of Twoness, in which we are always dissatisfied with how things are, and are always *striving* to make them different. In Threeness we accept everything as it is now.

And from this it follows that Threeness is also about *pleasure*. Because we are not trying to change things, we take pleasure in things as they are. Within Threeness, the purpose of life is to enjoy ourselves, and enjoy the world in which we live – in other words, to be happy.

The simplest aspect in Threeness is the trine, which is the 3rd harmonic. The trine is well understood in conventional astrology. Sue Tompkins says that the trine represents *ease* between the planets concerned: their energies flow well together.[4] This is because, when two planets are in trine, they share the same element. *They have the same environment.* However, in harmonic astrology the orbs allowed for the trine are much narrower than in conventional astrology: 4 degrees for a "wide" aspect, 2 degrees for a "close" aspect, and 40 minutes for a "very close" aspect. Thus, a Grand Trine (in which three planets are all in trine to one another) becomes a much rarer occurrence.

But in harmonic astrology there are also the 9th and 27th harmonics, which also represent pure Threeness (because 9 is 3 x 3, and 27 is 3 x 3 x 3). These aspects also represent the Threeness principle of acceptance and pleasure, but at a higher or more refined level. We can say, perhaps, that whereas in the 3rd harmonic the planets simply take pleasure in combining their energies, in the 9th harmonic there is *pleasure in pleasure* (3 x 3). That is to say, the planets are *aware* that they find pleasure in each other, and they find pleasure in this awareness. And in the 27th harmonic this awareness is taken even further: *pleasure in pleasure in pleasure.* Often this heightened pleasure – which we can call joy, or bliss – takes the form of love: love of oneself, of other people, of the whole world.

We can illustrate this from the chart of Mata Amritanandamayi, a spiritual teacher who is usually known simply as "Amma" (Figure 4.8). Amma has been described as "the most personally accessible, compassionate spiritual leader alive today". She always concludes her meetings by warmly embracing each person present. Deepak Chopra (another spiritual teacher) has said, "Amma is the embodiment of pure love. Her presence heals". At the head of her website (www.amma.org) there is the message: "May all beings in this world and in all the other worlds be peaceful and happy". In her natal chart, Amma has (MO-*27*-JU)-27/*27*-UR. If we include the asteroid Ceres (close to Venus at Virgo 2°39'), which is about loving and nurturing, the configuration becomes even stronger: ((UR-*9*-CE)-*27*-JU)-27/27/*27*-MO. Also she has SO-9-PL and an *exact* VE-*27*-SA. Thus we can see that, to a quite exceptional extent, Amma is filled with the highest and most refined form of Threeness. She loves and accepts everyone just as they

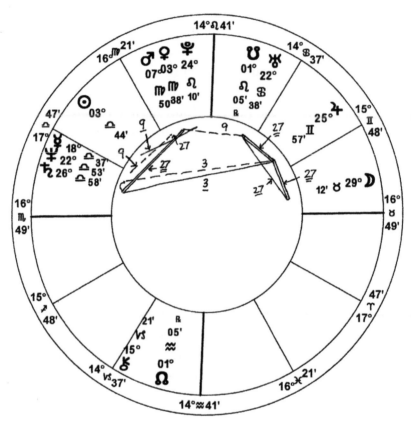

4.8 Amma: Pure Threeness Aspects

are. She is happy, and her happiness is contagious, affecting everyone she meets.

At a more basic level, Threeness links are concerned with the pursuit of pleasure. They denote a hedonistic, happy-go-lucky approach to life. I gave several examples of this in *TSON,* including several comedians, and the hedonistic brothel-keeper Cynthia Payne (p.64).

One way of looking at Threeness is to see it as *the quality which Hitler lacks.* Adolf Hitler's chart is strong in Twoness, Fiveness and Sevenness, but it has an almost total absence of Threeness, to a greater extent than any other chart that I have seen. Hitler was most certainly not "hedonistic" and "happy-go-lucky". And in fact politicians generally tend to be weak in Threeness, presumably because they have had to struggle to reach their positions of power, and Threeness people tend to be averse to this kind of struggle.

But one politician who is strong in Threeness is President George W. Bush (who, being the son of a former President, did not have to struggle so hard). Bush's Threeness aspects are shown in Figure 4.9. They can be listed as follows:

SO-_27_-PL
(MO*-_1_-JU*)-3/_3_-UR
(MO*-_9_-SA)-_27_/_27_-ME*
(MA-_9_-UR)-_27_/_27_-NE

The cluster (MO*-_9_-SA)-_27_/_27_-ME* is especially important because Moon is close to the IC and Mercury is close to the

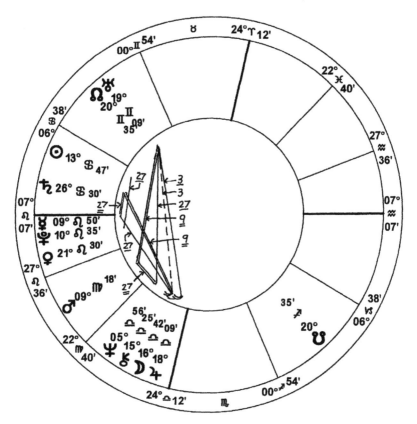

4.9 George W. Bush: Pure Threeness Aspects

Ascendant. The combination of these three planets in the pleasure-seeking harmonics shows Bush cheerfully accepting the world as he sees it, and communicating about it in an uncomplicated way. (In *Harmonic Charts* I mentioned "cheerful cynicism" as a characteristic of MO-9-SA.[5]) Meanwhile the cluster (MA-*9*-UR)-*27*/*27*-NE shows Bush as an outgoing character, rejoicing in his physicality and able to infect others with his enthusiasm for life. Of course this is not the whole of Bush's personality (ME*-*1*-PL* on the Ascendant shows a certain ruthlessness), but I think we can say that Bush coped with the Presidency in a more relaxed and easy-going way than most of the other occupants of the office, and that perhaps there was a tendency to not take his responsibilities seriously enough.

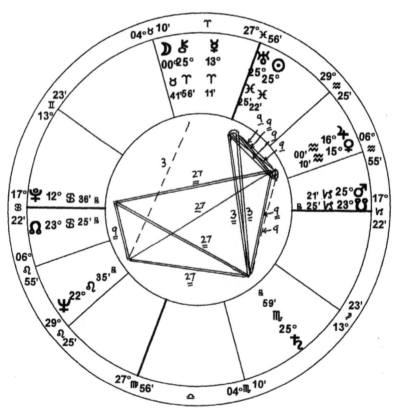

4.10 Jerry Lewis: Pure Threeness Aspects

I also gave the example (pp.59-62) of two people who were born within one day of each other, and so have almost identical patterns of Threeness: the comedian and film-maker Jerry Lewis (Figure 4.10), and the medium Pat Rodegast (Figure 4.11), who channelled the sayings of an "entity" called Emmanuel. These two cases offer an interesting study of how the expression of harmonic aspects is affected by the houses in which the planets are placed. Both Lewis and Rodegast have a very complex pattern of Threeness links, involving all the planets except Moon, Mercury and Chiron, and covering all the levels of Threeness (3, 9 and 27). But in Lewis's case Sun and Uranus (in Pisces) are close to the Midheaven, with Pluto near the Ascendant: this caused him to express his Threeness in original ways in his working career. As a film-maker he has been described as a "discoverer

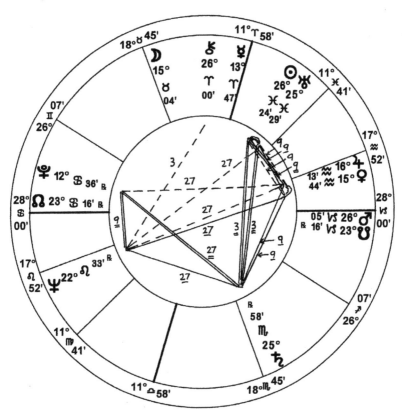

4.11 Pat Rodegast: Pure Threeness Aspects

of beauty", and as a purveyor of "pure pleasure"; also he has described himself as having "a love affair with humanity". Rodegast, on the other hand, has Mercury (in Aries) on the Midheaven, with Mars on the Descendant: but Mercury is not involved in the Threeness pattern, and this helps to explain why, in order to communicate to the world her message of pure love, she had to attribute it to a separate (male) identity which is represented by Mars.

So far we have been looking at pure Threeness (3, 9 and 27), but we also have to consider those harmonics (6, 12, 18 and 24) in which Threeness is combined with Twoness. If Twoness means *striving* and Threeness means *pleasure,* then these "Sixness" aspects can be described as *striving towards pleasure* or *pleasure in striving.* My impression is that these aspects are, in most cases, very beneficial,

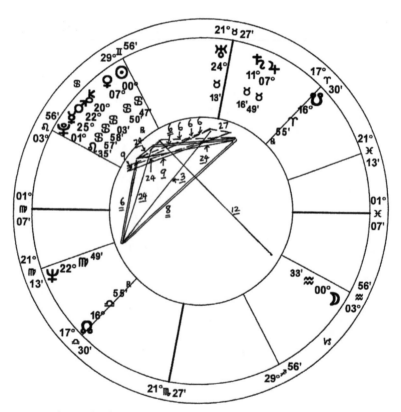

4.12 Charles Harvey: Twoness and Threeness Aspects

since they help the person to enjoy their work and to take pleasure in facing up to the challenges of life.

In *TSON* (p.75) I gave the example of the astrologer Charles Harvey, who has a very strong Sixness pattern: Charles's pleasure in his work was plain for all to see, and affected everyone whom he met. On Charles's chart (Figure 4.12) I have shown all his Twoness and Threeness aspects: this adds up to a very complex pattern, but we can see that it is built around an exact JU-*8*-NE (pure Twoness) and the pure Threeness aspects of UR-*3*-NE and SA-*9*-PL. These aspects are linked together by a large number of Sixness aspects involving Mercury, Venus, Mars and Uranus. Thus we can say that Charles's Twoness quest – the driving force of his life – is the search for a reconciliation between Jupiter and Neptune, which I see as the search for a spiritual vision which is both uplifting and life-enhancing and also (because Neptune is in Virgo in the 2nd house) realistic and grounded. Charles chose to pursue this through astrology, and the Threeness and Sixness links to all the other planets ensured that this pursuit brought enormous pleasure both to himself and to others.

I do not think that a clear distinction can be made between the meanings of the different Sixness aspects (6, 12, 18 and 24). They are all concerned with *pleasure in striving*. However, the *pleasure* element is very much stronger in the 18th harmonic (3 x 3 x 2) than it is in the 24th harmonic (3 x 2 x 2 x 2). H18 is closer to pure Threeness, whereas H24 is closer to pure Twoness.

I may so far have given the impression that Threeness is all sweetness and light. However, as I said in Chapter 3, no feature of the chart is, in itself, either good or bad; its "goodness" or "badness" depends on whether it is used well, or badly. The negative side of Threeness is to do with *negligence* and *carelessness*. *Carefree* (which is seen as positive) can easily become *careless* (which is seen as negative). Threeness, as I have said, is about accepting that everything is OK as it is now. But what if things are *not* OK, and action needs to be taken to put things right? The Threeness person may fail to take such action, or fail to see the need for it.

Thus, Threeness can manifest in the form of great love for other human beings; but it can also manifest as a lack of awareness of the other person's needs. The Threeness person believes that everyone has a right to be happy; but he or she may fail to understand that people also have a right to be *unhappy* if they have genuine problems.

Thus, Jerry Lewis was, as I have said, a very loving person, but he was also criticized for his lack of sensitivity towards disabled people, and his wife complained about his unthinking behaviour towards her. Also in *TSON* (pp.78-9) I gave the example of the Kray twins, Reginald and Ronald, who dominated the London criminal scene in the 1960s, and were eventually convicted of murder; their lives were spent in the pursuit of pleasure, and, although they inspired great affection, they could also behave callously and cruelly. We can see

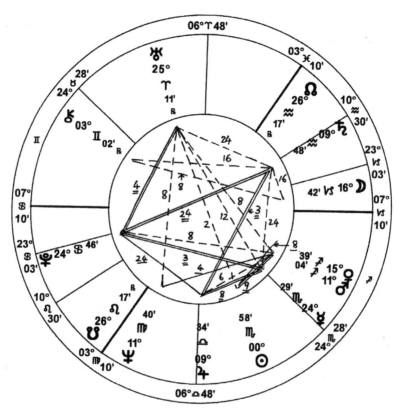

4.13 Ronald Kray: Twoness and Threeness Aspects

from Ronald Kray's "Twoness and Threeness Aspects" chart (Figure 4.13) how his pleasure-seeking activities are centred around an almost exact SA-24-PL, and this shows how he could easily turn to violence.

And also, there is the case of the entertainer Rolf Harris, who has a strong Sixness pattern. In *TSON* (pp.75-6) I described Harris as a person whose main desire in life was to give pleasure to others. This is how he was generally seen in 2010 when I wrote *TSON*. But since then it has emerged that Harris is also a paedophile, who has now been convicted and imprisoned on numerous charges of indecent assault against girls aged between 8 and 19. He appears to have had no understanding of the harm that he was doing to his victims. In his perception, he was still giving pleasure to others. We can see

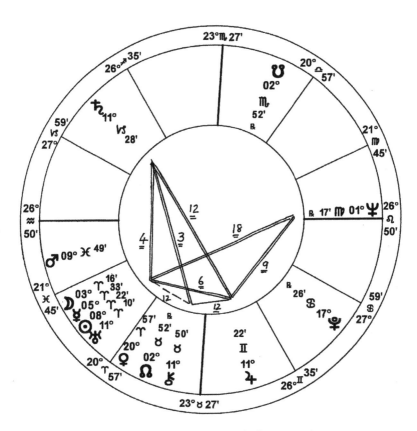

4.14 Rolf Harris: Twoness and Threeness Aspects

from his chart (Figure 4.14) how JU-_2_-NE, with Neptune in the 7th house near the Descendant, linked also to JU-_6_-UR and UR-_18_-NE, may have caused him to be carried away by his belief in his own "specialness" and in his freedom to relate to others in any way that he chose.

Thus, we can see that Threeness can be a potent force for either good or bad.

Fiveness

Three, as I have said, is the number in which we find our place in the world. After Three we come to Four, a higher manifestation of Twoness, in which we strive to achieve our goals within the world. But after Four we come to Five, a new prime number, and this is the number in which we can change the world, or create new worlds.

In Gareth Hill's typology, Fiveness corresponds to the *static masculine,* which he describes as "the tendency to create systems of order".[3] It may seem strange that a principle which is essentially creative should be described as "static," but the point is that Fiveness is concerned with the creation of things which, having been created, remain static. It is about the creation of *order out of chaos,* or *order out of flux.* Nature is not static; it is in constant flux. But in Fiveness we are able to take things from Nature and create things which remain static so that we can use them. We create man-made objects. We create towns and cities. We create technologies. We harness electricity for our own use. We create systems of distribution and exchange, and we invent money so that these systems work effectively. We create static roles for people to perform. We create abstract systems: religions, philosophies, political ideologies. We write books. We compose music. We paint pictures. We create the internet. The list is endless.

It is clear from this that Five is the number of Man. It describes what Man does to the world. Birds build nests, spiders build webs, beavers build dams, and social insects such as ants and bees have created elaborate hierarchies and systems of communication. But

Man, to a far greater extent than any other animal, has taken Fiveness and made it his own, shaping the whole world to fit in with his needs.

It is therefore appropriate that Man has also created the decimal system, which can be seen as a system of counting in fives. We can perhaps say that the decimal system (along with the alphabet) is one of the two basic systems on which all the other man-made systems depend. Through the decimal system Man has harnessed the numbers themselves and made them his own.

Thus, when two or more planets are linked by a Fiveness aspect, their energies are brought together in a *systematic* way. The person is engaged in creating some kind of *order* or *structure* which involves the energies of these planets. If there are a great many Fiveness aspects in the chart, this creation of order and structure will be a central feature of the person's life.

Thus, in *TSON* (pp.88-92) I showed that three of the strongest charts in terms of Fiveness were those of Bahá-u-lláh, the founder of the Baha'i faith; Frank Buchman, the founder of Moral Re-Armament; and the Indian sage Sri Aurobindo. All three of these, in different ways, were engaged in developing and presenting guidelines and rules by which people should live in order to reach the highest level of ethical and spiritual attainment. They were laying the foundations of a new moral order. This could be described as a very positive use of Fiveness.

I have found many cases of poets, novelists, painters, musicians and actors who were very strong in Fiveness, and many of these cases are described in *TSON*. In all these cases, the Fiveness refers to their skill in creating and assembling a work of art (a poem, a book, a painting, a musical or theatrical performance) in a satisfying and aesthetically pleasing way. For example, Sylvia Plath (*TSON* p.93) has, in addition to other Fiveness aspects, a cluster of ((ME-**5**-NE)-25/**25**-MO)-25/25/25-VE. In order to understand the emotional content of Plath's poetry, as well as her turbulent and ultimately tragic life, we would have to examine other harmonics. But the Fiveness refers to her skill as a poet, and to the fact that (as she said) she was "compelled towards perfection in everything she attempted".[6]

Thus, we can see that the "ordering and structuring" principle of Fiveness can be applied both *externally* and *internally*. Externally, it relates to the creation and construction of "things" outside oneself. But internally, it refers to the ordering and structuring of one's own life: the creation of patterns of behaviour. In the latter sense, a keyword for Fiveness is *style*. Fiveness aspects may provide insight into the *lifestyle* that the person chooses to follow.

Both of these tendencies are evident in the case of the poet Percy Bysshe Shelley (*TSON* pp.92-93), whose Fiveness aspects are shown in Figure 4.15. In Shelley's chart Sun-conjunct-Venus is connected by very strong Fiveness links with Mars-conjunct-Jupiter, and all these planets also have "25" links with Saturn on the Ascendant. Shelley is unusual in that all his Fiveness links are *pure* Fiveness; there is no Twoness or Threeness involved. Shelley was a brilliant poet, but also

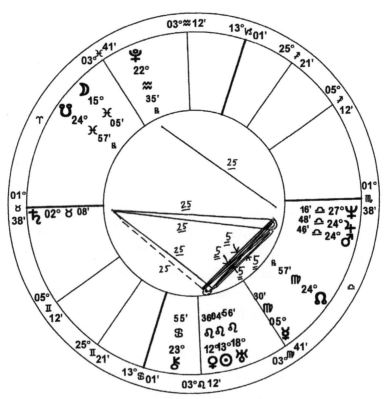

4.15 Percy Bysshe Shelley: Fiveness Aspects

he was a person who lived his whole life in accordance with his own rules, which were entirely different from those imposed by society. His life was governed by the principle of Fiveness.

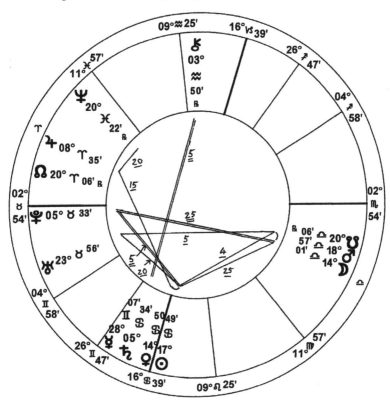

4.16 Nikola Tesla: Fiveness Aspects

Among scientists, strong Fiveness seems to be less common, but James D. Watson, the co-discoverer of the structure of DNA, has a very strong Fiveness cluster involving SO, MO, ME, MA, JU and UR. Also, we can note the remarkable case of the scientist and inventor Nikola Tesla, whose Fiveness links are shown in Figure 4.16. Tesla has a cluster of (SO*-5-PL*)-25/25-MO: this cluster is exceptionally powerful, because it unites the Sun with the Moon (when Sun and Moon come together in a particular harmonic, the quality of that harmonic pervades the whole personality) and also with Pluto which is on the Ascendant. Thus, Tesla is driven to develop a lifestyle, or a pattern of behaviour, in which Plutonian qualities are very strongly present and are displayed to the world. Also, Tesla has a Sun-Mars square with Fiveness links to Uranus - (SO-4-MA)-20/5-UR – which impels him to seek creative, original and striking (we could say "electric") ways of expressing his love of action. (Also there are ME-5-CH, VE-15-JU, and JU-20-NE.)

Tesla lived out these Fiveness characteristics to the full. He has been called "the greatest inventor the world has ever known," obsessively searching for ways of harnessing electrical power. But he was not only an inventor, he was also a showman. Charles Harvey paints a detailed and very vivid picture of how Tesla "delighted in putting on flashy, limelight-grabbing shows to awaken interest in his work".[7] The qualities of both Uranus and Pluto are very evident in Tesla's personality, but displayed in a systematic, structured, creative way which is typical of Fiveness.

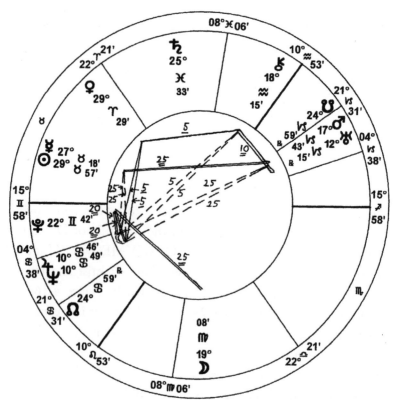

4.17 Laurence Olivier: Fiveness Aspects

An example of an actor with strong Fiveness aspects is Laurence Olivier (Figure 4.17), who was regarded by many as the greatest actor of his time. When he was just being himself, Olivier could seem rather colourless; but he came to life when he was "playing a part", *constructing* a personality for himself. Perhaps the most important aspect here is ME-*25*-MA, an *exact* aspect which shows Olivier's skill at conveying Martian forcefulness and vigour through his manner of speaking.

The negative side of Fiveness is the danger of becoming trapped or imprisoned within the structures and systems that one has created. Thus, in *TSON* (pp.84-88) I described in detail the case of June and Jennifer Gibbons, who are known as the "Silent Twins". Both June and Jennifer have an exceptionally strong cluster of Fiveness in their charts, involving all the planets except Chiron, and I wrote that they were "imprisoned by their Fiveness". They were always imposing rules on themselves, and allowing themselves to be trapped by their own rules. They refused to talk to other people except on the telephone, and they talked to each other in a special language which they themselves had devised.

Thus, Fiveness is prone to the development of *addictions* of all kinds. A person chooses a particular way of behaving, and then that way of behaving becomes ossified and develops into an addiction. An example is the singer-songwriter Kurt Cobain, whose Fiveness aspects are shown in Figure 4.18. I will not attempt here to summarize Cobain's complex life and personality, but will just say that he was extremely addiction-prone. He first took marijuana at the age of 13, but later developed addictions to various drugs including cocaine and heroin, as well as alcohol and substance abuse. He committed suicide with a gun at the age of 27, though he had previously tried to kill himself by overdosing on drugs.

Cobain's chart shows a very complex Fiveness pattern centred on the Sun. He has an *exact* SO-*3*-MA and a close VE*-3-JU, and these Threeness links are connected to each other by Fiveness and Fifteenness aspects (SO-*5*-JU, VE-5-MA, SO-15-VE and MA-*15*-JU). Fifteen (5 x 3) is about *enjoyment* of system-building, so this

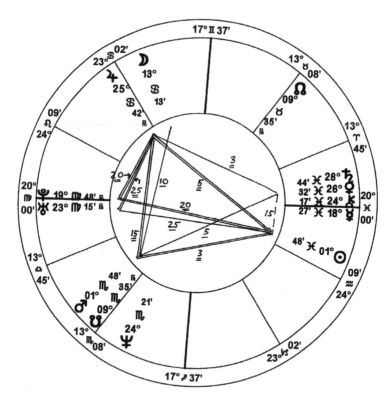

4.18: Kurt Cobain: Fiveness Aspects

pattern suggests that Cobain's initial experiments with drugs were the result of a natural exuberance and a desire to try out new experiences. But SO-*5*-JU is also involved in two other Fiveness clusters: (SO-*5*-JU)-*25*/*25*-UR* and (SO-*5*-JU)-*20*-PL* (with both UR and PL close to the Ascendant). These very powerful clusters will have caused Cobain (like the Silent Twins) to become imprisoned within his Fiveness, unable to escape from the habits he had formed. In fact, the Uranus cluster will have encouraged him to keep diving further into the addiction, experimenting with new drugs, while the Pluto cluster (with its double dose of Twoness, 20 = 5 x 2 x 2) is an indication of the self-punishment and torment to which he subjected himself, leading in the end to his suicide.

We could ask: Why did Cobain become a slave to his addictions, when other people with strong Fiveness have not done so? I believe that the answer lies, at least partly, in what I said in Chapter 3: *The chart shows only potential.* Every chart with strong Fiveness contains the *potential* for addiction, but not all Fiveness people become addicted. We should note that Fiveness actions always involve conscious choice: the person is *choosing* to re-shape the world (the external or the internal world) in one way rather than in another way. Thus, the person who takes drugs knows that he is choosing to do so, and that he could choose not to do so. But the paradox of Fiveness is that, while it gives people freedom of choice, it also takes that freedom away by forming habits that are difficult (and sometimes impossible) to break.

We can illustrate this by referring again to the Silent Twins, June and Jennifer. So long as both the twins were alive, they both found it impossible to break free from their habitual rule-bound behaviour. But, after Jennifer's death, June was able to break free and to live her life in a different way. She was still a Fiveness person with the same natal chart, but she learnt to use her Fiveness differently, by making different choices about how to re-shape her world.

In *TSON* (pp.94-5) I also gave the example of the novelist Graham Greene, whose chart contains a massive Fiveness configuration, and who seems to have used this Fiveness in a completely non-addictive way, by constantly creating fresh versions of himself. As I said in *TSON*, "a person who is strong in Fiveness is good at creating structures, and this means that he is able to create a whole variety of structures: if he is dissatisfied with one structure, he can knock it down and build another". Somehow - perhaps because of the centrality of Mercury in his Fiveness cluster: (ME-*5*-JU)-*5*/*5*-SA) - he was able to free himself from the habit-forming tendencies of his Fiveness and to use it in a more continuously creative way.

Thus, when two planets are linked by a quintile or bi-quintile aspect (5th harmonic), the tendency towards *ordering* and *structuring* comes easily and naturally. (Note that I mean *ordering* in the sense of "placing things in order", not in the sense of "giving orders".) If they are linked in the 10th or 20th harmonic (10 = 5 x 2; 20 = 5 x 2 x 2) there is also an element of Twoness: the person is *striving* to place things in order and to create systems and structures. If they are linked in the 15th harmonic (15 = 5 x 3) there is an element of Threeness: the person obtains *pleasure* from ordering and structuring (and so often the 15th harmonic carries the idea of *playfulness* and the enjoyment of playing games). If they are linked in the 30th harmonic (30 = 5 x 3 x 2), Twoness, Threeness and Fiveness are all present: *striving* towards *pleasure* in *structuring*.

Finally there is the 25th harmonic, which is 5 x 5. When we discussed Threeness, we said that the 9th harmonic (3 x 3) was about *pleasure in pleasure*. On this analogy, we can say that the 25th harmonic represents *structuring of structuring*. We have already given some examples of "25" aspects, but here we can mention some more cases in order to discover what this means in practice.

The film star Hedy Lamarr (Figure 4.19) has a cluster of (((SA-*1*-PL)-*5*-UR)-*25*/25/*25*-ME)-*25*/25/25/*25*-NE. Thus we can see that Mercury (which is in Scorpio in the 5th house) is linked in the 25th harmonic with four of the outer planets.

Lamarr was a brilliant actress (not afraid, in the film *Ecstasy* at the age of 18, to be filmed nude and to be shown facially in the throes of orgasm), but she said, "Any girl can be glamorous. All you have to do is stand still and look stupid". She was also a brilliant inventor (designing, among other things, a jam-proof radio guidance system for torpedoes), but she said: "The world isn't getting any easier. With all these new inventions I believe that people are hurried more and pushed more". She was an inspired wartime fundraiser (going on stage with a sailor and telling the audience that she would kiss him if enough people bought war bonds). She was married and divorced six times (she said, "I must quit marrying men who feel inferior to me"), but spent the last 35 years of her life living alone. She also said, "My favourite pastime is talking about myself. I love it."

From this it is clear that Lamarr was an exceptionally skilled operator at the level of Fiveness, brilliant at shaping both herself and the outside world in new and inventive ways, but that she was also unusually self-aware in relation to these activities. She was aware of

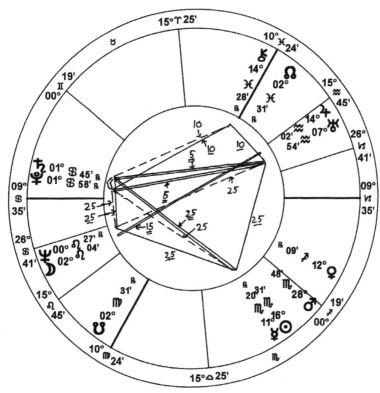

4.19 Hedy Lamarr: Fiveness Aspects

her own "structuring" tendencies and was able to direct, manipulate and comment incisively on them. This would seem to be the result of her Mercury-centred Twenty-fiveness.

Another person with very strong Twenty-fiveness is Harold Wilson (Figure 4.20), who was Prime Minister of the United Kingdom in the 1960s and 1970s. He has ((SO-25-MO)-25/25-NE)-25/25/25-PL (with Sun in Pisces 10th house, and Pluto rising in Cancer). Wilson has been described as "a master of exploiting the theme of Labour unity and finding the compromise formulas".[8] He himself said, "I'm at my best in a messy, middle-of-the-road muddle". That is to say, his skill was in finding ways of *creating order out of chaos*. This was very much in keeping with the spirit of Fiveness, and (as in the case of Hedy Lamarr) it seems that Wilson was very much aware of this "structuring" tendency in himself and was able to utilize it

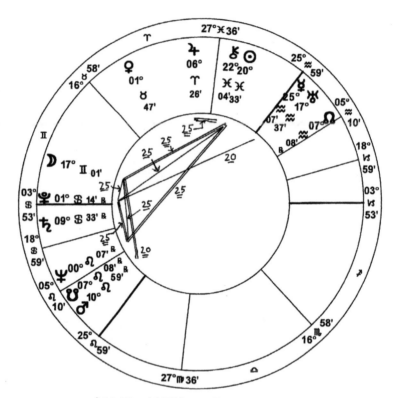

4.20 Harold Wilson: Fiveness Aspects

to maximum effect. This enabled him, despite his lack of personal charisma and lack of strong political principles, to win four elections and to hold the Labour Party together through very difficult times.

Sevenness

When we have used Fiveness to re-shape our world to fit in with our needs, we are able, in Six, to combine Twoness with Threeness in our dealings with the world: that is, to seek *pleasure* in our *actions,* and to *act* in pursuit of *pleasure.*

But then, after Six, we come to a new prime number, Seven: and in Sevenness we become able to *impose new meanings* on the world and on our relationship with the world. We learn to use our *imagination,* our *intuition* and our *insight* to probe beneath the surface appearance of the world and to interpret it in new ways.

In Gareth Hill's typology Sevenness corresponds to the *dynamic feminine*.[3] He says: "The tendency of the dynamic feminine is undirected movement toward the new, the non-rational, the playful. It is the flow of experience, vital, spontaneous, open to the unexpected, yielding and responsive to being acted upon". Here, the word *non-rational* is important. The movement from Fiveness into Sevenness involves a movement from the head into the heart. In the heart, we *know* what is right and true, without needing to work it out rationally.

Michael Harding in *Working with Astrology* says that the 7th harmonic describes "whatever turns you on": that is to say, whatever *inspires* you.[9] When two or more planets come together in a Sevenness aspect, the person is *inspired* by the idea of uniting the energies of those planets. He or she will be motivated to bring those energies together in new and creative ways. Harding reports on a remarkable research study in which "art students at various colleges were requested to give a short description of a painting for which they felt an immediate affinity". It was found that, for each student, the qualities of the chosen painting corresponded closely with the qualities indicated by the links between planets in the student's 7th harmonic chart.

Thus, it is clear that Seven is, like Five, a creative number; but it is creative in an entirely different way from Five. Sevenness is the inspirational force that motivates the creativity; Fiveness is the ability to direct this force into the actual process of creation. Thus, truly creative people tend to have strength both in Sevenness and in Fiveness.

But the creativity of Sevenness has to come from deep inside the person's inner world. Just as the mother gives birth to a baby whom she has nurtured within her body for nine months, so the artist, the writer, the musician, the dancer gives birth to a new creation which he or she has nurtured within the mind and the heart. Thus, Harding also says that "the truth of the 7th harmonic chart is the truth of an *inner reality*, which may or may not get to become imposed upon the world".[9] The planets that are connected by Sevenness aspects give us clues about the nature of this inner reality.

Thus, the person who has many Sevenness aspects will be a person who has an inner *vision* of how the world is, and of his own place in it. He *believes* this vision to be the reality. He may keep his vision to himself, in which case he may come across as quiet, introverted, wrapped up in his own private world. But he may be filled with a desire, or a passion, to share his vision, and impose it on the world. In this case he will, in one way or other, be creative. He will inspire others by his own inspiration.

An outstanding example of a person with a passion to share her vision is Malala Yousafzai, the youngest-ever Nobel Peace Prize laureate, who, both before and after the Taliban attempted to assassinate her, has inspired people throughout the world by her writing and campaigning for women's right to be educated and to be treated equally with men. Malala's Sevenness is exceptionally strong;

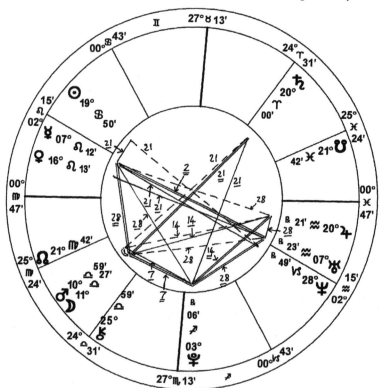

4.21 Malala Yousafzai: Sevenness Aspects

her Sevenness aspects (shown in Figure 4.21) can be listed as follows:

((MO-*1*-MA)-*7*/*7*-PL)-14/14/*14*-JU
         -*21*/21/*21*-SA
((MO-*7*-PL)-14/*14*-JU)-*28*/28/*28*/*28*/28/*28*-(ME-*2*-UR)
(SO-21-ME)-21/*21*-NE
VE-21-UR

It will be seen that all of Malala's planets (except Chiron) are involved in Sevenness aspects, but that the Sun is only weakly involved. Since the Sun is about one's own self-image, this shows that Malala's inner vision (to which she is striving to give creative expression) is not primarily a *personal* vision: that is to say, it is not primarily about how she wants her own life to develop. It is a vision of how she sees the external world; but, with the Moon's heavy involvement in the Sevenness pattern, she is happy to be a vehicle for the realization of this vision.

A different kind of creativity is shown by Eva Pierrakos, whose Sevenness aspects are shown in Figure 4.22. On the website of the International Pathwork Foundation (which she helped to found) it is stated: "Eva began to develop the gift of accessing an inner voice, at first through automatic writing and later by speaking in a trance state. In time the inner voice took shape as the authoritative, incisive and loving persona of the Pathwork Guide".[10] "Accessing an inner voice" is very much a characteristic of Sevenness, especially when Mercury is involved.

Eva's Sevenness pattern is less complex than Malala's, but the *almost exact* cluster of (ME-*1*-JU)-*14*-SO* (with Sun on the Midheaven) makes it very powerful. Eva's inner voice is telling her that her destiny is to share her personal vision with the world through expansive (Jupiterian) communication (but also with Saturnian self-control). (Mercury is also emphasized by being very closely -*8*-NE (with Neptune rising) and -*24*-MO.)

In very many cases (including Malala and Eva) the steadiness and powerfulness of the *inner reality* causes the Sevenness person to have a profound inner peacefulness and stillness, which they retain even

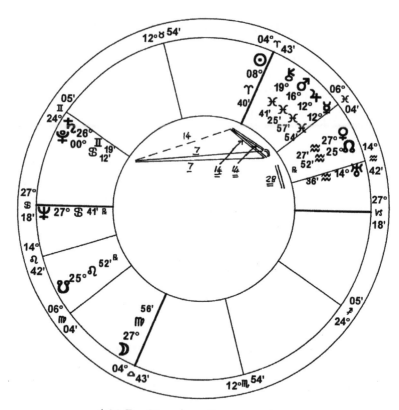

4.22 Eva Pierrakos: Sevenness Aspects

when they are acting energetically in the world. But there are also cases where this inner stillness is absent, because the *inner reality* itself contains elements of restlessness and conflict. This happens especially when there is a preponderance of "14" and "28" aspects: that is, aspects in which Sevenness is mingled with Twoness. An example of this is the writer Bruce Chatwin, whom I discussed in *TSON* pp.112-4, and whose Sevenness aspects are shown in Figure 4.23. These aspects can be listed as follows:

(SO*-_1_-UR*)-14/_14_-MO
(ME-_7_-VE)-_21_-MO
    -14/14/14/_14_-(NE-_7_-PL)
(UR-_3_-NE)-_21_/_7_-PL
JU-_14_-CH

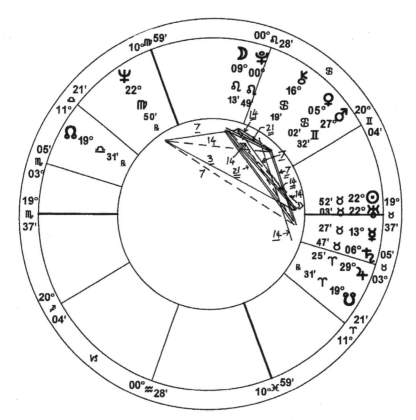

4.23 Bruce Chatwin: Sevenness Aspects

Chatwin's Sevenness pattern is extremely complex, and contains elements of Threeness as well as Twoness; but at its heart is (SO*-*1*-UR*)-14/*14*-MO, which shows that Chatwin's "inner reality" contains an unease, a conflict between his Sun and Moon. This manifested in an extreme restlessness (and in fact Chatwin wrote a book called *Anatomy of Restlessness*), a compulsion to be always on the move in search of new experiences. He talked incessantly, and was never at rest.

Chatwin's work is also an example of the *blurring between fact and fiction* which is sometimes the result of Sevenness. His travel books are not so much an objective report on the places he has visited, but rather an attempt to fit these places into his own inner vision of how the world is. The reader is never sure what is the truth, and what is a figment of the author's imagination.

Another example of this blurring between fact and fiction is Otto Dietrich (Figure 4.24), who was the Press Chief of the Reich under Hitler. Dietrich has an exceptionally strong Sevenness pattern involving all the planets except Moon and Pluto, and including an *exact* ME-Z-NE* with Neptune close to the Ascendant. (In Figure 4.24 "wide" aspects are omitted for the sake of clarity.) One website notes: "Dietrich was responsible for what newspapers printed, and he gained a reputation for never worrying too much about the truth when he wrote an article".[11] The nature of his "inner reality" can be gauged by his statement, "The individual has neither the right nor the duty to exist". However, after the war Dietrich was imprisoned for war crimes, and in prison he wrote a memoir, *The Hitler I Knew*, in which (alone among Nazi leaders) he expressed remorse for his previous actions.

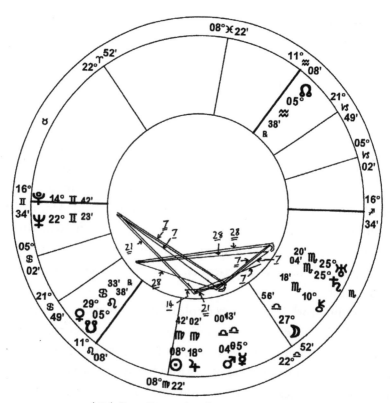

4.24 Otto Dietrich: Sevenness Aspects

Sevenness people sometimes report that they have had strange experiences. These experiences are real to them, because they are in accord with their "inner reality," but other people may be more sceptical. Thus, in *TSON* (pp.109-110) I reported on two people with strong Sevenness, George Van Tassel and Jean Miguères, whose aim in life was to pass on messages which they believed they had received from extra-terrestrial beings. Also there is the man whom AstroDatabank calls "Walk-in from Sirius," (*TSON* p.107) who has one of the strongest Sevenness clusters that I have seen, and who believed that an "entity from Sirius" had taken over his body.

Sevenness is sometimes linked with romantic love, especially when Venus is involved. Thus, the composer Hector Berlioz (*TSON* pp.114-5) has Venus on the Descendant, with Sevenness links to all five of the outer planets. Berlioz has been described as "innately romantic". He was exceptionally sensitive to, and emotionally affected by, physical beauty (easily falling in love) and stirring literature (weeping on reading Shakespeare), and this romantic sensitivity is evident in his music.

An important theme in Sevenness is the *communication of hidden knowledge,* especially when Mercury is involved. Sevenness people are often deeply involved in the study of ancient traditions, in subjects such as archaeology or Egyptology. And also, this includes astrology. It is notable that both John Addey, the "father" of harmonic astrology, and Reinhold Ebertin, the "father" of midpoint astrology, have very strong Sevenness patterns involving Mercury. Both of them devoted their lives to uncovering and communicating the hidden secrets of the universe, and both had a *vision* of how their work would transform astrology. We can also mention Alice Bailey (*TSON* pp.107-9), whose lifelong work was the channelling of spiritual information that she had received from an "entity" whom she called "the Tibetan". In Bailey's case, however, Mercury is not involved in the Sevenness: rather, it is centred on the Moon, which has Sevenness links with Venus, Mars, Saturn, Uranus and Neptune, and it is plain that Bailey saw herself as the *receiver* of the knowledge that she was transmitting.

In *TSON* (pp.117-9) I also described the cases of three murderers (Ira Einhorn, Charles Starkweather and Ian Brady), who all had very strong Sevenness patterns involving Pluto. I do not believe that their Sevenness drove them to murder (very many murderers are weak in Sevenness). But the common factor between these three murderers was that they all believed that they were "above the law," and so were able to murder with impunity. Yet they were all, in the end, caught by the law. Their "inner reality" caused them to have erroneous beliefs about their relationship to society. We could say that they were "living a fantasy": and this danger is always present with Sevenness. The Sevenness person may succeed in imposing his inner reality on society (as Hitler, who was strong in Sevenness as well as Fiveness, did), but it is also true that society may succeed in imposing *its* reality on him, and exposing his inner reality as a fantasy.

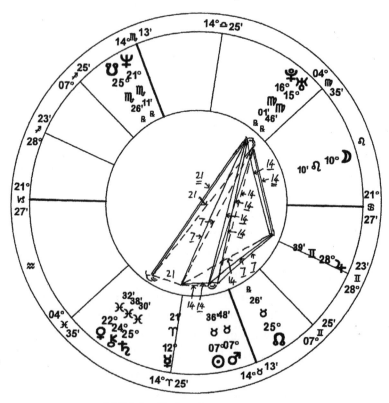

4.25 John Daly: Sevenness Aspects

In some cases Sevenness aspects seem to denote a natural fluency in some activity, which enables the person to perform the activity with an easy spontaneity. Thus, the tennis champion Roger Federer (*TSON* p.112) has (ME-Z-UR)-21-VE-21-PL. Another example is the golfer John Daly (Figure 4.25), who has a Sevenness pattern involving all the planets except Moon, Venus, Saturn and Neptune. One website says that Daly "has won 10 tournaments worldwide despite smoking around 40 Marlboros a day and drinking a dozen cans of diet coke. He has had five PGA Tour suspensions, has paid £65,000 in fines for various misdemeanours, and has been given seven Tour orders to undergo counselling or enter alcohol rehabilitation centres. He has 11 citings for conduct unbecoming a professional, and 21 for 'failing to give best efforts'".[12] It is plain that Daly wins tournaments by sheer Sevenness inspiration and flair, rather than by disciplined application. I have also found several examples of actors and singers with strong Sevenness patterns, whose skill seems to lie in throwing themselves into a performance with reckless abandon.

Thus, pure Sevenness aspects (7th harmonic) denote an *inspirational* link between the planets involved. If the link is in the 14th harmonic (14 = 7 x 2) or the 28th harmonic (28 – 7 x 2 x 2), there is an element of Twoness involved, and we can say that the person is *striving towards inspiration*. If it is in the 21st harmonic (21 = 7 x 3), there is an element of Threeness, and the person finds *pleasure in inspiration*.

It is clear that Sevenness, like other harmonics, contains great potential for both good and evil, and that this can be manifested in many different ways. But I think that one thing can be said with confidence about Sevenness links: they are never dull or boring. They are stimulating and exciting. They speak to the heart rather than the head.

Chapter 5
The Higher Prime Numbers

After Seven there is a break before we come to the next prime number. First we come to Eight, which is 2 x 2 x 2; then to Nine, which is 3 x 3; and then to Ten, which is 2 x 5. And then the sequence of prime numbers resumes with Eleven. This sequence goes on for ever, but we have to stop somewhere, and so in this chapter we will look at the first seven of these higher prime numbers: Eleven, Thirteen, Seventeen, Nineteen, Twenty-three, Twenty-nine, and Thirty-one.

Just as there are qualities of Oneness, Twoness, Threeness, Fiveness and Sevenness, so there are distinct qualities attached to each of the higher prime numbers: Elevenness, Thirteenness, and so on. But these qualities occur less frequently in the natal chart. They indicate something special or unusual in the personality, some way in which the person stands apart from the majority of his or her fellow human beings. So all of these higher prime numbers indicate some kind of *differentness* or *apartness.* But the particular flavour of this *apartness* varies from one number to another. Each of the higher prime numbers indicates a particular way in which a person can demonstrate his own uniqueness or individuality. So we can perhaps say that the sequence of the higher prime numbers represents a series of stages on the road towards human *individuality.*

In *Harmonic Charts* (pp.264-5) I suggested that "as we move along the sequence of prime numbers, we are proceeding further towards *internality:* that is, towards desires, thoughts and feelings which have their origins within the person's mind and are also increasingly introspective (concerned with the contemplation of the person himself), so that they bear no relation to the person's objective situation within his environment". However, I am no longer sure that this is the case. Certainly Two, Three and Five are especially concerned with the person's interaction with the outside world. But it seems to me now that many of the higher harmonics, such as 23 and 29, are not particularly internalized or introspective: they have effects which are very visible in the person's external behaviour.

Elevenness

The first prime number beyond Seven is Eleven, and a key word for Elevenness appears to be *defiance*. The person who is strong in Elevenness stands *defiantly* apart from other people.

In discussing Elevenness we can start with Colin Wilson (Figure 5.1), who clearly embodies this spirit of defiant apartness. Wilson has (SO-*11*-MO)-11-MA, with Sun rising and with Mars at the midpoint of Sun and Moon; also there is (SO-*11*-MO)-*22*-PL and

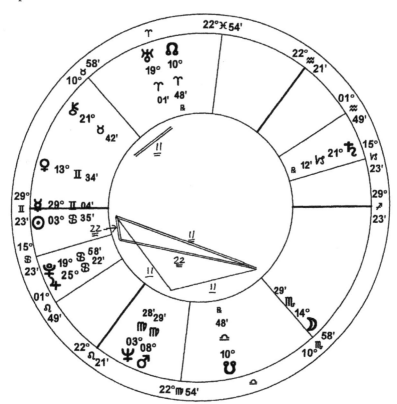

5.1 Colin Wilson: Elevenness Aspects

UR-*11*-CH. This pattern clearly shows how Wilson felt the apartness at the core of his being, and was disposed to express it in assertive and uncompromising ways. He said, "I would like my life to be a lesson in how to stand alone and thrive on it".[1] At the age of 24 he published his best-selling book *The Outsider,* which examined the theme of social alienation in the works of various cultural and literary figures. But, despite the fame that resulted from this book, he continued to lead an isolated life, writing more than 100 books, especially about the occult and paranormal. He described life in modern society as "the day-to-day struggle for intensity that disappears overnight, interrupted by human triviality and endless pettiness".[2]

The French writer Romain Rolland has an exceptionally strong pattern of Elevenness involving MO, MA, JU, SA, UR and NE. Rolland wrote, "Every man who is truly a man must learn to be alone in the midst of all others, and if need be against all others".[3] He also wrote, "We must always fight. God is a fighter, even He Himself. God is a conqueror, he is a devouring lion".[4]

Two racing drivers with very strong Elevenness are A.J. Foyt and Ralph Lee Earnhardt. Foyt's Elevenness cluster involves SO, MA, JU, SA, NE, PL and CH, whereas Earnhardt's involves SO, ME, VE, JU and PL. It would seem that motor racing is a sport particularly suited to the Elevenness temperament, since the driver is on his own, with no contact with his rivals, and yet striving to outdo them by defiant determination. Foyt said, "Determination that just won't quit – that's what it takes", and "You get out in front – you stay out in front".[5]

I have found two politicians with very strong Elevenness: Donald Trump (Figure 5.2) (*TSON* pp.128-9, written before Trump turned to politics) and Winston Churchill (Figure 5.3) (*TSON* pp.132-3). Churchill and Trump are clearly very different people, but they both have the same Elevenness spirit of *defiant apartness.* Churchill, as I wrote in *TSON,* "was sidelined for much of his life by his colleagues, who saw him as too aloof, too self-willed, not a good team player". It has been said of him that he was "wrong about nearly everything until he was right about Hitler". He came into his own during the war, when the qualities of Elevenness were greatly needed. Trump also sees himself as being at war with all the forces that oppose him, and his call to "make America great again" is reminiscent of Churchill's desire to restore the glories of the British Empire.

In Trump's chart there are two separate Elevenness clusters, one solar and one lunar. Firstly he has (SO-**11**-VE)-22/**22**/22/**22**-(ME-**11**-JU) (with ME at the SO/VE midpoint). This cluster shows Trump defiantly promoting himself, telling the world about his positive Venus/Jupiter qualities ("you've got to love me"). And secondly he has (MO-**11**-PL)-22/**22**/22/**22**-(MA*-**11**-SA), which shows him defiantly responding to people who criticize or attack him. In this case PL is at the MA/SA midpoint, showing the ruthlessness and thoroughness with which Trump responds to criticism.

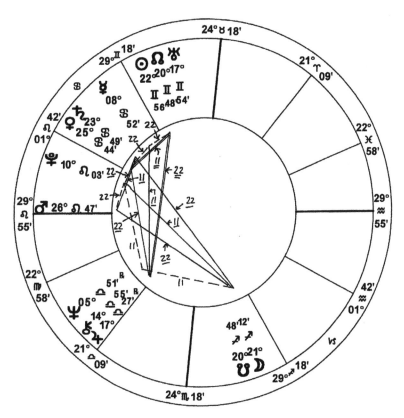

5.2 Donald Trump: Elevenness Aspects

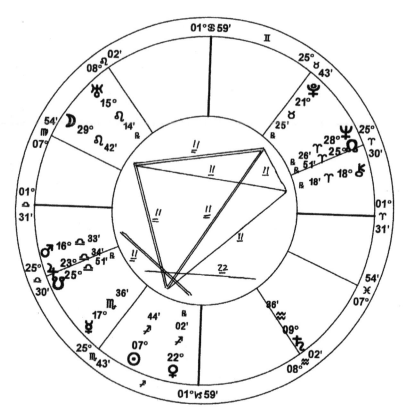

5.3 Winston Churchill: Elevenness Aspects

In Churchill's chart there is a single dominant cluster of (SO-*11*-MO-*11*-PL)-11-CH (with MO at the SO/PL midpoint). The almost exact coming-together of Sun and Moon in the 11th harmonic meant that people were able to see him as the complete embodiment of the Elevenness principle of defiance, united with Plutonian relentlessness and also with a sense that (with Chiron in the 7th house) Churchill would be able, through his defiance against Hitler, to heal their wounds and restore the peace. I feel that it was this cluster, more than anything else in Churchill's chart, which made him a great war leader.

The quality of defiance is evident also in the comedian Richard Pryor (*TSON* pp.127-8), who has an exceptionally strong Elevenness cluster, and also in the film star Jane Fonda, whose cluster of ((SO-*11*-NE)-*11*-UR)-*22/22/22*-ME (with NE at the SO/UR midpoint) motivated her strong opposition to the Vietnam war and her visit to Hanoi which caused her to be dubbed "Hanoi Jane".

The Elevenness person will tend to be solitary, preferring to do things his own way, and not good at working with others in a team. In *TSON* I gave the examples of the painter Paul Gauguin, who fled to Tahiti in order to escape from the expectations of society, and of the jazz trumpeter Humphrey Lyttelton, who went to extraordinary lengths to prevent journalistic intrusions into his private life.

Another quality of Elevenness is *perfectionism*. This is especially noticeable in the case of Fred Astaire (*TSON* pp.125-6), whose cluster of Elevenness involves eight of his planets, and who was notoriously perfectionist in his work, saying "I've never got anything 100% right". People who have strong Elevenness tend to be workaholic and doggedly persistent, never allowing themselves to be deterred by setbacks or by the judgements of others. They may (like Churchill) be subject to depression, or (like Trump) be thin-skinned and easily hurt, but they do not allow these setbacks to deter them from their chosen path. As Churchill said, "I have nothing to offer but blood, toil, tears and sweat," and "We will fight them on the beaches ... we will never surrender".

Thus, when two or more planets are conjunct in the 11th harmonic, their relationship will tend to have this quality of dogged defiance and persistence. If they are conjunct in the 22nd harmonic (22 = 11 x 2), there will also be an element of Twoness: the person will *strive* to unite the energies of the planets in a defiant and persistent way.

Thirteenness

The Thirteenness person, like the Elevenness person, feels himself to be separate and apart from other people; but he is far less confident and secure in his own identity. *He is on a journey in search of himself.* He is seeking an answer to the question "Who am I, really?" He may construct an elaborate mask (or a series of masks) to hide the fact that, underneath the mask, he does not know who he is; or he may withdraw from society, and spend his life in search of his true identity.

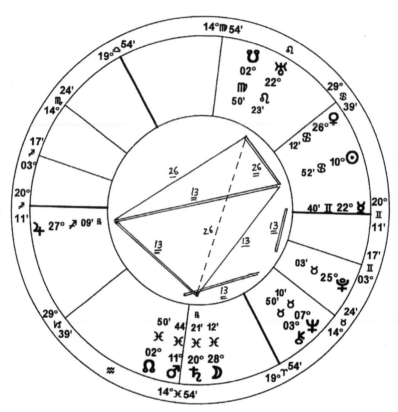

5.4 Hermann Hesse: Thirteenness Aspects

Perhaps the archetypal Thirteenness person is the German writer Hermann Hesse, whom I discussed in *TSON* pp.142-3. Hesse (Figure 5.4) has ((SO-*13*-JU)-*13*/*13*-SA)-*26*/26/26-UR, and also ME-*13*-PL and MA-*13*-NE. In *TSON* I wrote, "He attempted suicide at 15, and throughout his life struggled with manic depression, alcohol addiction, hypochondria and severe headaches. And yet Hesse achieved a degree of happiness and serenity by withdrawing into what Wikipedia calls 'a private life of self-exploration through journeys and wandering'". He wrote, "A man … is not made for life in the collective, but is a solitary king in a dream world of his own creation".[6]

In *TSON* I have given several other examples of Thirteenness people who, in one way or another, spent their lives searching for their own true identity. Some of them, such as the writer Truman Capote and the pop star Janis Joplin, were able to construct a flamboyant persona which can be seen as a mask concealing their uncertainty about who they truly were. In some cases the element of *risk-taking* is very prominent: thus, the list includes Antoine de Saint-Exupéry and Amelia Earhart, who were both pioneer aviators who gloried in risking their lives in the search for the limits of their own capabilities. Also there is Roberta Cowell, who was the first person in Britain (and perhaps the first in the world) to undergo a sex change from man to woman.

On the negative side there is the comic actor Peter Sellers (*TSON* p.140), who had a very close Thirteenness cluster of Sun, Moon and Saturn (Figure 5.5). It was said of Sellers that "he had an extraordinary sense of not being there. He genuinely felt that when he went into a

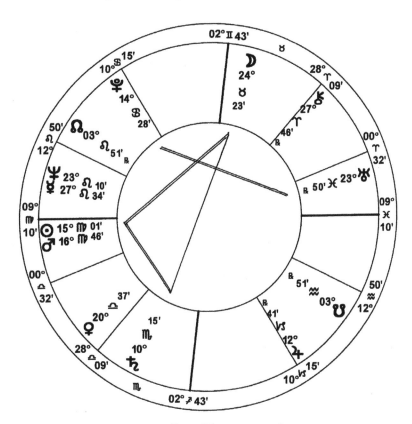

5.5 Peter Sellers: Thirteenness Aspects

room no one could see him".[7] Because of this, he was able to relate to people only by pretending to be someone other than himself. It would seem that, for Sellers, the sense of limitation imposed by Saturn meant that he despaired of finding his own identity; all he could do was construct masks, and his biography by Peter Evans has the title *Peter Sellers, the Mask Behind the Mask*.

For some people with strong Thirteenness, the challenge is to separate their own identity from that of the people who surround them. Also there is often a strong association with death (this is fitting, as the Death card is the 13th card in the Major Arcana of the Tarot pack). Mary Shelley, the author of *Frankenstein* (Figure 5.6), is an outstanding example of both of these tendencies, and so her case is worth studying in more detail. She has a Thirteenness cluster

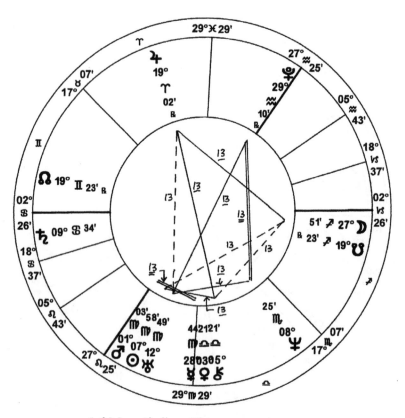

5.6 Mary Shelley: Thirteenness Aspects

involving Sun, Moon, Jupiter and Chiron; another involving Pluto (on the Midheaven), Uranus and Neptune; and also an *exact* ME-*13*-MA.

Mary Shelley was surrounded by famous people. She was the daughter of the political philosopher William Godwin, who is regarded as the first modern proponent of anarchism, and of the pioneering feminist Mary Wollstonecraft, author of *A Vindication of the Rights of Woman.* Twelve days after Mary Shelley's birth, her mother died of a septicaemia infection contracted during the birth. At the age of 17, Mary eloped with the poet Percy Shelley; their romance caused Percy Shelley's first wife, Harriet, to commit suicide. (Mary's half-sister Fanny Imlay also killed herself, and here again Mary may have felt she was partly responsible, as Fanny had pleaded with the Shelleys to be allowed to join them in Switzerland, but her request was turned down.) With Percy, Mary gave birth to four children, three of whom died in infancy. She wrote *Frankenstein* in the summer of 1816 while she and Percy were staying with Lord Byron in Geneva. (It rained every day: 1816 was known as "the year without a summer", as the air was full of debris from the 1815 eruption of the Tambora volcano.) And then on July 8, 1822, when Mary was only 24, Percy was drowned at sea.

Germaine Greer says that *Frankenstein* is about "the nameless female dread of gestating a monster",[8] but my feeling is that the novel is more about Mary's fear of herself *being* the monster; of being the strange, unnatural, nameless creature whose creation causes the deaths of those who created her and surround her. (In the novel the "monster" is never given a name, and we should remember that Mary, whose birth had caused her mother's death, was given her mother's name, so that she had no distinctive name of her own.) Thus, *Frankenstein* represents a dark moment in Mary's Thirteenness search for her own identity.

If we look at Mary's Thirteenness aspects, we see first the Thirteenness links connecting SO, MO, JU and CH, showing that this search for her identity is at the heart of Mary's personality (uniting the Sun and the Moon) and is the route by which she can heal her wounds through creative expression (Chiron in the 5th house) and become expansively involved in group activities (Jupiter in the 11th house). But, with Sun in the 4th house close to Mars and Uranus, her sense of her identity is inescapably bound up with her awareness of the very dynamic, striking and unusual background from which she sprang.

And secondly, we see the Thirteenness links between the three outermost (and most impersonal) planets, Uranus, Neptune and Pluto. This suggests that Mary's search for her own identity was also a search for the identity of the whole of mankind at a time of rapid, and little understood, change (it was the year after the final defeat of Napoleon). The subtitle of *Frankenstein* is *The Modern Prometheus*, because Prometheus had created mankind at the behest of Zeus, and the book raises profound questions about what happens when man becomes able to re-create himself.

Thirdly, Mary has an *exact* Thirteenness link between Mercury and Mars, and I feel that it was this aspect that enabled her, at the age of 18, to test her own limits by writing so forcefully about these issues.

After Percy's death Mary lived on for 28 more years, and never re-married. She wrote many novels and other works, but she never repeated the success of *Frankenstein,* and she was better known for her promotion of her husband's poetry than for her own writings. She died on February 1, 1851, having asked to be buried alongside her mother and father.

Thus, we can say that – although Mary had written, in *Frankenstein,* a work which is more famous, and has had a more lasting influence, than any of the writings of her father, her mother and her husband – she never succeeded in creating an identity for herself which is separate from theirs, and one always thinks of her as Mary Wollstonecraft's daughter and as Percy Shelley's wife.

In summary, then, we can say that, when two or more planets are conjunct in the 13th harmonic, the person will tend to spend his or her life searching for a way of bringing these planets together that helps to answer the question "Who am I, really?" If the planets are conjunct in the 26th harmonic (26 = 2 x 13), there will also be an element of Twoness: the person will be *striving* to bring the planets together in a Thrteenness way.

This search can be either external or internal. Externally, the person may be very adventurous, taking many risks, in an attempt to test his or her own limits. Internally, he or she may be adventurous in exploring their own inner life, and especially their "shadow" side, in an attempt to understand themselves in their totality.

Because he is so preoccupied with self-exploration, the Thirteenness person may tend (like the Elevenness person, but for different reasons) to be solitary. In so far as he has to relate to other people, he may construct a mask, or a false persona, which enables him to survive in the world, even though he knows that the mask is not who he really is. But the search for identity can also bring great rewards. Hermann Hesse, as I have said, achieved happiness and serenity through self-exploration. Also in *TSON* (p.142) I suggested that the German film director Rainer Werner Fassbinder, who had (UR-*13*-NE-*13*-PL)-13-MO and (NE-*13*-PL)-13-SA, was successful in finding the self-awareness which the Thirteenness person craves. Joe Ruffell wrote that Fassbinder's "self-awareness of his own tortuous personality is also the source of his undeniable genius".[9] Because he was so aware of the darkness in himself, he was able to portray it openly in his films. He had come to *accept* himself in his totality.

Seventeenness

After Thirteen, the next prime number is Seventeen. We should note at this point that 2 x 17 is 34, which is a higher number than 32; and, since we are looking only at the first 32 harmonics, this means that in the 17th harmonic we are looking only at conjunctions. Inevitably this means that the incidence of Seventeenness in the chart is lower than that for the prime numbers from 1 to 13. Although there are some charts that contain strong clusters of Seventeenness, it is very rare that Seventeen is the strongest number in the chart. Even if a person is very strong in Seventeenness, it is likely that he or she will be even stronger in one or more of the lower prime numbers.

Once again, Seventeen introduces a new quality. People who are strong in Seventeenness tend again to feel themselves to be *apart* from other people, but this time there is more of a spirit of *rebelliousness*. They feel dissatisfied with the world in which they find themselves, and they want to change it if they can. They feel themselves to be on a mission: they are campaigning for a better world. Often they are very clever with the use of words, using them with devastating effect in their campaigning. If they feel that they cannot change the world, they may rely on cutting humour, undermining their enemies through wit and satire.

In *TSON* I presented several examples of this. Among them were Madalyn Murray O'Hair, who has a Seventeenness cluster involving MO, ME, VE, JU and UR, and who spent her life campaigning for the cause of atheism and trying to prove the non-existence of God; the philosopher Bertrand Russell, who has (SO-*1*-MA)-*17*/17-SA (with an *exact* SO-*17*-SA), and who was imprisoned at the age of 86 as a result of his campaign against nuclear weapons; and the actress Vanessa Redgrave, who has two strong Seventeenness clusters, and has been a lifelong political activist. Also I presented the case of L. Ron Hubbard, the founder of Scientology, who has (JU-*17*-SA)-*17*-SO and also (MO-*17*-NE)-*17*/*17*-MA, and whose campaigning has been for the dissemination of his own ideas.

Here I will focus on two cases. The first of these is the Jungian psychologist James Hillman, whose Seventeenness links are shown in Figure 5.7.

Hillman has been described as "a US psychologist who concluded that therapy needed to change the world rather than focus on people's inner lives", and also as "a dedicated subversive – witty and original – and an heir to the Jungian tradition, which he reimagined with unceasing brilliance". In his many books (of which perhaps the best-known is *Re-Visioning Psychology*) he "proposed an 'archetypal'

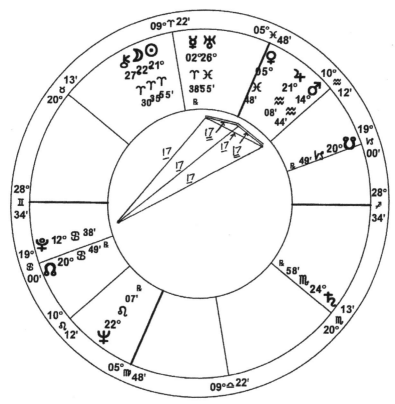

5.7 James Hillman: Seventeenness Aspects

or 'imaginal' psychology that would restore the soul, or psyche, to a discipline he believed to have been diminished by scientific and medical models .... His unrelenting cultural critique embraced everything from masturbation to plastic surgery, and the design of ceilings to US foreign policy".[10]

Hillman's chart shows a very strong Seventeenness cluster: ((VE*-_17_-MA)-_17_/_17_-UR)-_17_-PL. We should note that Venus is on the Midheaven and is at the midpoint of Mars and Uranus. We can see Venus on the Midheaven in Pisces as an indication of Hillman's goal of introducing "soul" as a key concept in psychology. (He wrote: "By soul I mean the imaginative possibility in our nature, the experiencing through reflective speculation, dream, image, fantasy – that mode which recognizes all realities as primarily symbolic or metaphorical".[11]) The Seventeenness links from Venus to Mars and Uranus in the 9th and 10th houses show that Hillman will pursue this goal in a forceful, original and ground-breaking way, campaigning to change society through his insights. And also, these planets are all -17- Pluto in the 1st house, showing the dedication and persistence with which Hillman devoted himself to these goals. The description of him as a "dedicated subversive, witty and original" is very fully borne out by these aspects.

Our second case is Dorothy Parker, who is remembered especially for her witty one-liners (very many of them at her own expense), but who was also a writer of poems, short stories, and film scripts. Her first collection of poems *Enough Rope* was described by a critic as "caked with a salty humour, rough with splinters of disillusion,

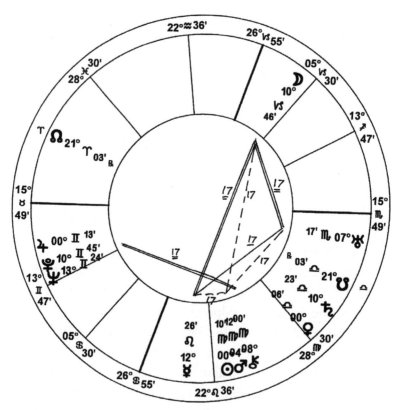

5.8 Dorothy Parker: Seventeenness Aspects

and tarred with a bright black authenticity".[12] However, Parker was dismissive of her wisecracking ability. In her later years she became a political activist, enthusiastically supporting various left-wing causes; she was suspected of being a Communist, and was blacklisted by the film industry during the McCarthy years. When she died, she left her estate to Martin Luther King, Jr.

Dorothy Parker's Seventeenness aspects are shown in Figure 5.8. She has a cluster of ((MO-*17*-ME)-*17*/17-UR)-17-MA. The close Seventeenness links between Moon, Mercury and Uranus are very descriptive of her quickfire wit: they show her responding to events with sharp, original and incisive communication, and with the Seventeenness quality of subversiveness. Her political activism is also very much in the spirit of Seventeeness: she wanted to change the world.

(There is also a very close NE-*17*-CH, but I feel that this isolated aspect between two of the outer planets is of only minor importance.)

Thus, we can say that, when two or more planets come together in the 17th harmonic, their relationship will have the quality of rebelliousness and subversiveness.

Nineteenness

The next prime number after Seventeen is Nineteen: and at this point I have to say that the quality of Nineteenness seems to me to be more elusive, more mysterious, and more difficult to capture in words, than that of any of the other prime numbers that we are considering. I will therefore discuss Nineteenness at greater length, in an effort to probe, and if possible to solve, the mystery of its meaning.

I will start (as I did in *TSON*) with the composer Jean Sibelius, because his Nineteenness is exceptionally strong. Sibelius's Nineteen-ness links are shown in Figure 5.9. He has a cluster of (SO-*19*-JU-*19*-SA)-19-MO-19-VE, and all of these planets except Moon are at the bottom of the chart, in the 2nd, 3rd and 4th houses.

Sibelius's earlier compositions, such as the first two symphonies

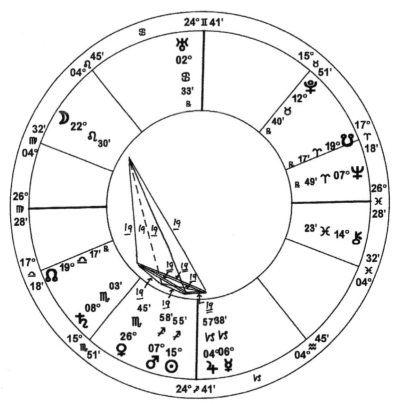

5.9 Jean Sibelius: Nineteenness Aspects

and the tone poem *Finlandia,* are rousing and inspiring, and may
have been born not so much out of Nineteenness but out of (ME-
1-JU)-2/*2*-UR* and other aspects in his chart. These compositions
caused Sibelius to be a national hero in Finland, but he did not
enjoy this fame, and retreated more and more into the solitude of
the countryside. It has been said of him: "Very few men have such
an intimate relationship with nature as he had, and all his life it was
a source of inspiration and joy".[13] His later compositions, such as
the Seventh Symphony and the tone poem *Tapiola,* are essentially
expressions of this "intimate relationship with nature": in them,
Sibelius is immersing himself completely in the rhythms of nature,
"going with the flow" of the natural world. For the last thirty years
of his life, Sibelius composed no music at all; he was content to live

in close communion with nature, without needing to give it creative expression.

We can now turn to another creative artist with exceptionally strong Nineteenness: Lita Albuquerque, who has been described as "an internationally renowned installation, environmental artist, painter and sculptor. She has developed a visual language that brings the realities of time and space to a human scale and is acclaimed for her ephemeral and permanent art works executed in the landscape and public sites".[14] Albuquerque's Nineteenness links are shown in Figure 5.10. She has a massive cluster of (SO-*1*-MO)-***19***/19/19/19/19/19-((SA-***19***-UR*)-19/***19***-PL) (with MO, UR and PL also -19-NE*).

It seems plain that Albuquerque, like Sibelius, has an "intimate relationship with nature", and that her artistic compositions can be

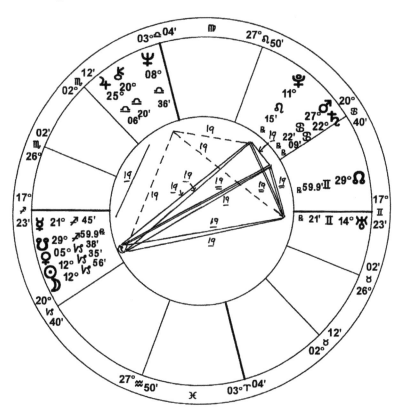

5.10 Lita Albuquerque: Nineteenness Aspects

seen as the visual equivalent of Sibelius's music. As with Sibelius, her instinctive feeling for the rhythms of nature is a "source of inspiration and joy". She has said, "Sometimes I'm amazed that I spend my days creating magic and fantasy and that people buy it. It's like connecting with the inner child in me. I'm just having a great time, and I'm chuckling to myself that this is really happening, that I can do this with my life".[15]

However, not all creative people with strong Nineteenness are in communion with nature. For some, it is more about immersing oneself in the human environment in which one finds oneself, and "going with the flow" of human interactions and human society. As an example, we can take Toni Collette, an Australian actress who has

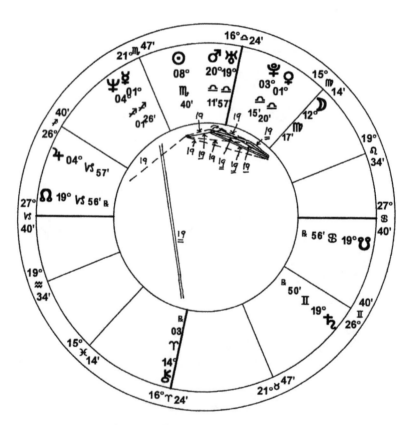

5.11 Toni Collette: Nineteenness Aspects

((MA*-*1*-UR*)-*19*/*19*/19/19-(MO-*19*-VE))-19/19/19/19-SO   (see Figure 5.11). Toni Collette has a great many quotes on the internet, which give a clear picture of her attitude to life.[16] Thus, she has said "I'm very happy with my lot" (this seems to be a frequent theme among Nineteenness people); also, "There are actors who are really fantastically talented at being natural on screen and appearing to be themselves, but I like the challenge of becoming someone else"; also, "I try to play real people who inspire me through something in their journey"; also, "If my boyfriend says 'You look gorgeous', I kinda feel funny. I don't know if I'm particularly comfortable with being attractive".

It seems clear that for Collette, as also for Sibelius and Albuquerque, there is no great interest in self-promotion. They are not interested in putting their own personalities on display, or on gaining recognition for their own qualities. Rather, their interest is in immersing themselves in their environment (either the natural or the human environment) and finding ways to express their appreciation of this environment. Thus, there are also people with strong Nineteenness who, in spite of their fame, present themselves as very "ordinary" people, without any strong personality characteristics. They are, one could say, extraordinary for their ordinariness.

An example of this is Gerald Ford, the 38th President of the USA. (38 is 2 x 19, but I expect this is a coincidence.) Ford's chart (Figure 5.12) shows a cluster of ((SO-*19*-MO)-19/*19*-JU)-19-SA.

Ford is the only person ever to have become President without having stood for election either as President or Vice-President. He was chosen as Vice-President by the Senate when Richard Nixon's Vice-President Spiro Agnew resigned, and then became President when Nixon himself resigned. Ford had not wanted to be President; his highest ambition had been to become Speaker of the House. But, having gained the Presidency, he seems to have enjoyed it.

One website says: "By all accounts, Ford was open, friendly, forthright, honest and considerate. He appeared to genuinely like people, and, although a more than 30-year veteran of political

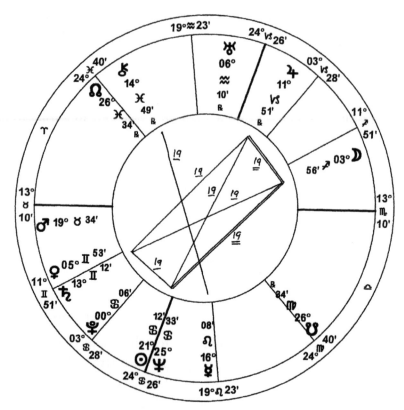

5.12 Gerald Ford: Nineteenness Aspects

wars, made remarkably few enemies along the way".[17] Ford's most controversial action during his brief Presidency was to grant a pardon to his predecessor Richard Nixon for all his crimes. This pardon caused outrage across America, and one website says that Ford "was stunned by the vehemence of the public's reaction. Forgiveness was so great a part of Ford's nature that he thought the American people would be forgiving, that they would accept Nixon's resignation as punishment enough".[18] *Forgiveness was a part of his nature:* I believe that this describes Ford's Nineteenness.

Another example is the film star Gregory Peck, who has a very close cluster of SO-*19*-UR*-*19*-PL, with Uranus close to the Midheaven. One would think that, in any other harmonic, the coming together of Sun, Uranus and Pluto would signify a very striking and unusual personality; but in the 19th harmonic this seems not to be the case. Peck has been described as follows: "Serious, restrained and intelligent, though never very exciting, he was one of Hollywood's most enduring stars ... A pillar of moral rectitude, standing up for decency and tolerance".[19] Like so many Nineteenness people, he gave himself no credit for his own success. He said, "I just do things I really enjoy. I enjoy acting. When I'm driving to the studio, I sing in the car. I love my work and my wife and my kids and my friends. And I think, 'You're a lucky man, Gregory Peck, a damn lucky man".[20]

Finally, we can mention the case of Eva Peron. I say this with some hesitation, because Eva Peron's birth chart is rated DD ("dirty data") by AstroDatabank, and some sources have given a different date and even a different year. However, the former mayor and publisher of

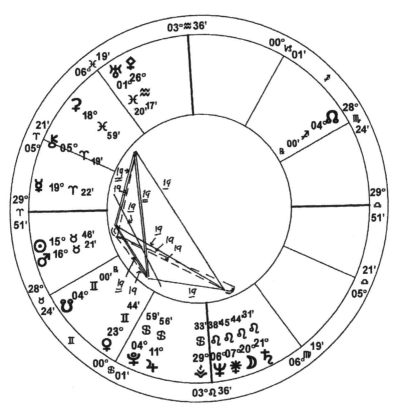

5.13 Eva Peron: Nineteenness Aspects, with Asteroids

the local paper has said, "I can assure you" that Eva was born at 5.00 a.m. on May 7, 1919. So this *may* be the correct data; and, if it is the correct data, it says something very important about the nature of Nineteenness.

In Figure 5.13 I have shown Eva Peron's Nineteenness aspects, and I have included the asteroids in order to show the links to the asteroid Ceres. The chart shows a cluster of (SO-*19*-VE-*19*-CE)-*19*-MO)-*1*/19/19/19-MA. (Also there is ME-19-JU.) Thus, in this chart, the Sun and the Moon (the two centres of Eva's personality) are united in Nineteenness with Venus, the planet of feminine beauty and attractiveness, and Ceres, the planet of mothering, caring and nurturing.

Eva Peron was a fighter, as befits a person with Sun closely conjunct Mars in the 1st house. She fought to get to the top from her humble origins, and, having arrived at the top, she fought for women's rights and for the rights of the poor and dispossessed. But I believe that the Argentinian people, in showering Eva with an almost religious adoration and in giving her the title of "Spiritual Leader of the Nation", were doing more than expressing gratitude for her work on their behalf. They were responding to something deeper in her personality. They could sense that she really cared for them, really empathized with them, and really accepted them for who they were. And these, in my view, are among the qualities of Nineteenness.

We have looked now at several cases of people with very strong Nineteenness, and I feel that they all share a quality which can perhaps best be described as *empathy*. They empathize with their surroundings and seek to immerse themselves in those surroundings, even if this means losing some of their own individuality. For Sibelius and Albuquerque this empathy is primarily with their natural surroundings, whereas in other cases it is with the people who surround them.

Nineteenness is in a sense the opposite of the rebellious spirit of Seventeenness. Nineteenness people *accept* the world as they find it, and do not seek to change it. They tend to be *forgiving* and *non-judgmental*. They tend to be happy with their present lot, and so are lacking in personal ambition. (In *TSON* I said that Nineteenness people tended to avoid fame, but I am not now sure that this is true. They may not seek fame, but, if they find it, in most cases they accept it, just as they also accept obscurity.) There is a receptivity to whatever life presents, allowing external circumstances to "just happen" to them, and being willing to learn from and be grateful for these experiences.

As I said in *TSON* (page 167), I think there may be a negative side of Nineteenness, in that the Nineteenness person may sometimes be so accepting of (we could say complacent about) their circumstances that they are reluctant to accept their responsibilities as an agent of change. This could be a problem, especially if he or she has responsibility for other people, for instance as a parent or as an employer.

We have been looking at people with many Nineteenness aspects. But what can we say about isolated Nineteenness aspects between two planets? For instance, in my own chart I have SO-19-PL. How should this aspect be interpreted?

Since we are saying that people with many Nineteenness aspects tend to be *accepting, empathic* and *non-judgmental,* it follows that the same qualities should be present in isolated Nineteenness aspects. Thus, we can take my own SO-19-PL. Sue Tompkins says that Sun-Pluto aspects are about the "hidden self": individuals with Sun-Pluto contacts "take pains to *hide* themselves".[21] I feel that SO-19-PL shows that I am *accepting* and *non-judgmental* about my own need for privacy and my tendency to "hide" certain aspects of myself, and also that I am *empathic* towards others who have the same need (this has helped me as a psychotherapist). Also, with Sun in the 6th house and Pluto in the 5th, I tend to want to immerse myself creatively and empathically in other people's inner worlds – which is what I am trying to do in writing this book. (I may seem to be painting a rosy picture of myself here, so I hasten to add that there are many other aspects in my chart that are much more problematic.)

So we can perhaps say that, when two or more planets come together in the 19th harmonic, their relationship has the quality of *acceptance* and *empathy*. The precise way in which this will be interpreted will vary from case to case.

Twenty-threeness

After Nineteen, the next prime number is Twenty-three, and this number again has its own unique quality. A key word for Twenty-threeness appears to be *inventiveness*. Many people who are strong in Twenty-threeness have a remarkable ability to invent new ways of behaving, new ways of living their lives, which cause them to stand apart from the crowd and to present themselves as unique and original individuals. Typically they are not withdrawing from society; rather, they are interacting with society in ways that are unique to themselves. They could be described as "character actors". It is as though they are telling a story, a story in which they themselves are the central characters.

I have presented several examples of this in *TSON*. One of the most striking is Marie Duplessis (*TSON* pp.169-70), whose real-life story was the inspiration for Dumas's novel *La Dame aux Camélias* and for Verdi's opera *La Traviata*. She was born into abject poverty, but she taught herself to read, write, dance, and play the piano, and she became fully accepted as a member of the Parisian aristocracy, with many lovers including the composer Franz Liszt; but she died of tuberculosis ("consumption") at the age of 23. Clearly (as one of her admirers said) she had an "incomparable charm", but it is also clear that she was used, and sexually abused, by the men whom she charmed. In a letter to Liszt (written not long before her death) she wrote:

> "I shall not live; I am an odd girl, and I shan't be able to hold on to this life which I don't know how not to lead and that I can equally no longer endure. Take me, take me anywhere you like; I shan't bother you, I sleep all day; in the evening you can let me go to the theatre; and at night you can do with me what you will."[22]

Her chart (Figure 5.14) shows that Marie Duplessis has SO-23-MO, showing that Twenty-threeness is at the core of her personality

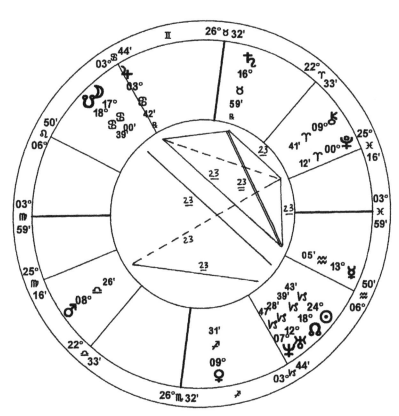

5.14 Marie Duplessis: Twenty-threeness Aspects

and she is naturally disposed towards "telling a story" about herself. Also she has a cluster of (ME-**23**-SA)-23-JU-23-PL, showing that the story which she is telling unites Mercury with Jupiter in the 11th house (expansion into society), Pluto in the 8th (sexual exploitation), and Saturn near the Midheaven (ultimate tragedy). (I suspect that actually she was born somewhat earlier than 8.00 p.m., bringing Jupiter into the 11th house and Saturn closer to the Midheaven.) And also she has MA-**23**-UR, perhaps denoting a story of sexual experimentation.

Another example is the serial murderer Charles Sobhraj (*TSON* pp.176-7), who is thought to have killed (mostly by poisoning) at least 20 people in seven Asian countries during the 1970s. "Handsome, charming and fluent in several languages, he was a skilled con artist who often targeted the young backpackers on the 'Hippie Trail'".[23]

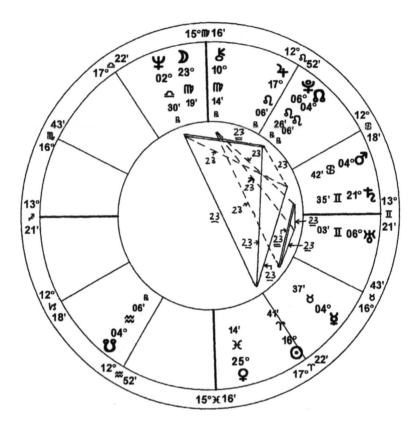

5.15 Charles Sobhraj: Twenty-threeness Aspects

He killed in order to rob his victims of their money and possessions and sustain his adventurous lifestyle, although he has also said that "he never kills good people, rather he rids society of all the evil".[24] Four books and three documentaries have been made about his life.

Sobhraj clearly displays to an outstanding extent the Twenty-threeness quality of *inventiveness*. He is telling a unique story, with himself as the hero or anti-hero. His chart (Figure 5.15) shows two strong Twenty-threeness clusters, one involving SO, MA, NE and PL, and the other involving ME, SA, UR* and CH. Perhaps we can say that the first cluster represents the story of himself as the ruthless and visionary action-man, and the second (with Saturn and Uranus straddling the Descendant) represents the story of the clever plotting by which he destroys his enemies and evades justice.

Many people with strong Twenty-threeness are inventive in telling stories, not only about themselves, but also about imaginary people. Among these we have:

- The short-story writer O. Henry (*TSON* pp.170-1), who has an exceptionally strong Twenty-threeness cluster of ((MO-**23**-SA-**23**-NE)-23/**23**/23-MA)-23/23/23/**23**-UR. O. Henry was a compulsive writer of stories, as well as having a highly original and opportunistic lifestyle.

- The poet Dylan Thomas (*TSON* pp.168-9), who, as well as living a wild life as a drunken poet, created in his radio play *Under Milk Wood* an array of extremely original and comical fictional characters. Thomas has three Twenty-threeness clusters: (SO-**23**-UR*)-23/**23**-MA; (VE-**23**-JU*)-23-CH; and ((SA-**1**-PL)-**23**/**23**-ME)-23-MO.

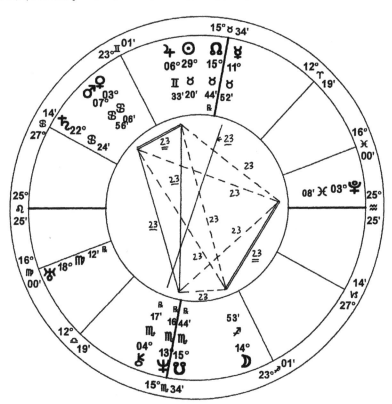

5.16 Honoré de Balzac: Twenty-threeness Aspects

- Hans Christian Andersen (*TSON* pp.173-4), the author of fairytales including *The Ugly Duckling* and *The Emperor's New Clothes,* has ((JU-**23**-UR*)-**23**/**23**-PL)-23-SO, and also (VE-**23**-MA)-23-ME and MO-**23**-CH.

- The novelist Honoré de Balzac (Figure 5.16) has a cluster of ((MA-**23**-JU)-**23**-NE*))-23-(MO-**23**-PL*) and also ME*-**23**-CH. One website describes his "efforts to set himself up as a dazzling figure in society ... He was avid for fame, fortune and love but was above all conscious of his own genius".[25] He was a compulsive writer, and his major work *La Comédie Humaine* is a sequence of almost 100 novels, short stories and plays, containing thousands of multi-faceted characters. Clearly, like the other people listed here, he was very inventive both in creating a story-line for his own life and in creating stories about the lives of others.

Finally I would like to mention the case of Tony Blair, who was Prime Minister of the United Kingdom from 1997 to 2007. As shown in Figure 5.17, Blair has a very tight cluster of SO-**23**-MO*-**23**-NE, with Saturn also involved because of the very close SA-NE conjunction. (If we include the asteroids, then Pallas, the planet of "feminine wisdom," is also involved: (SO-**1**-PA)-**23**-MO*-**23**-NE.)

In the U.S.A., the decision to invade Iraq in 2003 was the result of a collective policy consolidated by President Bush and his advisers over a period of time; but in the U.K., the decision to join in the invasion was very much Tony Blair's choice. He used his considerable powers of persuasion to obtain the consent of Parliament for the invasion, in spite of the opposition of many people in his own party, and in spite of the fact that two million people had demonstrated in London against the invasion. My belief is that this was the result of the Twenty-threeness in his chart. With SO-**23**-MO* he is very much a Twenty-threeness person, needing to show the world that he stands apart from the crowd and is capable of original, daring and inventive actions; and the close involvement of Neptune shows that this is tied in with a visionary tendency which is perhaps capable of delusion.

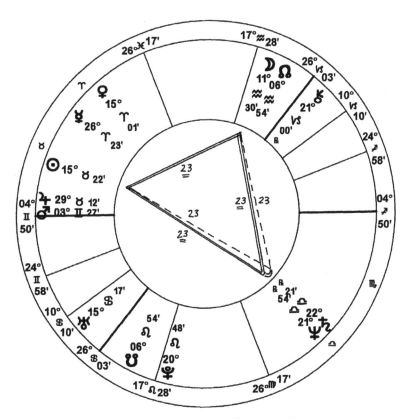

5.17 Tony Blair: Twenty-threeness Aspects

For a creative artist, Twenty-threeness can clearly be a very positive force, but for a politician it has its dangers, and, as I said in *TSON* (p.216), "I feel that the United Kingdom is lucky to have emerged relatively unscathed from ten years of being led by a Twenty-threeness person like Tony Blair".

In *TSON* (page 179) I said: "The Twenty-threeness person is a dreamer, a spinner of tales and fantasies. He or she dreams of living life to the full, playing a part in the fairytale, becoming the embodiment of the dream". However, I feel now that this is not entirely correct. Certainly the Twenty-threeness person has dreams and aspirations, but the people we have looked at have been remarkably successful in finding inventive ways of translating the dream into reality. Of course, by looking at the charts of famous people, we have been choosing the *most successful* Twenty-threeness people, and there may well be people with strong Twenty-threeness who live humdrum lives and find themselves unable to live their dreams. But my feeling is that the inventive spirit of Twenty-threeness is so strong that it will always break through in one way or another.

Thus, when two or more planets come together in the 23rd harmonic, we can say that the relationship between these planets will have this quality of *inventiveness*. The person will seek to express this relationship in original, startling and highly individualistic ways.

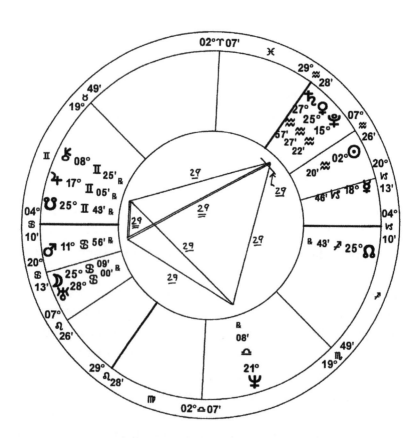

5.18 Lord Byron: Twenty-nineness Aspects

Twenty-nineness

After 23 there is a gap (because the next two odd numbers, 25 and 27, are not primes), and then we come to 29 and 31, which are the last two prime numbers that we will discuss in this book.

When we look at charts that are very strong in Twenty-nineness, it would be easy to conclude that the essence of Twenty-nineness is about sexual freedom, or lack of sexual inhibition. I gave several examples of this in *TSON*. One example is that of the poet Lord Byron (*TSON* pp.183-4). Figure 5.18 shows that Byron had a cluster of ((VE*-**29**-MA*)-**29**/**29**-JU)-**29**-NE, and also SA*-**29**-PL. Byron fled to Venice so as to be free to indulge his sexual desires, and he had innumerable affairs with both men and women, including (allegedly) his own half-sister. The involvement of both Venus and Mars in the

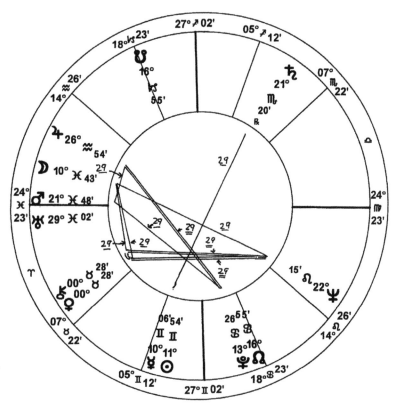

5.19 Allen Ginsberg: Twenty-nineness Aspects

Twenty-nineness cluster suggests that it is descriptive of his sexuality, rather than of other sides of his complex personality.

We can also look at another poet, Allen Ginsberg (*TSON* pp.184-5). Figure 5.19 shows that Ginsberg has two Twenty-nineness clusters, which we can call a Venus cluster and a Mars cluster: ((VE-*1*-CH)-*29*-NE)-29-MO, and (JU-*29*-PL)-29-MA*; also he has ME-29-SA.

Ginsberg has been described as "the embodiment of the ideals of personal freedom, nonconformity, and the search for enlightenment".[26] Although the search for sexual freedom was only a part of this, it was an important part. Ginsberg was aware of his sexual feelings from the age of seven. He was homosexual, and wrote openly about his homosexuality, at a time when this was rare. His best-known poem *Howl* was for a time banned as obscene, and his poem *Iron Horse* is partly a tantric meditation following masturbation in a train. Plainly Ginsberg, like Byron, felt himself to be free of the sexual inhibitions by which many people feel constrained.

However, I feel that, in spite of the prominence of the sexual theme in these and other cases, it is not central to the quality of Twenty-nineness. Rather, Twenty-nineness is more widely about freedom from the constraints imposed by society – the freedom to express one's own individuality. Thus, we can also look at some other cases of strong Twenty-nineness in which the issue of sexuality does not seem to be central.

We can, for example, look at yet another poet, Edith Sitwell (*TSON* p.182), who has a cluster of ((MO-*29*-PL*)-29-MA)-29/29/29-SO, and also SA-29-NE*. SO-29-MO shows that Twenty-nineness is central to her personality. Edith Sitwell gloried in her uniqueness, her difference from other people, although she said, "I am not eccentric. It's just that I am more alive than most people. I am an unpopular electric eel set in a pond of goldfish".[27] She dressed outrageously, and was, as the writer Elizabeth Bowen said, "like an altar on the move". She also said, "I have often wished I had time to cultivate modesty… but I am too busy thinking about myself".[28]

Another case is Diana Mosley (see Figure 5.20), who has a

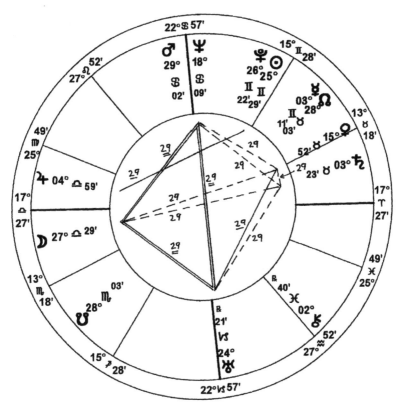

5.20 Diana Mosley: Twenty-nineness Aspects

very strong Twenty-nineness cluster of ((MO-_29_- UR*-_29_-NE*)-29/29/_29_-VE)-29-SA, and also SO-_29_-JU.

Diana was one of the celebrated Mitford sisters: her sisters were Nancy Mitford, the novelist; Unity Mitford, who was a member of Adolf Hitler's inner circle; Jessica Mitford, who became a Communist and later wrote *The American Way of Death;* and Deborah Mitford, who became the Duchess of Devonshire. When she was young, Diana was regarded as the cleverest and most beautiful of the sisters. She married Bryan Guinness, the heir to the brewery empire, and had two sons by him; but then she divorced him in order to marry Oswald Mosley, the leader of the British Union of Fascists, with whom she was madly in love. Diana and Oswald were married in Germany in the presence of Hitler and Goebbels. During the war she was imprisoned because of her pro-Nazi views. After the war she fled to France, where she lived until her death in 2003.

Diana Mosley never repented of her Nazi past. Michael Shelden has said, "Diana Mosley's stubbornness and aristocratic pride made her reluctant to admit that she had made a profound mistake".She continued to finance the British Union of Fascists, and attend its gatherings, until the death of its founder in 1994. She was not a Holocaust denier, and yet she continued to defend Hitler, saying: "Hitler was attractive, though not handsome, with great inner dynamism and charm ... I don't suppose I've met anyone quite so charming". On the Holocaust, she said, "I'm sure he was to blame for the extermination of the Jews. He was to blame for everything, and I say that as someone who approved of him".[29]

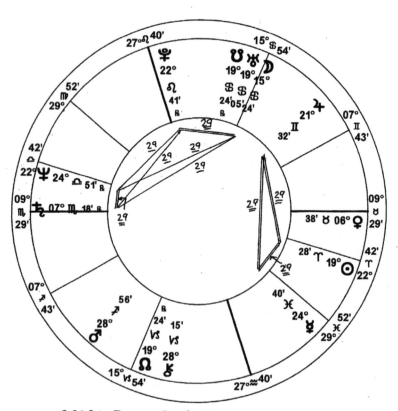

5.21 Iain Duncan Smith: Twenty-nineness Aspects

Before we consider the implications of this for the meaning of Twenty-nineness, I would like to look at another case: that of the British Conservative politician Iain Duncan Smith, who is generally known by his initials "I.D.S." Figure 5.21 shows that I.D.S. has two strong Twenty-nineness clusters: SO-_29_-ME-_29_-JU, and (MO-_29_-PL*)-_29_-(SA*-_29_-NE. Taken together, these clusters add up to one of the strongest Twenty-nineness charts that I have seen.

I.D.S. was unexpectedly elected as leader of the Conservative Party in 2001, during the premiership of Tony Blair. (He won this election largely because he was *not* Kenneth Clarke, the charismatic and controversial politician against whom he was standing.) I.D.S's two years as Leader of the Opposition were generally agreed to have been a total disaster, as he completely lacked the social skills and the "human touch" that were required of him. (He famously said about himself, "Do not underestimate the determination of a quiet man".) He also wrote a political novel, *The Devil's Tune,* which received universally bad reviews and has never been published in paperback.

However, I.D.S. has continued to believe in himself in spite of these setbacks. Since he was replaced as leader of the party, he has continued to work hard on its behalf and to show his commitment to its goals. For six years he was the Secretary of State for Work and Pensions. He claims to have been converted to a commitment to the eradication of poverty when he visited the poverty-stricken Easterhouse housing estate in Glasgow in 2002: but critics say that there is little evidence of this commitment in the policies that he has espoused. One critic has written:

> "How we must hunger for saints in our politics if we accept a man as good purely because he says he is good, while so much of what he does bespeaks falsehood and a perfect absence of empathy."[30]

It seems to me that the cases of Edith Sitwell, Diana Mosley and Iain Duncan Smith show that Twenty-nineness is essentially about having a strong and unshakeable belief in one's own uniqueness. These people have a pride in being themselves, which nothing is going to disturb. Even when the world is telling them that they ought not to believe in themselves, they stubbornly persist in doing so. And I believe that the same is true of Lord Byron, Allen Ginsberg, and other people whom I have found with strong Twenty-nineness.

Thus, we can say that when two or more planets come together in the 29th harmonic, their relationship will have this quality of unshakeable *pride* and *self-belief.* This self-belief is of course an admirable quality, and it can greatly help one to overcome setbacks, to achieve one's objectives, and to find happiness. But the downside is that it may make it hard for one to admit one's mistakes and learn from them, and hard to listen to and empathize with other people. Humility is also an admirable quality, but it is not a quality that one would associate with Twenty-nineness.

Thirty-oneness

Thirty-one is the last prime number that we will examine in this book, and, like the other prime numbers that we have looked at, it has its own distinctive quality. The quality of Thirty-oneness appears to be to do with *delving into the unconscious mind,* and especially into the aspect of the mind which Sigmund Freud called the "id".

According to Freud's theory of personality, "the id is the personality component made up of unconscious psychic energy that works to satisfy basic urges, needs and desires. The id operates on the pleasure principle, which demands instant gratification of needs ... The id is the only part of the personality that is present at birth, according to Freud ... The other components of personality develop as we age, allowing us to control the demands of the id and behave in socially acceptable ways".[31]

If Thirty-oneness is about delving into the unconscious, then it seems appropriate that Sigmund Freud himself should have very strong Thirty-oneness in his natal chart. Figure 5.22 shows that Freud has a cluster consisting of ((JU-*31*-PL*)-31-ME)-31/31/31-SO. Because all of these planets are clustered on the right-hand side of the chart near the Descendant, we could say this shows that Freud

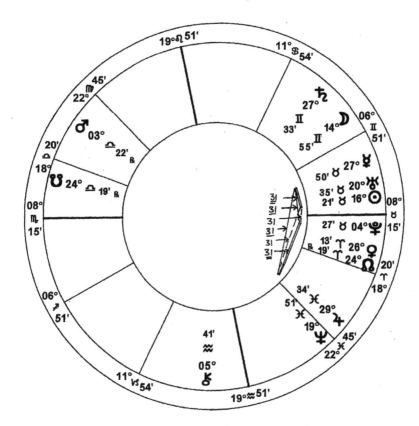

5.22 Sigmund Freud: Thirty-oneness Aspects

was primarily interested in probing the unconscious minds of other people; however, the inclusion of the Sun in the cluster shows how deeply he was himself involved in this search.

Carl Gustav Jung, who initially was a follower of Freud but broke away to found his own system of analytic psychology which is now (arguably) even more influential than that of Freud, also has strong Thirty-oneness. Figure 5.23 shows that Jung has (UR-*31*-PL)-*31*-SO*, also (MO-*31*-ME)-31-SA, and also VE-*31*-CH. Like Freud, Jung devoted his life to the exploration and understanding of the unconscious mind. The planets which are involved in the Thirty-oneness for both Freud and Jung are Sun (deep personal involvement), Mercury (thinking and communication), and Pluto (ruthlessness, persistence, transformation).

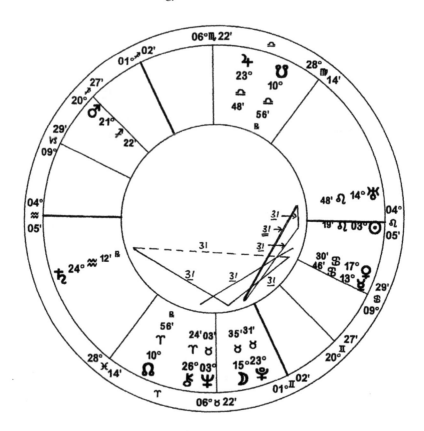

5.23 Carl Gustav Jung: Thirty-oneness Aspects

Thus, Freud and Jung show how the delving into the contents of the unconscious mind, which is facilitated by Thirty-oneness, can be hugely beneficial. It can help one both to understand oneself and to understand and help other people. But also, the ability to access unconscious material and bring it into consciousness can be very dangerous. It can mean that the person's ability to "control the demands of the id and behave in socially acceptable ways" is greatly weakened. The person becomes consciously aware of the id's demands, and may feel swamped by these demands and unable to resist them.

An example of this is the serial murderer John Wayne Gacy, who sexually assaulted, tortured and murdered at least 33 teenaged boys and young men between 1972 and 1978. Gacy's chart (Figure 5.24) shows that he has a cluster of ((SO-*31*-SA*)-31-MA*)-31/31/31-

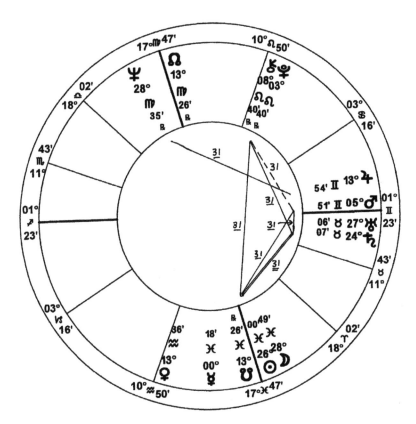

5.24 John Wayne Gacy: Thirty-oneness Aspects

PL, and also JU-<u>31</u>-NE. (Note that Mars and Saturn straddle the Descendant, with Uranus also between them.) One website says that Gacy "was widely respected in the community, charming and easy to get along with … He spent much of his time hosting elaborate street parties for his friends and neighbours, serving in community groups and entertaining children as 'Pogo the Clown'".[32] Yet underneath he had this dark secret, which was eventually uncovered.

In the late 1970s Gacy was the subject of an astrological experiment.[33] Tim Allen and Verle Muhrer gave Gacy's birth chart anonymously to five prominent astrologers, and asked them to comment on whether this person would be suitable for the youth ministry. All of these astrologers returned very positive reports, saying (for instance) that Gacy was "kind, gentle and considerate" and that he had "a marked capacity to uplift others". Allen and Muhrer regarded this as evidence that astrology does not work. But clearly, these astrologers were not using harmonic astrology and so had failed to discover the Thirty-oneness cluster in Gacy's chart. Without this, there was no evidence that Gacy would become a sadistic killer.

In *TSON* I reported on three other sadistic serial killers who, like Gacy, had strong Thirty-oneness clusters. These were:

- The Belgian paedophile murderer Marc Dutroux, who has an exceptionally strong cluster of (((ME*-**31**-MA)-**31**/31-UR)-31/31/31-SA)-**31**/**31**/**31**/31-PL*)-31/31/31/**31**/ 31-MO.

- The Scottish paedophile killer Robert Black, who has SO-**31**-VE-**31**-MA and also JU-**31**-NE-**31**-PL.

- The cannibalistic killer Jeffrey Dahmer, who has ((ME-**31**-MA)-**31**/**31**-NE)-31/31/**31**-MO*. Dahmer told a psychiatrist, "A compulsion with what I was doing overpowered any feelings of repulsion: it was the only thing that gave me satisfaction in life".[34] This is an illustration of how Thirty-oneness can cause a person to be overwhelmed by the id's desires.

The two sides of Thirty-oneness – the investigation of the unconscious mind, and the surrender to its desires – are found together in the case of the Marquis de Sade, whose name is the origin of the word "sadist". Figure 5.25 shows that de Sade has ((MO-**31**-VE)-31-NE)-31-MA, and also (JU-**31**-SA)-**31**-PL*. De Sade was concerned with investigating men's hidden desires (Simone de Beauvoir regarded him as a forerunner of Freud [35]), but also, both in his life and in his writings, he "pursued unrestrained and often violent and cruel sexual expression" (*TSON* p.192).

We can also mention the Spanish poet Federico Garcia Lorca (*TSON* pp.193-4), who has an exceptionally strong Thirty-oneness cluster involving SO*, MO*, ME, MA, SA* and PL*, and whose poems have been described as "disquieting in their projection of a

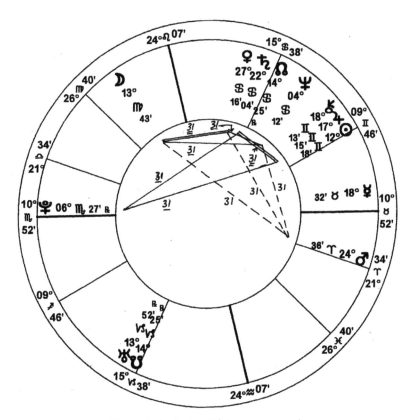

5.25 Marquis de Sade: Thirty-oneness Aspects

part-primitive, part-private world of myth moved by dark and not precisely identifiable forces".[36] Clearly Lorca was concerned with bringing to the surface the contents of the unconscious mind; and, since the planets in the cluster are close to the Midheaven and I.C., we can say that he regarded this as his life's work.

But of course, not all of us would commit sadistic murders, even if the darkest contents of our unconscious mind were brought to the surface and acted out. Thus, Thirty-oneness can also lead to less extreme forms of socially unacceptable behaviour. In *TSON* (pp.197-8) I reported on the comedian Carol Burnett, who had (SO-*31*-UR)-31-(MA-*31*-JU), and who loved to portray characters "with the lid off" – that is, as they would behave if they were able to cast off their inhibitions. Similarly, the mime Marcel Marceau (*TSON* pp.194-5), who had a Thirty-oneness cluster involving ME, MA, JU, UR and NE, excelled in showing how people would behave if they had no words with which to cover up their true feelings. Thus, Thirty-oneness, at its best, has a deep truthfulness which other harmonics lack.

But also, if we follow Freud in believing that we are born with the "id" and that the rest of the personality develops with age, then we can say that, in some cases, the Thirty-oneness person is like a child who refuses to grow up. Thus the French queen Marie Antoinette, who had (ME-*31*-PL*)-31-SO and also MA-*31*-JU and SA-31-NE, spent money recklessly on clothes, luxuries and gambling, apparently indifferent to her responsibilities as Queen and to the hostility of the French people, which was about to explode into revolution. She probably never said "Let them eat cake" (on being told that the people had no bread), but the fact that this phrase was attributed to her shows how she was perceived as being wilfully childish, caring only for instant gratification.

Thus, we can say that, when two or more planets come together in the 31st harmonic, their effect will be to bring into consciousness feelings and desires which would otherwise remain buried beneath the surface. The "shadow" side of the personality comes more easily into the open and is expressed in external behaviour. It seems that the effect of Thirty-oneness is to loosen and overcome the inhibitions and constraints which cause other people to keep their "shadow" side hidden.

The Higher Prime Numbers in Combination

At the start of this chapter we said that each of the higher prime numbers, from 11 to 31, represents some kind of *differentness* or *apartness*. Each of them shows a particular way in which the person feels himself to stand apart from the crowd and to display a marked *individuality*. So what if the chart shows strength in *many* of these higher prime numbers? How will these higher harmonics act in combination?

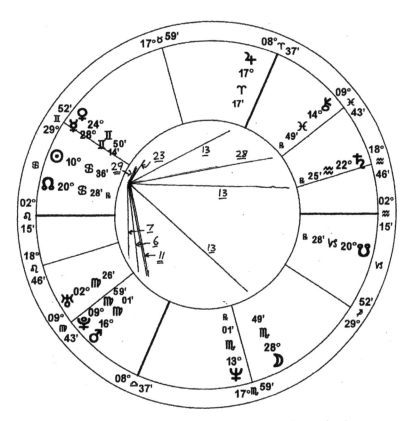

5.26 Tracey Emin: Harmonic Aspects involving the Sun

I would like here to look at the birth charts of two creative artists, Tracey Emin and Sophie Calle. Both Emin and Calle have an unusually high number of "close" or "very close" aspects linking the Sun to other planets in the higher prime numbers. Thus, Emin has: SO-*11*-MA; SO-13-MO, -13-JU, and -13-SA; SO-23-VE; and SO-*29*-ME. Calle has SO-*13*-UR*; SO-17-ME; SO-23-JU; and SO-*29*-SA. These aspects are shown on their charts in Figures 5.26 and 5.27.

Tracey Emin is a British artist known for her autobiographical and confessional artwork. Among her most famous exhibits are *My Bed* (her own dirty unmade bed, complete with used condoms and blood-stained underwear), and *Everyone I Have Ever Slept With 1963-1995* (a tent appliquéd with the names, not only of her sexual partners, but of relatives she slept with as a child). Among her later creations is a series of monoprints entitled *There Must Be Something Terebley Wrong With Me* (spelling mistakes are one of her "trademarks"). She became well known to the public in 1997 when she walked out of a live television discussion, slurring her words and swearing.

Sophie Calle has been described by a British critic as "France's answer to Tracey Emin". (A French critic would put it the other way round.) A recent article about Sophie Calle is entitled *A Woman Without Fear*, and states: "Sophie Calle makes art that is intimate, romantic, funny, dramatic and confessional".[37] Her "artwork" includes the book *Exquisite Pain*, in which she recounts her heartbreak to everyone she meets, asking them for the worst moment of their lives in return. Very many of her projects are about uncovering and exploring other people's pain and mixing it with her own, and yet completely without

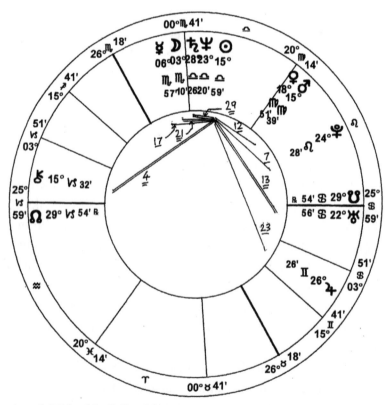

5.27 Sophie Calle: Harmonic Aspects involving the Sun

sentimentality. She has lived in the same house for 38 years and filled it with stuffed animals, including an enormous giraffe's head and neck which she has named after her mother.

The Sun represents one's self-image, one's sense of one's own identity, so it is not surprising that these two very unusual women should have many planets linked to the Sun in the higher harmonics which represent differentness and eccentricity. We can look in detail at the harmonic aspects:

- *Elevenness.* Emin has SO-**_11_**-MA, whereas Calle has no Elevenness aspects to the Sun. Elevenness is about defiance, and I feel that Emin is defiant in a way that Calle is not. Storming out of a live television debate was a classic enactment of SO-**_11_**-MA.

- *Thirteenness* is about taking risks in the search for one's own identity. Emin has Thirteenness aspects from the Sun to Moon, Jupiter and Saturn, which together make up a cluster of (MO-**_13_**-JU)-13-SO)-13/13/13-SA, and I feel that she is constantly taking risks in the exploration of her own feelings (MO), her own ability to grow and expand (JU), and her own limitations (SA). Calle, on the other hand, has a single very close Thirteenness aspect of SO-**_13_**-UR. With Uranus close to the Descendant, this shows how Calle takes risks by involving herself in other people's lives and inviting them to behave in original and startling ways.

- *Seventeenness.* Calle has SO-17-ME, whereas Emin has no Seventeenness aspects. Seventeenness is about campaigning for a better world, and Calle (unlike Emin) is doing this through her modes of communication. She is campaigning for a feminist cause, exposing some of the ways in which men use and abuse women.

- *Twenty-threeness*, especially when it involves the Sun, is about telling a story about one's own life. Emin has SO-23-VE, and the story which she is telling is primarily about her love-life and her relationships. Calle has SO-23-JU, and her story is mainly about her ability to break all the rules and to live her life as "a woman without fear".

- *Twenty-nineness* is about taking pride in one's own originality and eccentricity, and (as we might expect) both Emin and Calle have very close Twenty-nineness aspects to the Sun. Emin has SO-*29*-ME, and she takes huge pride in her ability to communicate. But Calle has SO-*29*-SA, and one feels that, despite all her risk-taking and fearlessness, Calle's pride is mainly in the control and discipline which she exercises over her own life. Eva Wiseman says, "Calle has been interviewed thousands of times and she's interested in the process, in what she chooses to withhold".[37] She is very much in control of her own boundaries.

It is also interesting that Tracey Emin has a twin brother named Paul. I have not been able to discover Paul's time of birth, but we can assume that it is close to Tracey's and that he shares most, if not all, of her harmonic aspects. Paul Emin has displayed none of his sister's artistic talents: he is an unemployed carpenter who suffers from epilepsy and survives on benefits. He has said that he is immensely proud of Tracey and is grateful for the financial support which she has sometimes given him, but once he attended one of her exhibitions and smashed one of her artworks (another enactment of SO-*11*-MA). The case of Tracey and Paul Emin shows once again that (as I said in Chapter 3) *the chart shows only potential,* and that some people are better able than others to make full use of the potential that the chart offers to them.

Prime Numbers Beyond Thirty-one

I have researched the meaning of the harmonics only as far as 32, and David Cochrane has also independently chosen to stop at the 32nd harmonic.[38] This means that (so far as I know) there has been no research into the meaning of the harmonics above 32. But for composite (non-prime) numbers we can deduce their meaning from the meaning of the prime numbers of which they are composed: thus, 33 (11 x 3) is a combination of Elevenness and Threeness, and 35 (7 x 5) is a combination of Sevenness and Fiveness. However, for the prime numbers above 32 – of which the first seven are 37, 41, 43,

47, 53, 59 and 61 – nothing is known about their meaning. So this would seem to be an excellent subject for future research.

My suggestion, to anyone who wishes to research the meaning of these numbers, is to take one harmonic at a time. Thus, if one wishes to investigate the 37th harmonic, one could cast the 37th harmonic chart for a large number of subjects. In each 37th harmonic chart, one could note the conjunctions (using the same orbs that I have used for conjunctions: 2 degrees for "very close" aspects, 6 degrees for "close", and 12 degrees for "wide"), paying special attention to "clusters", i.e. cases where three or more planets were in conjunction. If one did this for a large enough number of cases (probably more than 500), then it is likely that a pattern would begin to emerge: that is to say, it would begin to be apparent that the subjects with the strongest clusters of conjunctions in the 37th harmonic would have certain characteristics in common, and these characteristics could then be taken to be associated with the quality of Thirty-sevenness.

As it happens, I have (ME-*37*-NE)-37-SA in my own chart. What does this mean? I do not know. Maybe, before I die, someone will tell me.

Chapter 6
Guidelines for Harmonic Analysis

In Chapters 4 and 5 we have discussed the meaning of all the harmonics from 1 to 32, and we can briefly summarize these meanings here. (From what we have already said, it should be clear that the "keywords" that we are here using – words like *pleasure* and *inspiration* - are only pointers towards concepts or qualities that are far richer and more complex than these simple words imply.)

1: *unity, merging.*

2: *effort, striving.*

3: *pleasure, harmony.*

4 = 2 x 2: *effort towards striving (a more deliberate, or conscious, striving).*

5: *building, re-shaping (conscious creativity).*

6 = 3 x 2: *striving towards pleasure, or pleasure in striving.*

7: *inspiration, intuition.*

8 = 2 x 2 x 2: *even more effort-full striving.*

9 = 3 x 3: *pleasure in pleasure: joy.*

10 = 5 x 2: *striving towards creativity.*

11: *defiance, dogged persistence.*

12 = 3 x 2 x 2: *a more effort-full striving towards pleasure (or, pleasure in effort-full striving).*

13: *adventurousness (testing one's limits: the search for one's identity).*

14 = 7 x 2: *striving towards inspiration.*

15 = 5 x 3: *pleasure in creativity.*

16 = 2 x 2 x 2 x 2: *yet more effort-full striving.*

17: *rebelliousness, subversiveness, campaigning for change.*

18 = 3 x 3 x 2: *striving towards joy.*

19: *empathy, acceptance.*

20 = 5 x 2 x 2: *as 10, but with more effort.*

21 = 7 x 3: *pleasure in inspiration.*

22 = 11 x 2: *striving towards defiance.*

23: *inventiveness, story-telling.*

24 = 3 x 2 x 2 x 2: *as 12, but with more effort.*

25 = 5 x 5: *creating the conditions for creativity.*

26 = 13 x 2: *striving towards adventurousness.*

27 = 3 x 3 x 3: *pleasure in joy: bliss.*

28 = 7 x 2 x 2: *as 14, but with more effort.*

29: *pride in one's uniqueness.*

30 = 5 x 3 x 2: *striving towards pleasure in creativity.*

31: *openness to unconscious desires.*

32 = 2 x 2 x 2 x 2 x 2: *still more effort-full striving.*

We have also described how to compile a List of Significant Harmonic Aspects (LSHA) for a particular radical chart, whether natal or mundane, so that we know which of these harmonic aspects are found in the chart, and among which planets.

Our task now is to interpret the radical chart, making use of this information, and it is appropriate that I should offer some guidelines on how to do this.

I feel that the first and most important guideline is: *Continue to do what you already do.* I am assuming that you are an astrologer who has been using conventional astrological techniques, and that you now wish to add harmonic analysis to your existing techniques. (By "harmonic analysis" I mean here simply the analysis of interplanetary harmonic aspects.) You can do this without sacrificing any of your existing methods. Thus, you are free to interpret the planets, the signs, and the houses as you have always done; you are free to choose your preferred house system; you are free to adhere to conventional beliefs, for instance about rulerships, exaltations, and the effects of retrogression; you are free to use the Nodes, the Part of Fortune, or any other additional factors; you are free to use secondary or tertiary progressions. The harmonic analysis will provide *additional* information which will add to the richness of your interpretation.

There are, however, just two elements of conventional astrology which you must abandon if you wish to take up harmonic analysis. The first of these is the doctrine of *unaspected planets*. In harmonic astrology there are no unaspected planets, since every planet is linked to every other planet in one particular harmonic or another.

And the second element which you must abandon is the use of *wide orbs* for the traditional aspects of the opposition, the trine, and (especially) the square. In conventional astrology, these aspects are typically allowed an orb of 8 degrees on either side of exactitude. But in harmonic astrology, the orb allowed is *the conjunction orb divided by the number of the harmonic:* thus, if we allow a 12-degree orb for the conjunction, the maximum orb for the square (which is a 4th harmonic aspect) is 12 ÷ 4 = 3 degrees. A very close square aspect would be seen as very important, but, if the orb is more than 3 degrees, it is not counted as a square at all. Thus, for instance, in my own chart I have Moon at Sagittarius 0°46' and Saturn at Pisces 8°28': conventionally this would be counted as a Moon-Saturn square, but in harmonic astrology it is in fact an Elevenness aspect: MO-11-SA.)

So (with these two caveats) do what you have always done, but also use the List of Significant Harmonic Aspects (LSHA) to obtain *additional* information. How should you add this to your existing methods of astrological analysis?

There are no precise rules about how it should be done, and the way in which you use the list of harmonic aspects (just like any way in which you use other astrological techniques) will depend in part on your own inclinations and preferences, as well as on the particular questions which you are trying to answer. It is important to remember that the harmonic aspects contain an extraordinarily rich and complex portrait of a person (or of an event), and we cannot hope to analyse every detail of this level of complexity. Thus, I have of course been studying the harmonic aspects in my own birth chart for some time, and yet there are still some aspects that I have not really understood or tried to analyse. We must abandon any hope of trying to produce a perfect and 100% complete analysis.

So, we have to select the harmonic aspects which we see as among the most important. In compiling the List of Significant Harmonic

Aspects (LSHA) we have already removed some aspects which we saw as insignificant; but, even within the remaining aspects, we have to continue to be selective. Here are some suggested guidelines about how this should be done:

1. "Very close" aspects are always important.

2. "Close" or "very close" aspects in which one or more of the planets is close to the Angles of the chart (Asc, Desc, MC, IC) are always important.

3. Special attention should be paid to "clusters" of three or more planets in which at least one of the aspects in the cluster is "very close". If *all* of the aspects in the cluster are "very close", this is likely to be a dominant feature of the personality or the event (especially if the cluster involves the Sun or the Moon). Of course, the more planets there are in the cluster, the more important it will be. Occasionally one may find clusters of four, five, or even six planets: these clusters are likely to be very central to the personality or to the event.

The question remains of the *order* in which the different aspects and clusters should be looked at, and here, although there are no firm rules, I can say something about the procedure that I have followed in the case studies that are presented in Chapter 7 of this book.

At this point I would like to quote a passage from *Harmonic Charts* (p.137), since it helps to explain the way in which I interpret the Ascendant/Descendant and M.C./I.C. axes:

"The Ascendant/Descendant axis is concerned with one's relationship with other people and with the external world at the present time. People whose planets cluster around this axis tend to 'live in the present,' and to be little concerned with the past or the future. The Ascendant is particularly concerned with how one presents oneself to the world, and the Descendant is particularly concerned with the view which one has of the outside world. However, both ends of the axis are basically concerned with the same thing, which is the process of interaction between Self and Other.

The M.C./I.C. axis is concerned with the path which one follows through life, one's voyage out of the past and into the future. People whose planets cluster around this axis will tend to be greatly involved with the past and the future, and to be relatively little concerned with the 'here and now'. The I.C. is particularly concerned with the past (origins) and the M.C. with the future (ultimate goals), but both ends of the axis are basically concerned with the same thing, which is the development of Self through time."

In the case of Iris Murdoch (who is the subject of the first of these case studies), I started by noting that she has ME-2-MO on the horizontal (Asc-Desc) axis. Even though this traditional oppositional aspect is not "very close", its position on the ASC-DES axis makes it central to her personality. This particular observation is not dependent on harmonic analysis; probably any "typical" astrologer would also have started with this Mercury-Moon opposition. But in addition, now using harmonic analysis, I also looked at the harmonic aspects that link Mercury and Moon to other planets: Uranus, Jupiter, Mars, Pluto, Neptune and Saturn. In doing this I tried to present a fuller and more comprehensive picture of the side of Iris's personality which is centred around the ME-2-MO opposition on the horizontal axis.

Having done this, I might then have looked, in the same way, at any harmonic aspects and clusters that were connected to the vertical (MC-IC) axis, but it happens that Iris has no planets close to this axis. So next I looked at the harmonic aspects that were connected to the Sun. Leaving the Sun until so late in the analysis was perhaps unusual, but it was based on my judgment that Iris was living more out of her "lunar" personality than her "solar" one, and that the aspects to the Sun were therefore of somewhat lesser importance.

By looking at these two groups of aspects (the Moon-connected aspects and the Sun-connected ones) I did in fact cover nearly all of the "close" and "very close" harmonic aspects in Iris's chart.

In the case of Gerard Manley Hopkins, I again started with a traditional oppositional aspect, SO-2-SA, which is close to the horizontal axis. From this starting-point, I felt that in this case it was more appropriate to proceed upwards through the prime numbers, looking first at the Twoness and Threeness aspects in Hopkins's chart, then at the Fiveness and Sevenness aspects (which are the main clues to his creativity), and then at the higher prime numbers of Eleven onwards.

Of course, in some radical charts there are no planets close to the horizontal or vertical axes. In these cases I would probably start by looking at the harmonic aspects to the Sun. Especially, if there was a close harmonic link between the Sun and the Moon, I would make this my starting-point. If there is a close Sun-Moon link in a particular harmonic, then the qualities of that harmonic will tend to pervade the whole personality: thus, if there is SO-11-MO, then the personality will have the quality of Elevenness even if there are no other strong Elevenness aspects. If (as in the case of both Murdoch and Hopkins) there is no strong Sun-Moon link, there will tend to be a split between the solar and lunar sides of the personality.

Ultimately, you will have to make subjective judgments about which harmonic aspects are worthy of mention and which are not, and also about the ways in which you connect them together for purposes of interpretation. Astrological interpretation is an art, not a science, and, just as two artists looking at the same model will always produce two very different portraits, so two astrologers looking at the same chart will produce two different analyses: but, hopefully, each analysis will say something true and valuable about the chart and about its owner.

Until this point I have been assuming that the astrologer's task is to analyse the whole chart, with the aim of reaching a deeper understanding of the subject in his or her totality. But of course, this is not always the case. Very often, an astrologer is asked, not to analyse the whole chart, but to answer specific questions and to help the client to deal with specific problems, fears or difficulties. So we also need to look at the part which harmonic analysis might play in this.

To illustrate this, I would like to ask you to imagine that the year is 2010, and you are an established astrologer who has recently started to use harmonic analysis. A client comes to you and asks you to help her to understand and deal with her problems of alcohol and drug addiction and also with her issues about intimate relationships. This client is the singer-songwriter Amy Winehouse. What would you say to Amy, and how would you help her to deal with her problems?

I need at this point to say something about Amy's life story. Amy was a singer with a powerful contralto voice, a profound creativity and musicality, a deep commitment to making a success of her career, and a charismatic personality. Her album *Back to Black* was at that time the best-selling album in the UK in the 21st century. She was renowned for her kindness, and supported very many charitable causes. However, since her teenage years Amy had problems with alcohol and drug abuse. In 2007 she married Blake Fielder-Civil (born April 16, 1982), a school dropout with a history of criminality, who treated her violently and allegedly introduced her to cocaine and heroin. Amy and Blake were divorced in 2009, but Amy's problems continued. In June 2011 she was booed off the stage for being too drunk to perform. She died on July 23, 2011, thus joining the infamous "27 club" whose members (including Jimi Hendrix, Janis Joplin and Kurt Cobain) are all musicians who died at the age of 27. A coroner determined that her death was due to "accidental alcohol poisoning".

So, imagine that Amy comes to see you early in 2010. You look at her chart (Figure 6.1), and you see the very unusual fact that her ten major planets are in five separate close conjunctions: MA-1-VE in the 4th house, SO-*1*-ME in the 5th, PL-1-SA and JU-*1*-UR in the 6th, and NE-1-MO in the 7th. You see also that, apart from MO-SA and NE-PL sextiles, a ME-VE semi-sextile, and a wide VE-NE trine, there are (within harmonic orbs) no "traditional" aspects linking these conjunctions. So the question of how the conjunctions are linked by harmonic aspects becomes very important.

You use conventional astrology to explain to Amy the meaning of each of the five conjunctions (and also the opposition between Jupiter/Uranus and Chiron) within their signs and houses. Maybe

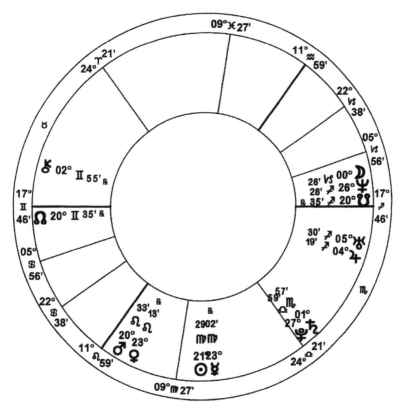

6.1 Amy Winehouse

you dwell especially on the tendency of Moon-Neptune in the 7th house to enter into unwise relationships based on false expectations. But none of this explains Amy's problems with addiction, which are her main reason for consulting you.

However, when you look at Amy's harmonic aspects, you see at once that she has a Fiveness problem. Her Fiveness links can be expressed as follows:

((SO-_1_-ME)-_5_/5/_5_/5-(JU-_1_-UR))-_10_/10/_10_/(10)-PL
(PL-5-CH)-_10_-SO
(MA-5-SA)-_20_-NE

The five-planet cluster might seem to be not very strong because it contains no "very close" Fiveness aspects, but it is greatly strengthened by the fact that Pluto is almost exactly at the midpoint of Sun and

Jupiter. Thus, we can see that three of Amy's five conjunctions (SO-ME, JU-UR, and SA-PL) are linked together in Fiveness, and there are Fiveness links also with the other two conjunctions through (MA-5-SA)-**20**-NE and with Chiron through (PL-5-CH)-10-SO. We can say that Fiveness pervades the whole of Amy's chart.

Fiveness is prone to addictions, because it creates structures and systems of behaviour which, once created, become ossified and hard to change. We saw this, for instance, in the case of the Silent Twins whom we discussed in Chapter 4, and who, as I said, were "imprisoned by their Fiveness". In Amy's case the central Fiveness cluster (around which the other Fiveness links are built) is (SO-5-JU)-10-PL, with Pluto at the SO/JU midpoint. This shows that Amy is constantly seeking ways of expressing herself in a free and uninhibited Jupiterian way, but that, in doing this, she always feels compelled to choose behaviours which have a Plutonian quality; and Pluto, especially since it is closely conjunct Saturn, is prone to choose actions which contain an element of danger and possible self-harm. This will have caused Amy, in the first place, to seek Jupiterian freedom through substances rather than other methods, and (because we are talking about Fiveness), once she has chosen this route, habits are formed which become difficult to break.

However, because Fiveness is about conscious choice, there is always the possibility of change. You cannot tell a Fiveness person to stop behaving in a Fiveness way, but you can perhaps help them to use their Fiveness differently. Thus, I feel that the important thing for you, as Amy's astrologer, would be to have extended discussions with her (she has plenty of money, so she can afford repeated sessions!) about how she might best use her Fiveness. Maybe the Plutonian theme of self-punishment will always be present, but Pluto does not inevitably mean substance abuse. It might be possible, for instance, for Amy to express (SO-5-JU)-10-PL through a rigorous programme of exercise, pushing her body to the limit, and punishing herself by forcing herself to endure the pain of withdrawal, but doing so in a way that was not ultimately self-harming.

And maybe her Elevenness aspects of ME-11-MA and JU-11-SA could help her here. Elevenness can be a valuable antidote to Fiveness, as is shown by the fact that Winston Churchill (whose dominant number was Eleven) was an effective adversary for Hitler (whose number was Five). ME-11-MA is important because of the very nature of the planets involved, and JU-11-SA is important because Saturn is conjunct Pluto, so that this aspect can modify the effects of JU-10-PL. These Elevenness aspects can help Amy to find the defiance and dogged persistence which will help her to stick to a new choice of lifestyle.

Amy also has a strong pattern of Sevenness, which is perhaps best observed, not from her List of Significant Harmonic Aspects (LSHA), but from her 7th harmonic chart: this shows that the midpoint of her natal VE-1-MA is almost exactly -7- the midpoint of her natal JU-1-UR, and also that this point is very closely -14-MO. This Sevenness pattern is, I feel, the main source of Amy's musical creativity. But I do not feel it is important for an astrologer to dwell on this, because Amy does not have a problem with it: this is not the area in which she needs help.

Amy would probably also be asking you to say something about your predictions for her future. Probably (because the use of harmonic aspects for prediction is in its infancy) you would respond to this by using conventional astrological methods. But you might possibly decide to look at the harmonic aspects in her Solar Return for September 2010, using the methods which I shall outline in Chapter 10 of this book. Remarkably, this Solar Return chart has VE-1-MA and JU-1-UR, just as in Amy's natal chart, and there is a -5- link from Venus to Jupiter and Uranus. If we look at the harmonic links between the Solar Return chart and the natal chart, we see that natal Venus is -5- transiting Jupiter, -5-transiting Uranus, and -25- transiting Pluto. All this suggests that, in the year between her 27th and 28th birthdays, Amy will be disposed to act out her natal JU-PL Fiveness link in a much more Venusian (loving, attractive?) way than before. This would seem to be very hopeful for the proposal that Amy should find new, less self-harming, ways of acting out her Fiveness. But the Solar Return chart also shows an *exact* square (-**4**-) between transiting Mercury and natal Uranus, coupled with a very close -**10**- between transiting Mars and natal Uranus, showing a danger of sudden and precipitate action, and the astrologer would need to warn Amy about this.

It seems to me just possible that working with Amy in this way, might have helped to save her life. I have no idea whether, in real life, Amy would have been receptive to this, but I do know that someone with a knowledge of harmonic aspects would have had more hope of helping her than an astrologer who did not have this knowledge.

Thus I believe that it is impossible to lay down rules about how to tackle a harmonic analysis, because the methods which one uses should always be tailored to the particular case.

For another example of how harmonic astrology might have been helpful for a client, I would refer you to the case of Alain Vareille, which I discussed in *The Spirit of Numbers* (pp.237-241). In that case study I showed how a harmonic astrologer might have helped Vareille to desist from killing his pregnant wife, his two children, and (later) himself. He might have been helped to see that there were other ways of dealing with the predicament in which he found himself, and other ways of finding outlets for the violent tendencies that were present in his chart.

Midpoints and Harmonics

As a postscript to this chapter, I would like to say something about the use of planetary midpoints in conjunction with harmonics. The principle of midpoints is that "a third planet at the midpoint of two others will act as a factor that brings these energies together and through which they will tend to be expressed".[1]

Historically, astrologers who have used harmonics have tended also to use midpoints. Thus, Harding and Harvey's book *Working with Astrology*[2] is concerned equally with harmonics and with midpoints, and the system of vibrational astrology which is taught by David Cochrane at the Avalon School of Astrology[3] uses both midpoints and harmonics.

As many readers of this book will already know, the seminal work on the interpretation of planetary midpoints is *The Combination of Stellar Influences* (affectionately known as *COSI*) by Reinhold Ebertin, which was first published in German in 1940 and was translated into English in 1960.[4] In Ebertin's system, the point which is halfway between Planet A and Planet B is known as the *direct midpoint.* However, Ebertin also uses *indirect midpoints,* in which (as Michael Harding explains) "the Moon falling at any multiple of 45° from the ME/JU midpoint is said to be 'on the ME/JU midpoint'"[5], and these indirect midpoints are seen to be just as powerful as the direct midpoints. In effect, this means that Ebertin is identifying *midpoints in the 8th harmonic chart,* and Harding explains: "The principle of the number 8 is, like all numbers based on multiples of 2, the principle of manifestation in the world. In the case of 8, this principle works particularly powerfully and almost always relates to concrete, tangible events".[5]

Readers of this book who wish to use Ebertin's midpoint system alongside the use of harmonics are, of course, welcome to do so. However, it is important to point out that Ebertin's system of indirect midpoints focuses entirely on Twoness at the expense of all the other prime numbers. It is true, as we said in Chapter 4, that Twoness is especially about striving to achieve in the world, and that Twoness aspects are always spurs to action. But to say that Twoness is "the principle of manifestation in the world" is to imply that other prime numbers do *not* manifest in the world; whereas I believe that harmonic astrology shows that *all* the prime numbers manifest in the world (that is, in a person's external behaviour), though the manner of manifestation is different for each number.

I would therefore like to suggest a simple method of identifying the *direct* midpoints in a chart, and relating these to *all* of the harmonic numbers. By "direct midpoint" I mean both the point which is midway between two planets (taking the shorter angular distance) and also its opposite point. Thus, if Sun is at 0° Aries and Moon is at 0° Gemini, both 0° Taurus and 0° Scorpio can be seen as the direct midpoint.

The procedure is as follows:

- Within the software that you are using, obtain a list of planetary midpoints. In the Kepler software that I use, this list can be customized by including only conjunctions and oppositions (i.e. direct midpoints) and by limiting the orb to a maximum of 1°00'.

- Make a list of these narrow-orb direct midpoints (there will only be a few of them).

- Alongside each midpoint, list the width of the orb, and also (from the Table of Harmonic Aspects) list the number(s) of the harmonic aspect(s) linking the pair of planets between which the midpoint is formed.

If we do this for Donald Trump, we come up with the following list:

SO/UR = MO	0°48'	1
SO/VE = ME	0°28'	*11*
SO/SA = ME	0°29'	12, 23
SO/MA = VE	0°53'	17
ME/CH = MA	0°07'	*15*
ME/PL = SA	0°38'	23
MA/SA = PL	0°15'	11
MO/PL = CH	0°43'	11

This shows that, in the natal chart. SO is -1- UR, and MO is at their midpoint; SO is -*11*-VE, and ME is at their midpoint; and so on.

The predominance of the 11th harmonic in Donald Trump's list of direct midpoints is not surprising, since (as we saw in Chapter 5) 11 is his strongest harmonic. In Figure 5.2 we showed Trump's

Elevenness aspects, and we said that he has two separate Elevenness clusters: a solar one (basically saying "you've got to love me") and a lunar one (showing him defiantly responding to criticism). SO/VE = ME belongs to the solar cluster, and refers to communicating about his own attractiveness. Ebertin says of this midpoint: "Idea or concept of love, thoughts of love, tendency to express one's ideas on love's problems".[6] In itself, this might seem inapplicable to Trump; but harmonic analysis shows that he will express this midpoint in an Elevenness way: that is, defiantly and with dogged persistence.

MA/SA = PL and MO/PL = CH belong to the lunar cluster. Ebertin, with reference to MA/SA = PL, speaks of "brutality, the rage or fury of destruction"[7], and we can see here the savagery with which Trump attacks his enemies such as Hillary Clinton. But again, we need to note that Trump will express this in an Elevenness way.

The list also contains some more unexpected midpoints. For instance, there is SO/MA = VE, about which Ebertin says: "Urge to beget children, development of creative faculties, intense love expression".[8] But Trump has SO-17-MA, with Mars rising, and so he will express this midpoint in a Seventeenness way (rebelliously, campaigning for change). I would relate this to Trump's expressed love of America and his drive to "make America great again".

Again, there is ME/PL = SA (Ebertin: "Quarrelsome nature, nagging character, irritability"[9]). Trump has ME-23-PL, so he will express this midpoint in a Twenty-threeness way: that is, inventively, telling stories. Maybe this is related to Trump's outbursts on Twitter, and to his penchant for creating "false news".

The "SO/SA = ME" midpoint can, I think, be ignored for this purpose, since there is no close harmonic aspect connecting SO and SA. It is still present as a midpoint, but it may not manifest in the manner of any particular harmonic.

If we were to do the same for Amy Winehouse (whose chart we presented earlier in this chapter), we would find that the *only* narrow-orb direct midpoints in her chart are:

SO/JU = PL	0°05'	5
SO/UR = PL	0°36'	5
ME/JU = PL	0°41'	5

This reinforces what we have already said about Amy's tendency to seek freedom and excitement through ruthless (Plutonian) actions, and to do this in a Fiveness way: that is, by building habit-forming patterns of behaviour which carry the danger of addiction.

Thus, the study of these direct midpoints can be a valuable adjunct to harmonic analysis.

Chapter 7
Case Studies

In this chapter I will present five case studies of the birth charts of famous (or infamous) people. The purpose of these case studies is to show how harmonic analysis can illuminate aspects of the personality which would otherwise have been hidden from the astrologer.

Therefore, it is important to stress that these case studies are not *complete* analyses of the charts. Any astrologer will be able to provide additional insights based on the sign- and house-placements of the planets, the Moon's nodes, and other traditional factors. Also any astrologer would be able to examine the development of the life through the study of transits and progressions, which I have not done here. But my aim here is simply to show that harmonic analysis can provide additional information which in some cases is *central* to an understanding of what makes this person distinctive, and of how and why they were able to behave in the way that they did.

As an example, we can take Gerard Manley Hopkins, who is the subject of the second of our case studies, and whose natal chart is shown in Figure 7.4. As "conventional" astrologers, we could comment on the fact that his Pluto is in the 10th house in Aries, which is ruled by Mars in Leo which is ruled by the Sun, and Sun is conjunct to Mars in the 1st house. This suggests that the Twoness aspect between Sun and Pluto (SO-32-PL) represents for Hopkins a deep-seated psychological struggle in dealing with his sexuality and his self-image, and with his father's expectations (seeing the 10th house as the father) that he should be more "manly". All this is perfectly valid, and shows how the harmonic aspects can be combined with conventional astrology to produce a more complete and rounded picture.

Iris Murdoch

Born 08.00 a.m., July 15, 1919, Dublin, Ireland. RR: A.

In 2001 the film *Iris* was released, starring Judi Dench, Kate Winslet, and Jim Broadbent. It tells the story of the relationship between the British novelist Iris Murdoch and her husband John Bayley, based on Bayley's book *Iris Murdoch, a Memoir* (published in America as *Elegy for Iris*). The film moves between the 1950s, when Iris was a young philosophy lecturer with a dashing and bohemian lifestyle, and the 1990s, when she was suffering from Alzheimer's disease and was dependent on her husband's care. It is a moving film, and was described by one critic as "the greatest love story of our time".

I have a special affection for Iris Murdoch, because as a philosophy student I attended her lectures at Oxford University in the 1950s. Her lectures on Ethics were always interesting and stimulating, dealing with important questions about how one should live one's life – such a contrast to the boring old male philosophy teachers who did nothing but play around with the meaning of words. Iris was then in her thirties, and was a very distinctive (and strangely lovable) personality. She was careless of her appearance, dressing scruffily and wearing no makeup. I have a vivid memory of seeing her cycling around Oxford, with her academic gown billowing in the wind and with a basket full of books attached to the handlebars.

She was born in Ireland to Irish parents, but her parents moved to London when Iris was still a baby. She was an only child, and she described her family as "a perfect trinity of love". Her parents made few friends in England, seeing themselves as exiles from Ireland, and always going to Ireland for holidays. But Iris was a gifted child, and won a scholarship to the prestigious Badminton School where she was a contemporary of Indira Gandhi. From there she proceeded to Oxford University, where she studied Classics and philosophy. During the war she worked as a civil servant in London, and then in 1944 she joined the United Nations Relief and Rehabilitation Administration (UNRRA), with postings in Belgium, Austria and the Netherlands, where she was involved in helping displaced persons return to their home countries. In 1946 she went to Cambridge University as a postgraduate researcher, and then in 1948 she returned to Oxford as a teacher of philosophy.

From her earliest adult years she led an extremely turbulent love life, with many brief affairs with both men and women. Her biographer A.N. Wilson has described her as "willing to go to bed with almost anyone",[1] but I believe that she did not sleep with anyone unless she was deeply in love with them, and indeed she fell in love (and out of love) very frequently. (She wrote, "Falling out of love is very enlightening. For a short while you see the world with new eyes".[2]) Most of her affairs were brief, but one longer-term affair was with the writer Elias Canetti (born 01.00 a.m., July 27, 1905, Ruse, Bulgaria, RR: AA) who later won the Nobel Prize for Literature. Canetti has been described as a "cruel" man who treated Iris sadistically and mocked her in public,[3] and yet Iris always defended him. She loved him for his authenticity, his *reality*, and he appears in some of her novels as a Magician or a Lord of Power.

Love was, indeed, the central theme of Iris's life. She wrote, "Love is the difficult realization that someone other than oneself is real".[4] As a philosopher her aim was to re-introduce the word "love" into the language of philosophy, from which it had long been absent. One of her philosophy books was *The Sovereignty of Good,* in which she sought to restore the concept of the "Good" to the pre-eminent place which had been given to it by Plato. In that book she writes:

"Love is the general name of the quality of attachment, and it is capable of infinite degradation and is the source of our greatest errors; but when it is even partially refined it is the energy and passion of the soul in its search for Good, the force that points us to Good and joins us to the world through Good. Its existence is the unmistakable sign that we are spiritual creatures, attracted by excellence and made for the Good. It is a reflection of the warmth and light of the sun."[5]

Her first novel *Under the Net* was published in 1954, and she continued to write novels for the rest of her life (until she was incapacitated by Alzheimer's), publishing 27 novels in all. Her novels brought her great fame; in 1978 she won the Booker Prize for *The Sea, The Sea,* and in 1987 she was made a Dame of the British Empire. Her novels deal with good and evil, sexual relationships, and the power of the unconscious. They have complex plots, which Iris would work out in great detail before she started to write.

Iris first met John Bayley (born March 27, 1925) in November 1953, and they were married on August 14, 1956. John was the opposite of Canetti: gentle, kindly and self-effacing. He was a virgin until he met Iris. Their mutual love seems to have been based on their ability to laugh together, and to play together like children. They stayed together for the rest of Iris's life, and had no children of their own. However, Iris, with John's consent, continued to have sexual liaisons outside marriage. In 1963 she had to resign from her post at Oxford University because of a scandal about a lesbian affair.

In 1997 Iris was diagnosed with Alzheimer's disease, and she died in an Oxford nursing home at 4.00 p.m. on February 8, 1999.[6] On that evening on the BBC, the report of her death had precedence over that of King Hussein of Jordan, who had died on the same day.

Her novels are now less fashionable than they were in the 1980s, and I feel it is regrettable that (because of Judi Dench's brilliant portrayal of her in her last years) Iris should now be better known as an Alzheimer's sufferer than as a novelist, philosopher and lover. Alzheimer's is a disease that affects many thousands of people, and it brings them all down to the same level. But, when she was in full possession of her faculties, Iris had unique and remarkable qualities, and it is these qualities that I want to examine in this analysis.

Iris's birth chart is shown in Figure 7.1. Her List of Significant Harmonic Aspects is as follows:

1: SO-1-JU
    MA-1-PL

2: SO-8-VE
    MO*-2-ME*

11: ME*-11-CH

13: MO*-13-MA
     ME*-26-PL

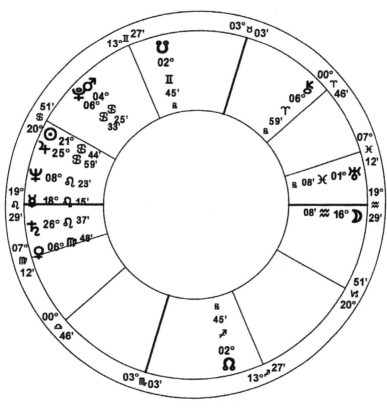

7.1 Iris Murdoch

ME*-_16_-JU
(MA-_1_-PL)-4/_4_-CH

3: SO-_27_-ME*
MO*-_9_-JU
MO*-_24_-UR
(SO-_8_-VE)-_24_/_24_/6/_4_-(PL-_4_-CH)

5: (JU-_5_-UR)-10/_10_-CH
(PL-_4_-CH)-20/_10_-UR

7: (SO-_21_-MA)-21-NE
(MA-_1_-PL)-_7_/7-SA*
ME*-_28_-UR
MO*-_7_-CH

17: MO-_17_-SA*

19: none

23: (UR-_23_-PL)-23-SO
MO*-_23_-PL
VE-_23_-JU

29: JU-_29_-NE

31: (SO-_31_-SA*)-31-CH
VE-_31_-UR

If we look first at Iris's natal chart, the first thing to notice is that the planets are clustered around the horizontal (Asc-Desc) axis rather than the vertical (MH-IC) axis. Eight of her planets are in the 1st, 6th, 7th and 12th houses, which are the houses that adjoin the Ascendant and Descendant; and there are no planets (apart from Chiron) in the houses that adjoin the MH and IC. This suggests that Iris's overwhelming preoccupation is with the relationship between Self and Other, rather than the relationship between past and future. The question which Iris is trying to answer is: "How do I relate to my environment – and in particular to other people – in the present moment?" Questions such as "What are my goals? Where have I come from, and where am I going?" are of far lesser importance to her.

And the two planets that are closest to the horizontal axis are Mercury and Moon, so the opposition between them (MO*-2-ME*) is of paramount importance. Moon and Mercury are the planets through which Iris sees the world, and through which the world sees her. On the front cover of A.N. Wilson's book *Iris Murdoch as I Knew Her* there is a photograph of Iris as a young woman, looking straight at the camera, and one can clearly see MO*-2-ME* in this photograph. One can see in her eyes the clear, cool, steady, observant detachment of Moon in Aquarius, and behind it one can sense the fierce, fiery intelligence of Mercury in Leo, making sense of what she sees. Looking at this photograph one feels: This is a woman who really *sees* me for who I am, and who understands what she sees.

Since Moon and Mercury are central in Iris's personality, we need to look at the harmonic aspects that connect Moon and Mercury to other planets. In harmonic astrology it is always important to look for aspects that are *exact* (or very close to exactitude), and in Iris's case we find such an aspect in MO*-**24**-UR. (Moon is at Aquarius 16°08' and Uranus is at Pisces 1°08': exactly 15 degrees apart, and 15 degrees is one twenty-fourth of the circle.)

Exact aspects such as this will tend to have a compulsive effect on the personality. So, with the Moon, Iris coolly sees people as they are; but, with Uranus in the 7th house in Pisces, she seeks variety, excitement and emotional involvement in relationships, and, with MO*-_**24**_-UR, she compulsively seeks out these relationships, even when they cause her emotional pain. 24 is 2 x 2 x 2 x 3, so there is great effort involved, and yet the goal is pleasure. Always she is seeking something new and original, something different from herself. ("Love is the difficult realization that something other than oneself is real.") Thus she is able to fall in love with people as diverse as John Bayley and Elias Canetti, and it has been said that even her long-term relationship with John was based on their ability constantly to find something new in each other. And yet also, there is always *acceptance* of the other person: she does not try to change them, because she values their originality.

We have looked at the links between Moon and Mercury and between Moon and Uranus: but what of the link between Mercury and Uranus? If we look down Iris's list of harmonic aspects, we see that she also has ME*-_**28**_-UR. This aspect also is extremely close (within 2 minutes of exactitude), so again it will have a compulsive effect. 28 is 2 x 2 x 7, so it is about *striving towards inspiration.* It shows Iris striving to verbalize and communicate, in creative and imaginative ways, her search for variety and originality in relationships. I believe that it was this aspect, more than any other, which caused Iris to write novels in which the huge variety and complexity of human interactions, especially in intimate relationships, is explored. It was not enough for her to carry out the MO*-_**24**_-UR search in her own life; she also had to write about it, to theorize about it, to use her imagination to explore it in other people's lives. She gave huge love and empathy to her partners; but the price they had to pay was that they might find themselves portrayed, not always flatteringly, in her novels.

Thus I believe that a great part of Iris's originality can be traced to this relationship between these three planets, Moon, Mercury and Uranus, which can be expressed as (MO*-_2_-ME*)-_**24**_/_**28**_-UR, and which is shown in Figure 7.2.

But other planets also play a part. First, we can bring Jupiter into the picture by looking at its links with Moon, Mercury and Uranus.

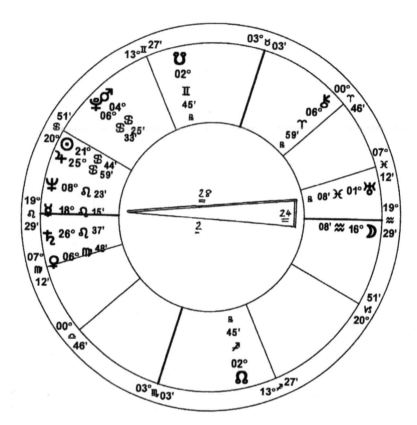

7.2 Iris Murdoch: MO-ME-UR Aspects

Jupiter is in the 12th house close to the Sun, so it is about exploring one's own subconscious in an open-minded, optimistic, Jupiterian way, in order to achieve a deeper sense of self-realization. If we look down the list of aspects, we find that Jupiter is -9- Moon, -16- Mercury, and -5- Uranus. MO*-9-JU is very close, and shows Iris obtaining a deep sense of pleasure and joy from this expansive self-exploration: it is something with which she feels very comfortable. But ME*-16-JU shows that she will also put tremendous *effort* into thinking about it, making sense of it, communicating about it. And finally JU-5-UR brings in the Fiveness element of ordering and structuring: she will be motivated to do all this in a systematic and ordered way. All this contributes to her skill as a writer and to the fact that her novels are so readable and enjoyable.

I think also that MO*-_9_-JU is related to a certain mischievousness or playfulness, which was certainly part of Iris's character, and seems to have been very important in her relationship with John Bayley.

We can note also some other very close links involving Moon and Mercury. Firstly, both Moon and Mercury have Thirteenness links: MO*-_13_-MA and ME*-_26_-PL. But Mars and Pluto are conjunct in the natal chart (in Cancer in the 11th house), so this configuration can be expressed as (MA-_1_-PL)-_13_/_26_-(MO*-_2_-ME*). We have seen that Thirteenness is about going on a journey of discovery in search of one's own identity. This brings a further element of adventurousness and risk-taking into the picture, especially in relation to 11th house matters such as groups and organizations. We can relate this to Iris's bravery in taking on a position as a philosophy lecturer within Oxford University and yet rejecting the "received wisdom" within that organization and striking out on a path of her own (in a very thoroughgoing Mars/Pluto way) in pursuit of her Moon-Mercury goals; and, more generally, we can relate it to her willingness to defy conventional *mores* and to openly practise bisexual promiscuity, in an age (the 1950s) when such behaviour was generally frowned on and kept hidden.

Also she has a very close Seventeenness link between Moon and Saturn: MO*-_17_-SA*. Saturn is also angular, because it is in the 1st house within 8 degrees of the Ascendant in Leo. This is a very confident and assertive position for Saturn: it is the kind of Saturn that imposes limitations, both on oneself and on other people, rather than feeling constrained by the limitations imposed by others. And Seventeenness is about campaigning for a better world, and is often associated with great verbal dexterity. I see this MO*-_17_-SA* as being related to Iris's lifelong concern with *morality*. Saturn is always concerned with morality, because it says that some things are right, other things are wrong, and people should control their behaviour by sticking to the right things. So Iris was campaigning for a deeper understanding of morality, and this aspect (together with the closeness of Saturn to Mercury on the Ascendant) will have helped her to write books such as *Metaphysics as a Guide to Morals*.[7] And she imposed this morality on herself. Her letters show that, in writing to her numerous friends and lovers, Iris was often very self-critical, asking herself whether her actions had been morally correct.[8] And in the last paragraph of *The Sovereignty of Good* she writes about the importance of *humility* as an element of the Good.[9] "Humility," she writes, "is a rare virtue and an unfashionable one and one which is often hard to discern. Only rarely does one meet somebody in whom it positively shines, in whom one apprehends with amazement the absence of the anxious avaricious tentacles of the self."

And she also has MO*-**23**-NE. Neptune is in Cancer in the 12th house, balancing Saturn in Leo in the 1st, on either side of Mercury and the Ascendant. And Twenty-three is itself a very Neptunian number. Whereas Seventeenness people *campaign* for a better world, Twenty-threeness people *dream* of a better world. Often they are very creative, because they are able to bring life to their fantasies and convert them into reality. Thus I relate this MO*-**23**-NE to the inventiveness of Iris's novels and to the fact that many of her characters are in a state of dissatisfied longing. Also I relate it to some of her own sayings. For instance, she said:

> "We live in a fantasy world, a world of illusion. The great task in life is to find reality."

> "I daresay anything can be made holy by being sincerely worshipped."

> "People from a world without flowers would think we must be mad with joy the whole time to have such things about us."

> "We can only learn to love by loving."[10]

So far I have barely mentioned the Sun: and it seems to be true that, with her angular Moon, Iris lived her life more out of her lunar personality than her solar one. (There is no close harmonic link between the Sun and the Moon.) However, the Sun is still there, representing Iris's deeper sense of who she really is; and I feel that, in looking at Iris's photograph one can sense that, despite her airy Moon and her fiery Mercury, she is, deep down, a Water person, with all the profound caring for herself and for the rest of humanity that comes from having Sun in Cancer in the 12th house. Thus, I also need to mention the cluster of harmonic aspects involving the Sun:

(SO-**8**-VE)-24/24/**6**/**4**-(PL-**4**-CH)

SO-**8**-VE is a very common aspect (because the planet Venus spends a disproportionate amount of time at an angle of 45 degrees from the Sun), and it often represents the feeling that one is unloved and that one needs to find love in order to find oneself. But I do not think that Iris felt unloved or unlovable: she said, after all, that her birth family was "a perfect trinity of love". Nevertheless, as an adult she was still searching for love. Unlike many (perhaps most) novelists who deal with psychological issues, Iris did not write about the overcoming of childhood traumas. Rather, she wrote about adults who, after a trauma-free childhood, find themselves searching for love in the strange, unfamiliar and "unreal" world outside their family of birth.

So SO-**8**-VE is tied up with Pluto and Chiron (Pluto in the 11th house, Chiron in the 9th) in a pattern of Twoness combined with Threeness: striving for pleasure. We can relate this again to Iris's willingness to enter into intimate relationships with people who were very different from herself. (She wrote: "No love is entirely without worth, even when the frivolous calls to the frivolous and the base to the base".) I feel that this relentless searching for love anywhere and everywhere contains the qualities of both Pluto and Chiron: through love, she is aiming to transform the world and also to heal it.

And, I should add, she was in search, not only of love, but also of beauty. Venus is in Virgo on the cusp of the 2nd house, and is the only Earth planet in her chart. Iris was, as I have said, careless about her appearance; she was careless also about money; and (judging from the film *Iris*) she seems also, at least in her later years, to have been careless about cleanliness and tidiness in her home. It may seem strange that Venus on the 2nd house cusp should be careless about these things, but Venus in Virgo can (as I know from my own chart) be very "choosy" about the beauty which it appreciates, and Iris was in search of *true* beauty: the beauty of nature, the beauty of humanity when people are behaving naturally and spontaneously. Her Venus is -23-MA and -31-UR, so that the VE-MA-UR relationship can be expressed as (MA-**28**-UR)-23/31-VE: these are all very creative harmonics, showing Iris seeking beauty in passionate and original ways. At the age of 19, she wrote, "My religion is a passionate belief in the beautiful".[11]

She also has SO-**31**-SA*. Thirty-oneness seems to be about the willingness to plumb deep into the unconscious and to expose the workings of the *id* as well as the ego, so this aspect will have helped Iris to be ruthless and determined in exploring her own failings and limitations.

Finally I would like to add that the inclusion of the asteroids Ceres, Pallas, Juno and Vesta in the chart (as I have done in Figure 7.3) adds further to the understanding of Iris's personality. Figure 3 shows that the asteroids add further to the emphasis on the horizontal axis, since three of the four asteroids are in houses adjacent to the Ascendant and Descendant. In particular we find that Saturn is closely conjunct to Vesta, the planet of purity, and closely opposite to Pallas, the planet of feminine wisdom. If, as I have said, Saturn is connected with Iris's exploration of morality, this can give further insight into the type of morality that she was trying to define. Also, Ceres, the planet of caring and nurturing is conjunct to Chiron and so is linked into the SO/VE/PL/CH cluster that I described: this suggests that her caring instincts, which never found an outlet in the mothering of children, were devoted instead to her wide-ranging search for love. And finally, Juno, the planet of faithfulness in marriage, is closely opposite to Uranus, which reinforces what I have said about the nature of her marriage. We could also study the harmonic aspects involving the asteroids (which are included in the "Table of Harmonics 1-32" provided by www.astrosoftware.com), but I will not attempt to do that here.

Of course, not everyone born at the same time as Iris Murdoch would have been able to do all the things that she did. We can say

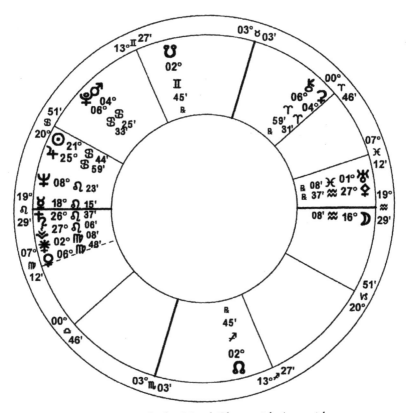

7.3 Iris Murdoch: Natal Chart with Asteroids

that, for most of her life, Iris succeeded in fulfilling the potential of her birth chart to a remarkable extent. And we should remember that, even in her last years, when she was suffering from Alzheimer's and was reduced to watching the Teletubbies on television, she was still the same person and still had the same birth chart; but her body and her mind were no longer able to make use of the chart's potential. The chart is there to help us, but we vary in the extent to which we are able to receive that help.

Gerard Manley Hopkins

Born 04.15 a.m., July 28, 1844, Stratford (London), England. RR: B.

Gerard Manley Hopkins has been described as the third greatest Victorian poet, after Tennyson and Browning. For me, however, Hopkins is the greatest Victorian poet – except that his poetry, unlike that of Tennyson and Browning, does not have a "Victorian" quality at all. It is unique and timeless, belonging to our own age as much as to Hopkins's own.

For readers who are unfamiliar with Hopkins's work, I will reproduce here his poem *The Windhover,* which is headed "To Christ our Lord". ("Windhover" is another word for "kestrel".)

> I caught this morning morning's minion, king-
> dom of daylight's dauphin, dapple-dawn-drawn Falcon, in his riding
> Of the rolling level underneath him steady air, and striding
> High there, how he rung upon the rein of a wimpling wing
> In his ecstasy! then off, off forth on swing,
> As a skate's heel sweeps smooth on a bow-bend: the hurl and gliding
> Rebuffed the big wind. My heart in hiding
> Stirred for a bird, - the achieve of; the mastery of the thing!
>
> Brute beauty and valour and act, oh, air, pride, plume, here
> Buckle! AND the fire that breaks from thee then, a billion
> Times told lovelier, more dangerous, O my chevalier!
>
> No wonder of it: shéer plód makes plough down sillion
> Shine, and blue-bleak embers, ah my dear,
> Fall, gall themselves, and gash gold-vermillion.

Also I will reproduce a simpler poem, *Spring and Fall,* which is headed "To a Young Child".

> Margaret, are you grieving
> Over Goldengrove unleaving?
> Leaves, like the things of man, you

With your fresh thoughts care for, can you?
Ah! as the heart grows older
It will come to such sights colder
By and by, nor spare a sigh
Though worlds of wanwood leafmeal lie;
And yet you *will* weep and know why.
Now no matter, child, the name:
Sorrow's springs are the same.
Nor mouth had, no nor mind, expressed
What héart héard of, ghóst guéssed:
It is the blight man was born for,
It is Margaret you mourn for.

I feel that the extraordinary vividness and vitality of Hopkins's poetry is based on two things. First, it is based on his use of what he called "sprung rhythm," in which the first syllable is stressed and may be followed by a variable number of unstressed syllables. Hopkins claimed that this imitated the rhythm of natural speech.

And secondly, it is based on his exceptional receptivity to the *essence* of what he is describing, together with his remarkable facility in finding (and sometimes inventing) words to describe this essence. Hopkins invented the term *inscape,* by which he meant "the unified complex of characteristics that gives each thing its uniqueness",[12] and he believed that a glimpse of the inscape of a thing shows us why God created it: 'Each mortal thing does one thing and the same ... Myself it speaks and spells, crying What I do is me: for that I came."[13] That is why *The Windhover* is headed "To Christ our Lord". In praising the windhover Hopkins is praising God who created it.

So, Hopkins was an inspired, innovative and creative poet, full of enthusiasm for the task of writing poetry as it had never been written before. Surely it must have occurred to him that his own personal inscape – that for which God had created him – was the writing of poetry. So why is it that he burnt his early poems, believing that that was what God required of him? The attempt to answer this question is one of the challenges facing an astrologer when looking at his chart.

Gerard Hopkins hated his middle name "Manley" and never used it, and yet somehow the name has stuck to him, a perpetual reminder of how he had let his father down by not being sufficiently "manly".

He was born in Stratford, east London, and a word needs to be added about the birth time. His biographer Norman White[14] gives the time of 4.15 a.m., but does not state the original source, so that one might be inclined to question whether this time is correct. However, I find that the placement of the planets in the 4.15 chart is totally convincing, and I am reasonably sure that the time is (approximately) accurate.

Gerard was the eldest of nine children. His father was a marine insurance adjuster who was also a compulsive writer. (Among other things, he wrote a history of Hawaii which became the standard work, even though he had never been there.) Gerard did well at school, and proceeded to Oxford University where he studied Classics. He seems at this time to have been fairly typical of middle-class young men of his time. Sexually he was homosexual but celibate. His biographer R.B. Martin explains how "normal" this was at the time: the word "homosexual" had not yet been invented (nor, of course, had "gay"), and, although homosexual *acts* were unlawful, it was expected that young men would fall in love with one another.[15]

But Gerard was different from the others in two ways. Firstly, he was very short of stature (5'2"). And secondly, he was already writing poetry. The poetry was the result both of his sensitivity to physical beauty (in human beings and in nature) and of his sensitivity to the beauty of words. In writing poetry, his aim was to find words whose beauty matched the beauty of what they described.

While he was at Oxford he converted to the Catholic Church. He had been brought up as a High Church Anglican (the equivalent of Episcopalian in America), but he was "in search of a religion that could speak with true authority".[16]

After graduating with brilliant first-class honours, he immediately joined the Society of Jesus and began training to become a Jesuit priest. This required a vow of celibacy: this was easy for Gerard as he was already celibate, but he seems to have felt that he also had to abstain from poetry precisely because he loved it so much. On November 6, 1865, he wrote in his diary: "On this day by God's grace I resolved to give up all beauty until I had His leave for it", and he burnt his early poems.

Over the next twenty years, first as a novitiate and then as an ordained priest, he moved wherever his superiors told him to move. Mostly he worked in grimy industrial cities, far from the natural beauty which he loved. As a parish priest he was not a success. He found the work stressful and exhausting. He did not know how to relate to ordinary people. A fellow Jesuit described him as "a man who in his shyness felt enormously awkward when he had to perform any public task".[17] He was especially ineffective as a preacher: on one occasion he reduced his congregation to mocking laughter when he tried to introduce lofty poetic imagery into one of his sermons.

In 1875 he was greatly moved to hear of the foundering of a German ship, the *Deutschland,* in which a hundred people, including five Franciscan nuns, had drowned, and this caused him to write his longest and most ambitious poem, *The Wreck of the Deutschland.* From then onwards he continued to write poetry, but not for publication. He sent some of his poems to his friend, the poet Robert Bridges, but, almost certainly, many of his later poems have been lost. (After Hopkins's death, a fellow Jesuit, who did not even know that Hopkins was a poet, came into his rooms and burnt all the papers that he found.)

In 1884 Hopkins was appointed Professor of Latin and Greek at University College, Dublin, but he found this work too gruelling and exhausting. He was not happy in Ireland, which at the time was in a state of political turmoil. He felt that his prayers were no longer reaching God, and he wrote his "terrible sonnets," of which his biographer says: "These highly personal sonnets make us feel that Hopkins is speaking for all of terrified humanity".[18] He came close to a mental breakdown. And then he contracted typhoid fever, and died in Dublin at 1.30 p.m. on June 8, 1889, at the age of 44.[19] His last words, which he was heard to repeat several times, were: "I am so happy, so happy".

Queen Victoria, who had been on the throne when Hopkins was born, was still there when he died; and for the rest of the Victorian age, and for a long time afterwards, Hopkins was completely unknown. It was only in 1918, 29 years after his death, that Robert Bridges, to whom Hopkins had entrusted some of his poems, took them to a publisher.

Hopkins's natal chart is shown in Figure 7.4. His List of Significant Harmonic Aspects is as follows:

1: (SO*-1-MA*)-1/1-ME
    -1-VE*
JU*-1-UR*

2: ((SO*-1-MA*)-1-VE*)-2/2/2-SA*
SO*-32-PL

3: (SO*-1-MA*)-3/3/3/3-
    (JU*-1-UR*)
(SO*-3-UR*)-9/**9**-MO
(SO*-1-MA*)-2/2-SA*)-3/3/**6**-JU*
(JU*-**6**-SA*)-**18**/**9**-PL
VE*-18-CH

5: MO-**15**-VE*
MO-25-MA*
MO-20-SA*
(ME-10-PL)-**20**/20-UR*
UR*-25-NE

7: (MO-7-ME)-14/14-JU*
ME-21-SA*

11: MO-11-PL

13: none

17: ME-**17**-NE
JU*-17-CH

19: (SA*-**19**-NE)-19-CH

23: VE*-23-PL

29: SA*-29-UR*

31: VE*-**31**-SA*

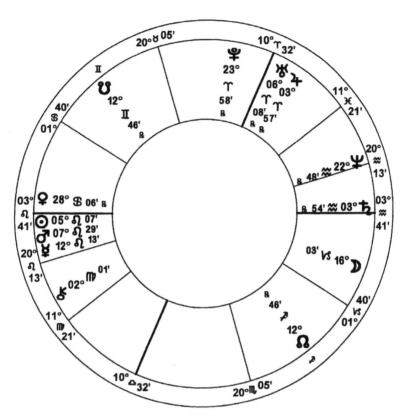

7.4 Gerard Manley Hopkins

When we look at Hopkins's chart, the first thing we notice is Sun, Mercury, Venus and Mars all close to the Ascendant in Leo/Cancer, facing Saturn which (if the birth time is right) is exactly on the Descendant in Aquarius. An image comes to my mind of an irresistible force coming up against an immovable block. There is so much fiery (and watery) power contained in SO, ME, VE and MA, seeking to express itself across the horizontal axis which represents the relationship between Self and Other, but when it reaches its destination it comes up against Saturn which says: No, you cannot express yourself freely, you must be controlled and disciplined.

But Saturn is itself part of Hopkins's make-up; it indicates what he is seeking in relationships. Saturn in the 7th house is often interpreted as the search for stability in marriage. But Hopkins was not seeking marriage. For him, Saturn represents his "search for a religion that could speak with true authority". It represents his willingness to take a vow of obedience, and to allow his whole life to be directed by others who had authority over him.

The closest opposition here is SO*-2-SA*. If we see the Sun as Hopkins's sense of his own identity, we can relate this aspect to his view of himself primarily as a priest, and only secondarily as a poet. VE*-2-SA* and MA*-2-SA* are "wide" aspects, but they gain strength from their closeness to the horizontal axis, and also from the fact that SA is at the VE/MA midpoint. We can perhaps see MA*-2-SA* as Hopkins's vow of celibacy, and VE*-2-SA* as his vow to "give up all beauty until he had [God's] leave for it".

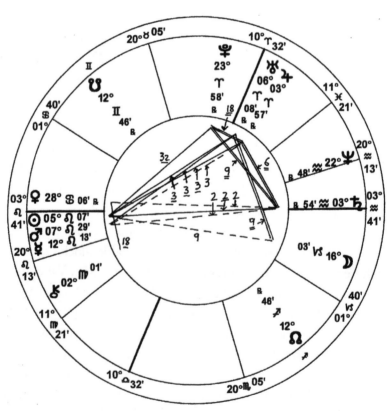

7.5 Gerard Manley Hopkins: Twoness and Threeness Aspects

But Mercury is outside this pattern. Although it is close to Sun and Mars, it is outside the orb for opposition to Saturn. So, although Hopkins has surrendered Sun, Venus and Mars to the authority of the Church, he is still free to *think* independently. Although he has resolved to live his life as a priest, he does not think, talk and communicate as a priest should. Hence some of his difficulties in carrying out his role.

However, these oppositions between SA and SO/VE/MA are almost the only pure Twoness aspects in Hopkins's chart. In Figure 7.5 I have shown all the Twoness and Threeness aspects in the chart, and we can see that the chart contains far more Threeness than Twoness. In fact, it is quite unusual to find a chart with so little Twoness. The chart contains no squares, no semi-squares or sesquiquadrates, no "16" aspects, and only one "32" aspect (SO-32-PL). But this last aspect is important. With Pluto in the 10th house, it shows a determination to deal ruthlessly with oneself – to punish oneself, almost – in relation to one's work in the world, and I believe this is connected to Hopkins's decision to join the most severe and most disciplined of all the Catholic orders.

In fact, I think that his lack of Twoness is one of the important features of his chart. Twoness aspects, as I have said, are *spurs to action:* they cause one to take action in the world to resolve one's problems. But Hopkins did not know how to do this. Once he had made his decision to become a Jesuit priest, he allowed his external behaviour to be directed by other people. He never took action to resolve his problems.

However, Hopkins has a very strong and complex pattern of Threeness, involving SO, MO, MA, JU, SA, UR and PL, and we need to try to unravel this pattern. To do so, we must first look at the planets that compose it.

Hopkins has no planets in the houses adjacent to the IC, and his parents (who were still alive when he died) and his numerous siblings seem to have been very unimportant to him. But in the houses adjacent to the Midheaven he has Jupiter and Uranus, which are conjunct each other near the Midheaven, and Pluto in the 10th house. These planets are descriptive of his goals – what he is working towards.

Jupiter in the 9th house in the first degrees of Aries seems to represent his desire to experience the grandeur of the universe – to expand into it, to feel himself to be part of it. "The world is charged with the grandeur of God," he wrote. And Uranus close to Jupiter represents his awareness of the diversity of this grandeur and the uniqueness of every element within it. "Each mortal thing does one thing and the same ... Myself it speaks and spells, crying What I do is me: for that I came."

The Threeness pattern shows that Jupiter and Uranus are linked by trines to Sun and Mars: (SO*-1-MA*)-3/3/3/3-(JU*-1-UR*). Hopkins delights in his awareness of the world's grandeur and diversity, it brings him pleasure, it arouses his Martian vitality.

But also, we see that Sun and Uranus are linked by "9" aspects (pleasure in pleasure) to his Moon, with the MO-UR link being very close: (SO*-3-UR*)-9/9-MO. The Moon is in Capricorn in the 6th house, and in conventional astrology it would be regarded as an "unaspected planet," since it has none of the traditional aspects (except for a sesquiquadrate to Chiron and a very wide square to Pluto). But in harmonic astrology we can see that it has this Nineness link to Sun and Uranus, as well as other aspects that we shall look at later. Moon in Capricorn denotes an "earthy" way of responding to events, and I feel that these Nineness links increase Hopkins's sensitivity to his physical environment, and therefore his skill as a poet of nature: he *delights* in the uniqueness of each object that surrounds him. Also Moon in the 6th house shows a desire to be of service in the world, and we should remember that Hopkins, despite all his difficulties, never deviated from his commitment to his work as a priest.

Thirdly, we can see that there is a cluster of very close aspects linking Jupiter, Saturn and Pluto: (JU*-6-SA*)-18/9-PL. The precise meaning of these aspects is difficult to put into words, but I feel that they show Hopkins *rejoicing* (Threeness) in the totality of his situation:

rejoicing in the bringing-together of his awareness of God's grandeur with his awareness of the restrictions imposed by Saturn, and using this as a vehicle for Plutonian self-cleansing and transformation. They are an indicator of the depth of his Christian faith.

Thus, we can see that Hopkins is more of a Threeness person than a Twoness person; and Threeness is about accepting the world as it is. At the end of his life, while wracked by pain, he was able to say: "I am so happy, so happy". He was able to surrender to (JU*-*6*-SA*)-*18/9*-PL and to joyfully welcome death.

But we have still not explained Hopkins's skill and originality as a poet; and for this we must turn to the higher harmonic numbers, and especially to Five and Seven, which are especially concerned with creativity.

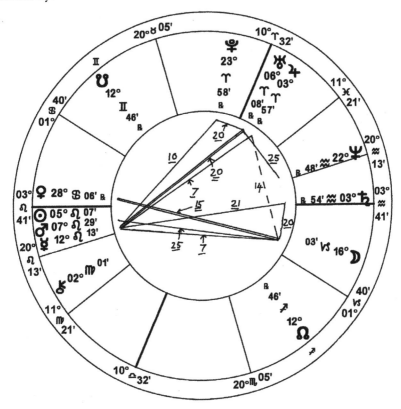

7.6 Gerard Manley Hopkins: Fiveness and Sevenness Aspects

Figure 7.6 shows Hopkins's Fiveness and Sevenness aspects. Here we can see that, whereas his Twoness and Threeness aspects were centred around the SO-SA opposition on the horizontal axis, the Fiveness and Sevenness aspects are centred around Moon and Mercury. Moon and Mercury are not angular, and so are less visible in how Hopkins presents himself to other people, but their Fiveness and Sevenness links show a profound creativity. We can say, perhaps, that in his solar personality (which includes Saturn) Hopkins is a priest, but in his lunar personality (which includes Mercury) he is a poet.

We will take the Sevenness links first, because Sevenness denotes creative inspiration, whereas Fiveness denotes skill in the process of creation. Mercury has three Sevenness links, all close: ME-7-MO, ME-14-JU*, and ME-21-SA*. These Mercury links show that Hopkins's creative inspiration is essentially *verbal:* he is inspired to communicate verbally about his emotions and his responses to events, and he is inspired to write both about Jupiterian themes ("The world is charged with the grandeur of God") and about Saturnian ones ("It is the blight man was born for, it is Margaret you mourn for"). ME-21-SA* suggests a certain *pleasure* in being inspired by misfortune, and I believe that, although Hopkins was genuinely grieving for the nuns who had drowned on the *Deutschland,* he also found pleasure in the way that their fate aroused his creativity.

And the Fiveness links are even stronger. Here we can see a very important cluster: (ME-10-PL)-*20*/20-UR*, with ME-*20*-UR* only 5 minutes from exactitude. 20 is 2 x 2 x 5: *striving* to create *structure and order.* So ME-*20*-UR* shows Hopkins working very hard to find the words which will best describe the uniqueness of what he observes, and the links to Pluto show that he will do this in a thoroughgoing and ruthless way. I believe that this well describes the skill which Hopkins displays in a poem such as *The Windhover.* It is related to his use of "sprung rhythm" and to his invention of the term *inscape,* which we mentioned earlier. And also there is a "25" link between Uranus and Neptune, which will increase his ability to use these skills in an imaginative and uplifting way.

Figure 7.6 also shows three separate Fiveness links to the Moon: MO-_15_-VE*, MO-_20_-MA*, and MO-_25_-SA*. These links show Hopkins's skill in creating poems which describe his innermost feelings and responses to events. In particular, the very close MO-_15_-VE* shows his pleasure in creating things which are both beautiful in themselves and are also descriptive of the beauty of the world.

There are also some links in the higher harmonics that we need to mention. There are two aspects involving Pluto, MO-_11_-PL and VE*-_23_-PL, and these should be considered together with MO-_15_-VE* which we discussed in the last paragraph. (MO-_15_-VE*)-_11/23_-PL shows that Hopkins's pleasure in creating things of beauty is tinged also with a spirit of defiance (11) and of longing for a better world (23) in relation to his desire (Pluto in the 10th house) to pursue his

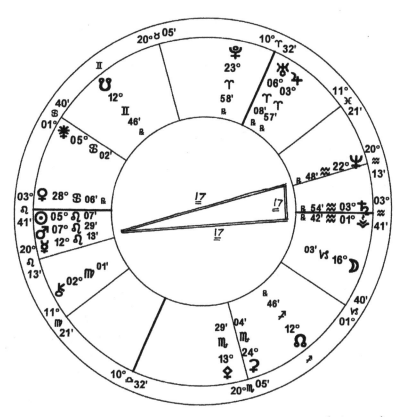

7.7 Gerard Manley Hopkins: Seventeenness Aspects, with Asteroids

goals with great focus and determination. This is a complex thing to describe, but I feel that Hopkins is saying: "These beautiful poems are my account of how I see the world: I wish that everyone could see the beauty that I see; but I am going to stick defiantly to my perceptions, even if no one else can share them".

And then there is ME-_17_-NE. This is an *exact* aspect, and I feel it is one of the most important aspects in Hopkins's chart. If we include the asteroids in the chart, we find that both Mercury and Neptune also have very close "17" links to Vesta, which is close to the Descendant, so that we have ME-_17_-NE-_17_-VT*. This is shown in Figure 7.7.

Seventeenness is about campaigning for a cause in which one believes, in an attempt to make the world a better place. ME-_17_-NE shows that Hopkins was campaigning for the deeper spiritual understanding of language, and the involvement of Vesta shows that this is also about the desire for *purity* in the use of language. This is exactly expressed by R.B. Martin who says that Hopkins was attempting to "scrape clean the bones of language and restore its purity".[20] His "campaigning" was not done in public, it belonged to his lunar "poetic" personality which he kept hidden, and yet it seems clear that he was on a mission, even if he had no expectation that his theories and beliefs would ever see the light of day.

In fact, Hopkins's Seventeenness is even stronger than this. If we look at his 17th harmonic chart, we see that it contains close trines from Mercury, Neptune and Vesta to both Sun and Venus. Thus (because 17 x 3 = 51) we have a mammoth cluster which can be expressed as follows:

((ME-_17_-NE-_17_-VT*)-_51_/_51_/51-SO*)-_51_/_51_/51/_51_-VE*

This shows that his "mission" was about enhancing the *beauty* of language (Venus) as well as its transcendence (Neptune) and its purity (Vesta); also that he was himself deeply committed to this mission (Sun); and also that he obtained great pleasure from it (17 x 3).

It may sometimes be worthwhile to look at the harmonic charts in search of aspects in harmonics higher than 32, but my suggestion is that these aspects should not be used for interpretation unless (as in this case) they form part of a very strong cluster.

Then there is (SA*-*19*-NE)-19-CH. Nineteenness people tend to shun fame and to prefer not to put themselves in the limelight, and these aspects will have contributed to Hopkins's choice to lead what his biographer calls "a very private life", and not to attempt to publish his poems.

And finally there is VE*-*31*-SA*. We have already noted that Venus is widely opposite to Saturn (VE*-2-SA*), and we suggested that this was connected to Hopkins's renunciation of beauty when he burned his early poems. But here we see that Venus also has a very close "31" link with Saturn. Thirty-oneness is often connected with violent and impulsive actions arising from deep emotions coming to the surface, so this link suggests that his burning of his poems was an impulsive act of violence against himself – what, in modern parlance, we would call an "act of self-harm". And it could be that this aspect contributed also to the despair which Hopkins experienced in his last years, when he felt that God had abandoned him, and he wrote his "terrible sonnets".

It would be easy to see Hopkins's life as a tragedy, and it would be easy to bemoan the fact that so many of his poems have been lost. But for me, the important thing is that he lived his life in his own unique way, and so increased the range of human diversity; and that he was a good man, who felt deeply for his fellow human beings and who never did anyone any harm; and that he has given us some of the finest poems in the English language. For this, we should be grateful.

René Magritte

Born November 21, 1898, 07.30 a.m., Lessines, Belgium. RR: AA.

René Magritte is, along with Salvador Dali, one of the two most famous Surrealist painters of the early twentieth century. One of his best-known paintings depicts a pipe, and beneath it the words *Ceci n'est pas une pipe* ("This is not a pipe"). Well, of course it's not a pipe, it's a *painting* of a pipe, it has two dimensions whereas a pipe has three;

and yet the painting still has the power to shock, as though Magritte was saying something controversial. His work is a constant reminder that the depiction of a thing is not the thing itself. And because it is not the thing itself, it can be placed alongside the depiction of other things, with which the "thing itself" would never be associated. That is what "surrealism" means: "if you describe something as surreal, you mean that the elements in it are combined in a strange way that you would not normally expect, like in a dream".[21]

Magritte's mother attempted suicide many times, causing her husband to lock her into her bedroom. But one day she escaped and was missing for several days; then, on March 12, 1912, her body was found drowned in a local river. It is said that Magritte himself (who was 13 at the time) was present when the body was found, and that she was found with her dress covering her face. It seems that Magritte never spoke about his mother's suicide, nor about the effects of having been reared by a mother who was mentally ill and who (one imagines) could give him very little love or support. Even though he was influenced by Freud's theories, he never sought psychotherapeutic help for himself. But clearly, his mother's fate had its effects on his painting – not only in that many of his figures have cloths covering their faces, but more generally, in that in his paintings he seems to be exploring the *mystery* of his mother's (and his own) identity. The appearance, he is saying, is not the reality, and yet the reality is mysterious and unknowable. Thus, he paints the *appearance* of a thing faithfully and realistically, and yet he said: "Everything we see hides another thing, we always want to see what is hidden by what we see".[22] Again, he said: "Art evokes the mystery without which the world would not exist".

My assumption is that Magritte's mother, behind her *appearance* as an ordinary woman, had never revealed the reality of her inner world which drove her to suicide. In the same way, Magritte himself preserved an *appearance* of ordinariness. He dressed conventionally (often wearing the bowler hat which is worn by many of the male figures in his paintings), and lived a conventional suburban life with his wife Georgette and their dog. He said, "Life obliges me to do something, so I paint". He also spoke of himself "dragging a fairly drab existence to its conclusion". Thus, the only clues to the inner reality behind the ordinary appearance lie in his paintings. He said, "I make use of paintings to render thoughts visible".

It is sometimes said that, because they are so well-known and because of their influence on later artists such as Andy Warhol, Magritte's paintings have now lost their power to shock. But in fact, Magritte's paintings can still be genuinely shocking. One of his earliest works is an extremely gruesome painting entitled *Young Girl Eating a Bird*. Magritte had seen his wife eating a chocolate bird (a *depiction* of a bird), so he decided to create a *depiction* of a woman eating a live bird. Also there are later paintings such as *The Rape,* in which the woman's facial features are replaced by her breasts and genitals, turning the

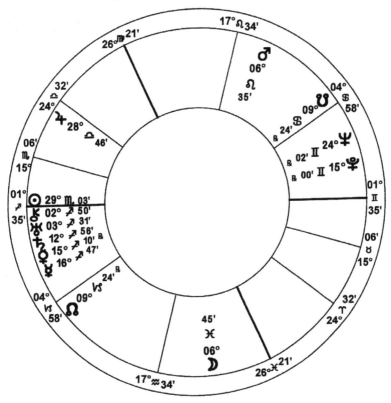

7.8 René Magritte

face into a sexual object. Thus, the thoughts which Magritte "renders visible" through his paintings can be extremely disturbing.

Magritte's chart is shown in Figure 7.8. His List of Significant Harmonic Aspects is as follows:

1:	(UR*-*1*-CH*)-1-SO* (ME-*1*-VE)-1-SA	**11:**	((MO-*11*-PL)-11-SO*)- *22*/*2*/*22*-VE
2:	((ME-*1*-VE)-1-SA)-*2*/*2*/2-PL ((VE-1-SA)-*2*/2-PL)-8-JU SO*-*16*-MA	**13:**	SO*-*26*-SA JU-*26*-NE ME-*26*-CH*
3:	SO*-*12*-JU (MO-*9*-ME)-*27*/*27*-UR* MO-*12*-MA UR*-*9*-NE	**17:**	MA-*17*-NE
		19:	none
		23:	MO-*23*-CH*
5:	SO*-*20*-ME ME-*15*-JU ME-*25*-NE PL-*15*-CH*	**29:**	VE-*29*-CH*
		31:	(VE-*31*-JU)-*31*/31-UR* MA-*31*-CH*
7:	SO*-*7*-NE (VE-*2*-PL)-*14*/*7*-MA JU-*21*-CH*		

We do not need harmonic astrology to see that, with Sun, Uranus and Chiron tightly bunched around the Ascendant, Magritte's task is to present himself to the world as a highly original and provocative healer. Healing is what Magritte's work is essentially about: healing of himself, and healing of the world. By "rendering thoughts visible", and presenting them to the world in a straightforward and unemotional way, he helps to make those thoughts acceptable, and to lessen the anguish that they create in our minds. Yes, we have these thoughts, and yes, that's OK. It is notable that, at the time of his mother's death on March 12, 1912, transiting Chiron was conjunct his natal Moon.

It is as though this was the moment when Magritte received the wound which enabled him to become the Wounded Healer.

Also, we can note the triple conjunction of Mercury, Venus and Saturn which is also in the first house, and which enables him to communicate his thoughts in a beautiful but also controlled and disciplined way (we should not forget Magritte's sheer skill as a largely self-taught painter). These two triple conjunctions are linked to each other, and also to Jupiter, by the Thirty-oneness cluster of (VE-*31*-JU)-*31*/31-UR*, and there is also MA-*31*-CH* linking Chiron to Mars which is the closest planet to the Midheaven. Thirty-oneness links are about delving into the subconscious mind, so these aspects will have helped Magritte to develop his skill in "making thoughts visible", presenting to the world the mystery that lies below the surface of things.

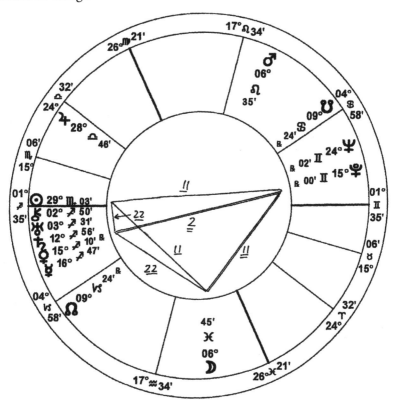

7.9 René Magritte: Elevenness Aspects

However, I feel that the most important harmonic cluster is the Elevenness cluster of ((MO-*11*-PL)-11-SO*)-22/*2*/22-VE which is illustrated in Figure 7.9. The importance of this cluster lies in the fact that:

(a) It brings together the Sun and the Moon, meaning that the quality of Elevenness pervades the whole of Magritte's personality: there is no conflict between his "solar" and his "lunar" nature;

(b) It unites Sun and Moon with the very close Venus-Pluto opposition between the 1st and 7th houses. This VE-PL opposition is clearly a driving force for Magritte. In itself it might seem to describe him as a charming and attractive person who was easily drawn into intense, powerful and transformative relationships. But the links binding these planets to Sun and Moon are Elevenness links; and the keywords for Elevenness include *defiance* and *dogged persistence*. This defiance was certainly a characteristic of Magritte's. He said:

> "I despise my own past and that of others. I despise resignation, patience, professional heroism and all the obligatory sentiments. I also despise the decorative arts, folklore, advertising, radio announcers' voices, aerodynamics, the Boy Scouts, the smell of naphtha, the news, and drunks. I like subversive humour, women's knees and long hair, the laughter of playing children, and a girl running down the street. I hope for vibrant love, the impossible, the chimerical. I dread knowing precisely my own limitations.".[22]

For me, this quotation is a very vivid description of the dynamic of VE-*2*-PL as modified by the Elevenness links with Sun and Moon. Magritte loves things which are purely Venusian. He projects Pluto out onto the outside world, and despises, and stands defiantly against, all the external pressures and expectations which constantly threaten to undermine his enjoyment of beauty and laughter. Having rejected Pluto, he is thrown back into (ME-*1*-VE)-1-SA in which he has to face up to this own limitations. And yet (because Twoness is always striving towards Oneness, even when the Oneness is out of reach) he longs for the union of Venus with Pluto: "vibrant love, the impossible, the chimerical".

Certainly, Elevenness defiance and persistence were dominant in Magritte's character. Like most Elevenness people, he was a workaholic, sticking resolutely to his preferred painting style and often repeating the same themes. He had to do things in his own way, not in the expected way. (As a young man he attended art school, but left because he felt that the teachers had nothing to teach him.)

Magritte also has great strength in both Fiveness and Sevenness. For a creative artist, Five and Seven are the numbers that say most about the creative process: Sevenness describes the inspiration which gives rise to the creation, and Fiveness describes the actual process of creating something new. So we can look at these two harmonics together in order to understand the nature of Magritte's artistic talent.

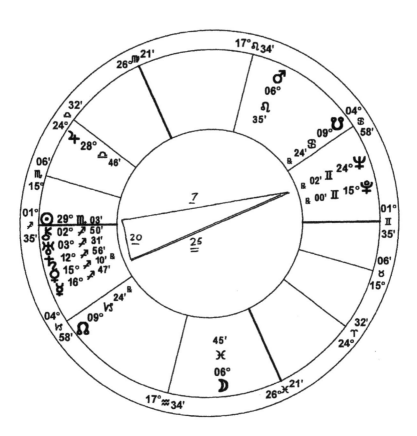

7.10 René Magritte: SO-ME-NE Aspects

In Figure 7.10 I have shown the harmonic aspects linking Magritte's Sun, Mercury and Neptune. From this we can see:

(a) Sun on the Ascendant is -7- Neptune, showing that Magritte is inspired by whatever has Neptunian qualities. This relates, I believe, to his fascination with the *mysterious* and the *dreamlike*. He said, "Art evokes the mystery without which the world would not exist," and "If the dream is a translation of waking life, waking life is also a translation of the dream". He has been described as the "enigmatic master of the impossible dream".[23] Especially, because Neptune is in the 7th house, Magritte is inspired by the Neptunian qualities of other people: their mysteriousness, their unknowability, their unfulfilled longings. He will try to convey these qualities in his art.

(b) Mercury is -**25**- Neptune. This almost-exact aspect gives Magritte an exceptional ability to use his rational mind to create Neptunian images. I see this aspect as the origin of his extraordinary skill in juxtaposing "ordinary" images so as to create a Neptunian effect. We have defined 25 (5 x 5) as *structuring of structuring*, or as *creating the conditions for structuring*. With this aspect, Magritte is able to structure his thoughts in such a way as to create the opportunity for Neptunian works of art.

(c) Sun is -20- Mercury. 20 is 5 x 2 x 2, denoting *striving towards structuring*. Magritte is struggling to make sense of his own life through rational thought. This completes the triangle, and shows how Magritte will devote his life to using his ME-**25**-NE skill to create images which express his SO-7-NE inspiration.

And Mercury is also -**15**- Jupiter. 15 is 5 x 3: pleasure in creativity. So Magritte will obtain great pleasure from doing this in an expansive, uninhibited Jupiterian way. This helps to explain the lightness and playfulness of his style, even when his subject-matter is dark and disturbing. One always has the feeling that Magritte *enjoyed* creating his paintings.

Also, the Venus-Pluto opposition (which we have already discussed) has very strong Sevenness links with Mars: (VE-**2**-PL)-**14**/7-MA. This shows how Magritte is *inspired* to express the Venus-Pluto dilemma through vigorous action: and, since Mars is in the 8th house, these actions will be connected with 8th house themes of life and death, relationships, and sexuality. Together with the SO*-7-MA link, this explains much about his choice of subjects for his paintings.

Since both Mars and Neptune are involved in the Sevenness links, we can note also MA-17-NE. Seventeenness is about *campaigning for a better world*, and this aspect might lead us to expect Magritte to be politically active, campaigning for a visionary future. He did in fact have strong political views; he was strongly anti-fascist, and after World War II he joined the Communist Party, but it seems that other features of his personality held him back from political activism.

Then there is SO*-**26**-SA. Thirteenness links involving the Sun are about the quest for one's own identity, and "26" links are the same but with a greater sense of effort and struggle. If Saturn is the planet linked to the Sun, we can say that the search is for one's *limitations*, and I believe we can relate this to Magritte's saying (which we have already quoted): "I dread knowing precisely my own limitations". Also there is SO*-**16**-MA, which suggests a struggle to express himself in action – a struggle, perhaps, against laziness and inertia.

There are also some harmonic links involving Chiron (which is important because of its position on the Ascendant).

- ME-26-CH* suggests an adventurousness in mentally exploring ways in which he can be of service to others.

- MO-**23**-CH*. We have already suggested that Moon/Chiron is about Magritte's response to his mother's suicide. Twenty-threeness is about story-telling, so Magritte (through his paintings) is telling a story about his mother's fate. I feel this is one of the ways in which he distanced himself from emotional involvement.

- VE-29-CH*. Twenty-nineness is about pride in one's uniqueness, so this aspect suggests that Magritte is proud of the beauty of his images and of their capacity to heal.

Finally we can note the strong Threeness pattern in (MO-**9**-ME)-27/**27**-UR* and also UR*-**9**-NE. This shows that, in spite of all the "darkness" in his thoughts, Magritte remained essentially cheerful, with a light-hearted, easy-going attitude to life, and with a sparkling and original sense of humour. In fact, for some critics this is his most outstanding characteristic. Terry Gilliam (a member of the Monty Python comedy team) describes Magritte as "this wonderfully dry joke-teller," and says that he walked round an exhibition of Magritte's paintings "laughing uncontrollably".[23]

But one harmonic number which is absent from Magritte's chart is Nineteen. We have said that Nineteenness is about *empathy,* and this was a quality which Magritte lacked. In fact, this lack of empathy has been cited as one of his strengths. Thus, Jonathan Jones, in writing about Magritte's painting *Man with a Newspaper* (in which the man is there, and then he is not there), points out that "the painting is not mournful or sad. That's because the man is portrayed *without a shred of empathy* ... that's why his disappearance is not that big a deal. Perhaps that is part of Magritte's point. We exist, and then we don't. The world will be there when we are gone"[24] (my italics). (And yet I need to add a caution here. Iris Murdoch was also lacking in Nineteenness aspects, and yet she was not lacking in empathy. There are dangers in assuming that these keywords, such as *inspiration, defiance* and *empathy,* are the exclusive property of one particular harmonic number – in assuming, for instance, that a person who is weak in Sevenness is uninspired, or that a person without Elevenness is incapable of defiance. Life is never as simple as that.)

Magritte died on August 15, 1967, after a long battle with pancreatic cancer. In my view, he was one of the most innovative, profound and thought-provoking painters of all time. I have tried to do justice to him in these pages, and yet I feel that, if he is watching me from beyond the grave, I owe him an apology. I believe that he would not have welcomed this attempt to analyse his mind; he would prefer it to remain mysterious. "The meaning of the mind", he said, "is unknowable".

Whitney Houston

Born August 9, 1963, 08.55 p.m., Newark, NJ, USA. RR: AA.

"Spectacular". That is a word that is often used to describe Whitney Houston, and it seems to suit her exceptionally well: not only because of her striking appearance, and the brilliance of her three-octave voice, but also because of the way in which she threw herself, with total enthusiasm, vitality, passion and dedication, into her performances.

Whitney first sang in public at the age of 12. Her mother, Cissy Houston (born September 30, 1933), a successful gospel singer, taught Whitney to sing and carefully nurtured and directed her career, and also instilled in her the Baptist faith. As a teenager, Whitney sang in various nightclubs alongside her mother. Then, at the age of 21, she produced her first album, *Whitney Houston,* which became the best-selling debut album in history. From then on, there was no holding her back: she became a global superstar.

On July 18, 1992, she married the singer Bobby Brown (born February 5, 1969, 05.21 a.m., Boston, MA: RR: AA): she cried throughout the ceremony. Bobby was known as a "bad boy" and had had three children by two different women, but Whitney said that she felt safe with him and could just "be herself". Their daughter Bobbi Kristina was born on March 4, 1993; later, Whitney had two miscarriages.

Whitney and Bobby stayed together until 2006, when they were divorced; but Whitney's use of cocaine gradually became more and more addictive, and she began cancelling engagements and behaving unpredictably. But she continued to perform until the very end, and her performances were still described as "spectacular". She died at 3.55 p.m. on February 11, 2012, in the Beverley Hills Hilton Hotel, CA. The autopsy report stated that she had drowned accidentally in the bathtub, and that heart disease and chronic cocaine use were contributory factors.

In 2017 a documentary was released entitled *Whitney: Can I Be Me?* The message of this very moving film is that Whitney suffered from low self-esteem. Although she was proud of her voice (which she saw as God-given), she *did not believe that her identity as a famous singer was who she really was.* Hence her repeated cry, "Can I be me?" She longed to be loved and accepted for herself, not for her performances. She was uncomfortable with her fame, and with the expectations put on her by the public and the media that she should be happy because she was rich and famous. She was lonely. She needed to feel safe and protected.

As a child she had felt loved and accepted by her father, but not by her mother. As an adult she became very dependent on a close friend, Robyn Crawford, who became a substitute mother for her, shielded her from the world, and helped her to make decisions. (The media misunderstood their relationship, and speculated that they were having a lesbian affair.) She also initially felt loved and accepted

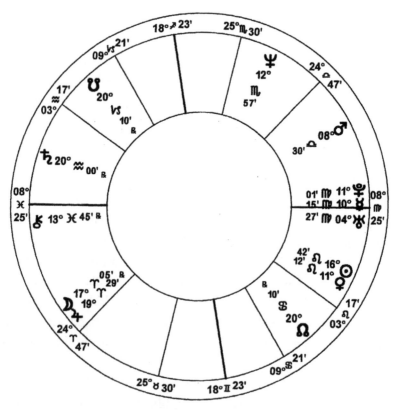

7.11 Whitney Houston

by Bobby. But Bobby and Robyn hated each other, and eventually Bobby drove Robyn out. Then Bobby was unfaithful to Whitney, and started to behave violently towards her, causing the break-up of the marriage. And then the last straw for Whitney was when her father, by whom she still felt loved, filed a lawsuit against her, demanding that she paid him a million dollars which he said she owed him. When she died, a friend said she was sure that she had died of a broken heart.

Whitney Houston's chart is shown in Figure 7.11. Her List of Significant Harmonic Aspects is as follows:

1:	SO-1-VE	**11:**	VE-22-CH*
	MO-1-JU		
	(ME*-1-PL*)-1/1-UR*	**13:**	SA-26-NE
2:	(ME*-1-PL*)-2/2-CH*	**17:**	none
	JU-8-UR*		
3:	(MO-1-JU)-3/3-SO	**19:**	MO-19-SA
	ME*-9-SA		UR*-19-CH*
	JU-6-SA		
	NE-3-CH*	**23:**	(JU-23-NE)-23-ME*
5:	(SO-3-MO)-15/15/5/5-	**29:**	VE-29-JU
	(ME*-1-PL*)		NE-29-PL*
	SO-25-NE		
	(JU-6-SA)-10/15-CH*	**31:**	VE-31-UR*
7:	((SO-7-MA)-3/21/21/21-(MO-7-NE))-(21)/21/21/21-UR*		
	VE-21-SA		

Perhaps the most important aspect in Whitney's chart is the very close Sun-Moon trine (SO-3-MO) in Fire signs. (It may also be important that the Midheaven is close to the Sun-Moon midpoint, so that it forms a Grand Trine with Sun and Moon, and also with Jupiter.) Because in conventional astrology we are accustomed to allowing orbs of up to 8° for the trine, we may regard such trines as common and unremarkable. But in harmonic astrology *everything depends on the closeness of the aspect to exactitude*. Thus, Whitney's Sun-Moon trine, with an orb of only 0°23', is far more exceptional, and is a very important determinant of the personality.

In Chapter 6 I said: "If there is a close Sun-Moon link in a particular harmonic, then the qualities of that harmonic will tend to pervade the whole personality". Thus, Whitney's SO-*3*-MO shows that her personality is pervaded by Threeness. She is a seeker of pleasure. She naturally has the happy-go-lucky, easy-going attitude to life of someone for whom Threeness is the most important principle. She wants to be free to take life as it comes. And, because Sun and Moon are in Fire signs (and also because of MO-1-JU), she will tend to express this in a fiery, dramatic, outgoing way.

In contrast, Twoness is rather weak in Whitney's chart. There is the not-very-close opposition between Mercury/Pluto descending and Chiron rising, which shows, perhaps, that she feels driven towards using her Mercury/Pluto abilities (which I will come back to later) for the purpose of healing both herself and others. But, apart from this, the only Twoness aspect is JU-*8*-UR*: this aspect is almost exact, and is indicative of how, in her performances, Whitney sometimes seems to be pushing herself very hard, holding on to each note for as long as she possibly can, forcing herself to express every last gram of emotion.

This relative absence of Twoness shows that Whitney is lacking in the basic Twoness ability to *take action to resolve one's problems*. As I said in *The Spirit of Numbers* (p.56), "the positive side of Twoness is that it can spur us into action to resolve our problems". Whitney was not good at this. She became very dependent on Robyn Crawford to advise her on how to cope with difficulties, and how to organize her life in general. In Robyn's absence she left difficult decisions to other people, thus becoming their victim; and she coped with unhappiness by taking cocaine, knowing full well that this would not solve the problems, but would only provide temporary relief.

There are, however, strong patterns of Fiveness and Sevenness: but these are tied in with the Sun-Moon trine, so that they are in fact

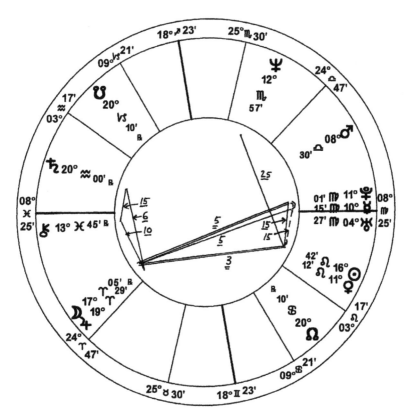

7.12 Whitney Houston: Fiveness Aspects

patterns of Fifteenness (15 = 5 x 3) and of Twenty-oneness (21 = 7 x 3).

Figure 7.12 shows the Fiveness links in Whitney's chart, and here the most important cluster is (SO-*3*-MO)-15/15/5/*5*-(ME*-*1*-PL*). In fact, if we include the asteroid Ceres (which is in Libra in the 7th house), this cluster becomes even stronger, since Ceres has Fifteenness links with all four of these planets. Thus we have:

$$((SO\text{-}\textbf{3}\text{-}MO)\text{-}15/\underline{15}/5/\textbf{5}\text{-}(ME^*\text{-}\textbf{1}\text{-}PL^*))\text{-}\underline{15}/15/\underline{\textbf{15}}/15\text{-}CE.$$

This cluster is, I believe, the most important indicator of how Whitney was able to develop her amazing gifts as a singer. Fiveness always involves *conscious creation*: the re-ordering and re-shaping of the world to create something that was not there before. And, if the Sun and Moon are involved, the thing that is being re-ordered and re-shaped is one's own personality, and the way one lives one's life. Thus, the Fiveness and Fifteenness links between SO-*3*-MO and ME*-*1*-PL* (with MO-*5*-PL* almost exact) show how Whitney was able to harness her natural SO-*3*-MO exuberance to her ME*-*1*-PL* ability to communicate with the world in a powerful, dedicated, transformative Plutonian way. This cluster may not explain the power of Whitney's God-given voice, but it does help to explain the "spectacular" quality of her performances and the power which she exerted over her audiences.

The involvement of Ceres adds to the power of this created personality. Jessica Adams[25] says that the placement of Ceres shows where one can find *abundance,* and there was certainly abundance in the face which Whitney presented to the world. But Ceres also carries the connotation of *caring and nurturing.* With Ceres (as well as Mercury and Pluto) in the 7th house, Whitney developed an intense relationship with her audiences. She is communicating with them (Mercury), transforming them (Pluto), and caring for them (Ceres).

But the problem for Whitney was that this re-ordering and re-shaping was directed, not by Whitney herself, but by her mother. It was her mother who taught her to sing and who carefully controlled and directed her career until it took off of its own accord. It has been said that Whitney lived the life that her mother had wanted for herself. Thus, Whitney became saddled with a public personality that was not of her own making. Left to herself, she would still have had the Fiveness tendencies, but she would probably have used them in a different way.

It is important to stress that Whitney was not *resistant* to being controlled by her mother. The Fifteenness links (pleasure in creativity) show that she responded enthusiastically, and took great pleasure in doing what her mother wanted. Nevertheless, by doing this, she went to a place where she had not planned to go. She acquired fame, which was what her mother wanted for her, but not what she wanted for herself. With Mercury, Mars, Pluto, and all four asteroids (Ceres, Pallas, Juno, Vesta) in the 7th house, Whitney was an extremely sociable person. Close one-to-one relationships were what mattered to her, what she lived her life for. She needed relationships that were diverse, intense, and authentic. But fame took her to a place where she was unreachable by ordinary people, and where close one-to-one relationships (uncontaminated by issues of power, money and reputation) were virtually impossible. Whiney did her best for her friends: she bought them cars, she bought them houses, she regaled them with her infectious laughter, but she could no longer have authentic relationships with them. She was too rich and too famous.

Thus (like many people with strong Fiveness) Whitney ended up being imprisoned by her Fiveness. Fiveness is about *building*. You build yourself a palace, and then the palace turns out to be a prison from which you cannot escape.

Figure 7.12 also shows SO-25-NE. I believe that (with Neptune in the 8th house) this increases Whitney's ability to present herself in a way that arouses people's sexual fantasies. (This was, in fact, one of her difficulties. She suffered greatly from stalkers who pursued her.)

Also there is the cluster of (JU-6-SA)-10/15-CH*. This cluster combines elements of Twoness, Threeness and Fiveness, and its precise effects are difficult to determine. But let me give a tentative interpretation of its meaning. With Chiron rising, Whitney identifies with the Wounded Healer archetype.[26] This gives her a great vulnerability: she is easily wounded, and is seeking ways to heal her wounds. The Fiveness links with Jupiter and Saturn cause her to seek ways which combine Jupiterian expansiveness (Jupiter in the 1st house: look at me, I'm free, I can do whatever I like) with Saturnian limitation (Saturn in the 12th house: I'm inadequate, I'm full of self-doubt). This somehow expresses the paradox of Whitney's life: how she was able to go on stage and, in a very uninhibited way, express all of her inner sense of inadequacy. This was a healing process for her, and potentially also for her audiences. And yet the healing is never complete: the vulnerability is still there.

Whitney also has a very strong pattern of Sevenness, which is shown in Figure 7.13. Here the main cluster is:

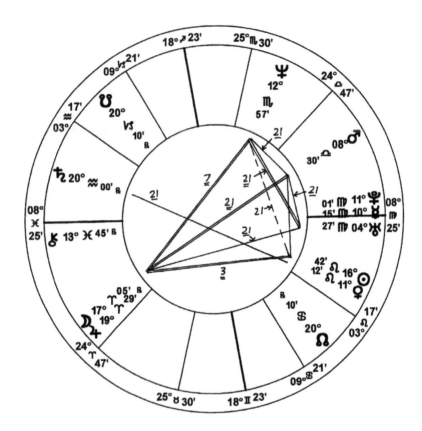

7.13 Whitney Houston: Sevenness Aspects

((SO-7-MA)-*3*/21/*21*/21-(MO-7-NE))-(21)/*21*/*21*/*21*-UR*.

Once again, we can see how this cluster is built around the Sun-Moon trine. Thus, Sun and Moon (whose aspect is Threeness, *pure pleasure*) are linked to Mars, Neptune and Uranus by aspects which are either Sevenness (*pure inspiration*) or Twenty-oneness (*pleasure in inspiration*).

These aspects point to the immense exhilaration and emotionality which is a major part of Whitney's charisma. She is *pleasurably inspired* by whatever has the qualities of Mars, Neptune and Uranus, and this inspiration is conveyed to us through her singing. Since Mars is in the 7th house, Neptune in the 8th, and Uranus close to the Descendant, the inspiration is aroused especially in relationships, and comes out in songs such as *I Will Always Love You,* a song which was composed by Dolly Parton but which Whitney made her own by singing it with an immense passion. But the passion is also evident in Whitney's personal relationships, and especially in the emotionality of her attraction to Bobby Brown, in whom she found a kindred spirit (he himself has MO-*21*-NE).

There is also VE-21-SA, and this aspect is linked to the asteroid Juno: thus, if we include the asteroids in the chart, we have (VE-Z-JN)-21/21-SA. Juno is the planet of marital faithfulness, so VE-Z-JN suggests that Whitney is inspired by the idea of fulfilling her femininity through a long-term relationship with a single partner. But the involvement of Saturn suggests that she is also aware that there will always be sadnesses and disappointments around this. Whitney's Saturn is strongly placed in the 12th house but does not have very strong harmonic aspects; it is a kind of looming presence in the chart, suggesting that underneath the wild enthusiasm there is always the sadness; and this too is present in the quality of Whitney's singing. MO-19-SA suggests a great ability to empathize with the suffering of others.

Another harmonic cluster is (JU-*23*-NE)-23-ME*. Twenty-threeness is about inventiveness and story-telling, so this cluster suggests that Whitney was adept in inventing stories which combine the qualities of Jupiter and Neptune. I am not sure how this manifested in her life. Maybe this was an ability that she would have expressed more strongly if she had chosen a different lifestyle. (We should always remember that the chart shows only potential. A person does not always fully manifest all the potentialities of their chart.)

Also there are a number of higher-harmonic aspects affecting Venus: VE-22-CH*, VE-29-JU, and VE-*31*-UR*. Venus is conjunct the Sun and so is about her awareness of her own femininity and her attractiveness. VE-22-CH* suggests a certain defiance about her awareness of her vulnerability as a woman: it is as though she was saying "I know I am vulnerable, I defy you to wound me". VE-29-JU suggests a great pride in the unique Jupiterian quality of her beauty.

And VE-*31*-UR*, which is an almost exact aspect, suggests a tendency (which was evident in her relationship with Bobby) to suddenly erupt in surprising ways, imposing her feminine qualities on other people and challenging them to respond.

The 17th harmonic, which is associated with political activism, is absent from Whitney's chart. She was in fact socially active in certain ways, founding the Whitney Houston Foundation for Children (which helps kids with cancer and AIDS) and joining in protests against apartheid in South Africa, and yet one website says that she was "primarily an entertainer ... she was not an activist".[27]

Other astrologers may disagree with me, but I personally believe that there is nothing in Whitney's chart which shows that she *had* to be born to a controlling mother. Thus, I believe that, if Whitney had been born with the same chart but to a different mother, her life would have developed differently. She would have been able to use her Fiveness to create a personality of her own choosing, not of her mother's choosing. She would still have been an amazing person, but she would probably not have become famous. She would probably have been happier, and she would probably have had a longer life.

Whitney Houston brought joy to millions of people through her singing. But in a televised interview, she was asked, "How would you like to be remembered?" Whitney did not reply that she wanted to be remembered as a singer. Rather, she said: "I just want to be remembered for being a real nice person. Somebody who cared, somebody who tried to do everybody righteously".[28] So let us remember her that way. It's what she wanted, and it's what she richly deserves.

Patricia Columbo

Born June 21, 1956, 11.52 a.m. (standard time), Chicago, IL, USA. RR: B.

I am including this case study because I believe it is an excellent example of a case where an examination of the harmonic aspects is *essential* for an understanding of the chart.[29]

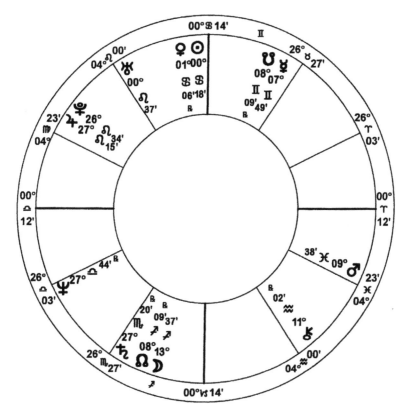

7.14 Patricia Columbo

At 10.30 p.m. on May 4, 1976, 19-year-old Patricia Columbo, together with her boyfriend 36-year-old Frank DeLuca, murdered Patricia's father Frank, her mother Mary, and her 13-year-old brother Michael, in their home at Elk Grove, Illinois. All three victims were shot by DeLuca, but they were also repeatedly stabbed and mutilated, and it is said that most of the stabbing and mutilation was carried out by Patricia.

It is thought that Patricia was motivated by a desire to inherit her parents' money, but there are also reports of tensions in the family. For the first six years of her life Patricia had been her father's "princess", but when Michael was born her father had transferred his affections to his son and heir, and Patricia had felt discarded. When Patricia reached puberty she was sexually precocious and had a number of lovers. (She claimed that she had been sexually molested by a family friend.) At the age of 17 she formed a liaison with DeLuca, who took her to live with him at his home, along with his wife and children. This aroused the anger of Patricia's father, who went to DeLuca's place of work and smashed his teeth in with a rifle butt.

It was alleged that Patricia had been planning the murders for several months, and that, before approaching DeLuca, she had tried to persuade two other men (who were also her lovers) to assist her in the killings.

She and DeLuca were both sentenced to 200 years in prison. In effect, this meant that they could both expect to die in prison. In 1979 it was reported that Patricia had been organizing sex orgies in the prison, and several prison officers were forced to resign. Since then, however, Patricia has repeatedly (and unsuccessfully) applied for parole, claiming that she is full of remorse and is no longer a danger to society. She has studied for a degree, and has become a model prisoner, teaching arts and crafts, and helping other inmates.

Patricia's birth chart is shown in Figure 7.14. However, before we look at the chart, we need to discuss a problem about the time of birth. Patricia's biographer Clark Howard reports that he had obtained the time of 11.52 a.m. from Patricia's stepmother who was present at the birth.[30] This is, I feel, an adequately trustworthy source. However, there is a problem about daylight saving time.

At the time of Patricia's birth, daylight saving time was in operation, but all the hospitals in Illinois were required by the state government to record births in standard time, not in daylight saving time. I have therefore followed AstroDatabank in assuming that the time given is in standard time (on the assumption that the stepmother was reporting the time officially recorded by the hospital, or else that she was observing the hospital clocks which were set to standard time).

But of course, this may not have been the case, and Patricia may have been born an hour earlier. If we cast the chart for 11.52 DST, we find that the Ascendant is now at 18° Virgo and the MH at 16° Gemini. Sun and Venus are no longer on the MH, but the Moon is now within 4 degrees of the IC. Most of the harmonic aspects remain the same, but the Elevenness aspects linking the Moon to Sun and

Saturn are no longer present. The DST chart is, I feel, less convincing, and I am therefore using the standard time chart.

Her List of Significant Harmonic Aspects is as follows:

1:	SO*-_1_-VE*	**11:**	(SO*-_11_-MO)-22/_22_-SA
	JU-_1_-PL		(JU-_1_-PL)-_11_/11-CH
2:	(SO*-_16_-ME)-_32_-PL	**13:**	((SO*-_1_-VE*)-_13_/13-
	(JU-_1_-PL)-_4_/4-SA		MA)-13/_13_/13-PL
	(JU-_4_-SA)-32/_32_-VE*		
	MO-_8_-NE	**17:**	MA-_17_-SA
3:	(SO*-_1_-VE*)-_12_-UR	**19:**	(JU-_1_-PL)-_19_/19-SO*
	((JU-_1_-PL)-_4_/4-SA)-_6_/6/_12_-NE		
	-_6_/6-NE)-_9_/9/_18_-ME	**23:**	MA-_23_-UR
	JU-_27_-UR		
	VE*-_18_-CH	**29:**	none
5:	(JU-_6_-NE)-_15_/30-MA	**31:**	(MO-_31_-ME)-31/_31_-VE*
	(MO-_25_-CH)-25/_25_-MA		
7:	SA-_4_-PL)-_7_/28-MA		

The challenge for an astrologer, in analysing Patricia's chart, is to find clues in the chart which might help to explain how she was able to plan and execute the murder of her family. One can see, from her family history, how she might well have fantasized about killing her parents and her brother, and might well have wished them dead; but to turn this fantasy into reality is a different matter.

And I do not think that conventional astrology offers satisfactory answers to this question. One can, of course, see some clues. Firstly, there is Sun very closely conjunct Venus on the Midheaven. With this placement, we can say that Patricia's whole goal in life is the promotion of herself as the personification of Venus-Aphrodite. She was clearly intoxicated by her own beauty and her power to attract men, and she believed that this enabled her to get away with anything. (She flirted

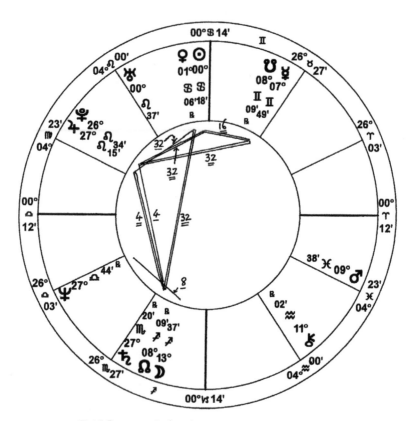

7.15 Patricia Columbo: Pure Twoness Aspects

"outrageously" with the police officers who questioned her about the murders, in the belief that this would help to secure her release.)

And secondly, we can note the very close Jupiter-Saturn square (orb 0°05') with Jupiter also very closely conjunct Pluto ((JU-*1*-PL)-*4*/*4*-SA). Saturn is in the 3rd house and seems to represent her feeling of being constrained and restricted by her family. So the square aspects from Saturn to Jupiter and Pluto show that there is a very strong desire to find ways of breaking free from these restrictions in a dramatic, drastic, thoroughgoing Jupiter-Pluto way.

But I feel we must turn to the harmonic aspects to find a full explanation for Patricia's behaviour. And, if we look at her List of Harmonic Aspects, we see that she has four very strong clusters of aspects which offer vital clues. These clusters are listed under the headings 2, 11, 13 and 31.

Firstly, Twoness. Patricia has two strong clusters involving the higher levels of Twoness (16 and 32).

(SO*-*16*-ME)-*32*-PL
(JU-*4*-SA)-32/*32*-VE*

If we enter these aspects onto the chart (Figure 7.15), we see that (because of the Sun-Venus and Jupiter-Pluto conjunctions) these two clusters are in fact one single cluster, uniting SO*-*1*-VE* with (JU-*1*-PL)-*4*/4-SA, and also with Mercury, in a single complex pattern of Twoness.

Twoness aspects are always *spurs to action*. The person is driven to find *ways of acting* that will resolve the conflicts between the planets involved. So Patricia is strongly motivated to find ways of using her Sun-Venus attractiveness to resolve the Jupiter-Saturn-Pluto problem. And especially important are the "16" and "32" aspects linking Mercury to Sun and Pluto. These aspects (which are *exact*) show Patricia compulsively using her Gemini mind to plan ways (ruthless Plutonian ways) of resolving her problems. We can see how this will have caused her to obsessively plan the murder of her family, blinding her to all the reasons (both moral and practical) why this was not a sensible thing to do.

Secondly, Elevenness. Patricia has a cluster of (SO*-11-MO)-22/*22*-SA. The harmonic that brings the Sun and the Moon together is always important, and in Patricia's case Elevenness unites the Sun not only with the Moon but also with Saturn. We have said that the keywords for Elevenness include *defiance* and *dogged persistence:* the person who is strong in Elevenness stands defiantly apart from other people, and doggedly pursues his or her own path. So these aspects will have helped Patricia to pursue a path that was so markedly in contrast to what was expected of her. I have a feeling that, with Saturn involved, and with both Moon and Saturn in the 3rd house, there is a sense of fatalism about these aspects – as though Patricia was aware that, by destroying her family, she would also destroy her own freedom, and would bring herself down with them, and yet felt compelled to carry her actions through.

Thirdly, Thirteenness. Patricia has a cluster of ((SO*-*1*-VE*)-*13*/13-MA)-13/*13*/13-PL, which includes very close Thirteenness aspects between Sun and Mars and between Venus and Pluto. These Thirteenness links are very much tied in with the Twoness pattern which we showed in Figure 7.15, since Venus and Pluto are two of the planets involved in that pattern. So this brings a further element of adventurousness and risk-taking into the picture. Thirteenness people are prone to taking risks in their search to test their own limits, and this is perhaps especially true of SO-*13*-MA, which is inclined to reckless and impulsive actions. It is as though Patricia is saying to herself, "Can I really stab my father, my mother and my brother to death? I need to prove to myself that I can do it."

And finally, Thirty-oneness. Patricia has a cluster of (MO-*31*-ME)-31/*31*-VE*, including very close Thirty-oneness links between Moon and Mercury and between Mercury and Venus (the Moon-Mercury link is almost exact). As I have already reported, I have found several examples of sadistic murderers (as well as the Marquis de Sade himself) with strong Thirty-oneness patterns, and it would seem that there is a connection between Thirty-oneness and sadistic violence. In Patricia's case the Thirty-oneness is centred on the Moon, and so is to do with how she *responds* to events. If unpleasant things happen to her, she tends to respond in a violent and uncontrolled manner. This helps to explain the savagery with which she attacked her relatives, as though she was not content merely to see them killed: she wanted them to suffer as much pain as possible before they died. I think that this savagery was probably unpremeditated: she had probably *planned* simply to have DeLuca shoot her family to death, but, in the heat of the moment, raw emotions arose, to which she gave vent.

All these harmonic aspects support each other and add to the picture, and I feel that, taken together, they add up to a fairly comprehensive explanation of why Patricia Columbo was able to commit her appalling crime.

Chapter 8
Harmonics in Mundane Charts

Harmonic aspects are of course present in mundane charts, just as much as in natal charts. In *The Spirit of Numbers* I presented several cases of mundane charts, and showed how the study of harmonic aspects could enhance and illuminate one's understanding of those charts. The general theory that I was proposing was as follows: *When an event occurs, the chart for that event very often reflects the mindset of the person or people who caused the event to happen.* We can say that, at that moment, a particular pattern of interplanetary aspects is "in the air", and may cause people to act in ways which reflect the nature of that pattern.

Thus, for instance, I presented the charts for several rail crashes, and showed that:

- The chart for the Nuneaton crash of 1975 (June 6, 1975, 01.55 a.m., Nuneaton, England), in which six people died, contains an extremely strong pattern of Twoness, indicating stress and tension. This crash appears to have been caused by the very great stress (desperately trying to make up for lost time) which the train driver was experiencing at the time.

- The chart for the Paddington crash of 1999 (October 5, 1999, 08.09 a.m., London, England), in which 31 people died, contains a very strong pattern of Threeness, indicating a carefree (careless) attitude to life. This crash was caused by the carelessness of the driver of one of the trains that collided: he failed to notice a series of red signals, and continued on when he should have stopped.

- The chart for the Ufton Nervet crash of 2004 (November 6, 2004, 06.12 p.m., Ufton Nervet, near Reading, England), in which seven people died, contains an exceptionally strong pattern of Fiveness.

This crash was deliberately caused by a car driver who parked his car on a level crossing and waited for it to be hit by a train. Fiveness, as we have seen, is about Man's power to affect and change his environment. (The time of this crash, when Jupiter, Saturn, Uranus and Pluto were all quintile to one another, was also the time of the U.S. Army's attack on the town of Fallujah, known as the Second Battle of Fallujah (November 7, 2004, 07.00 p.m.[1]), which was the bloodiest and most brutal event of the Iraq war. Fiveness can cause tremendous *de*struction as well as *con*struction.)

It is important to note that, in these rail crashes, *the chart describes the causes of the crash, not the effects.* This is especially clear in the case of the Paddington chart, which appears to be a cheerful, happy-go-lucky chart, because this was the train driver's state of mind at the time. And yet this was the moment when 31 people died a terrible death: but the chart says nothing about their suffering.

In *Harmonic Charts* I discussed the chart for the time when Picasso was inspired to create his most famous painting *Guernica*. Because this book is now out of print, it seems worthwhile to retell this story here.

The aerial bombing of the Basque town of Guernica started at 04.30 p.m. on April 26, 1937, during the Spanish Civil War. This was the first time in history that civilians had been deliberately targeted in an aerial attack. However, news of the bombing did not reach Picasso in Paris until April 29. Roland Penrose in his biography of Picasso reports:

> "On 29 April 1937 news reached Paris that German bombers in Franco's pay had wiped out the small market town of Guernica, the ancient capital of the Basques. This gratuitous outrage, perpetrated at an hour when the streets were thronged with people, roused Picasso from melancholy to anger. Acting as a catalyst to the anxiety and indignation mingled within him, it gave him the theme he had been seeking".[2]

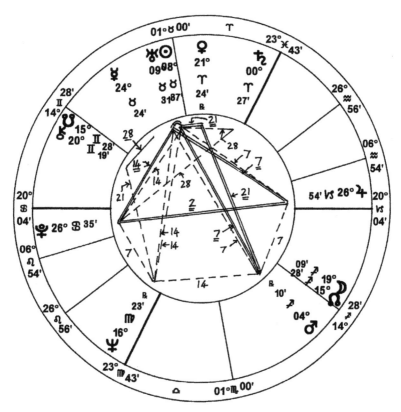

8.1 Guernica news reaches Picasso: Sevenness Aspects

Penrose does not give a time, but Wikipedia states that an eye-witness account of the Guernica bombing was published in the French daily *L'Humanité* on 29 April, and it seems likely that Picasso read this paper during the morning. I have therefore cast a chart for 10.00 a.m. on April 29, 1937, in Paris (Figure 8.1). This chart shows an immensely strong pattern of Sevenness, in which SO-*1*-UR and JU-*2*-PL are linked to each other and also to VE, MA, SA and NE by Sevenness aspects. Sevenness is about inspiration, and this chart seems highly appropriate as the "birth chart" of a painting which has been described as "modern art's most powerful anti-war statement".[3]

We can also note that, if we include the asteroids in the chart, the asteroid Ceres (signifying caring and nurturing) is at Aquarius 22°20' and is closely involved in the Sevenness, being -*7*-PL, -*7*-NE, *14*-

UR, -14-JU, and -14-SO. I feel that this represents Picasso's intense compassion for the victims of the Guernica bombing. (One of the images in the painting is of a wailing mother holding her (possibly dead) baby, directly under the head of the bull which Picasso said represented "brutality and darkness".[4])

The chart can also be seen as a map of the transits affecting Picasso's birth chart at the time when he was inspired to paint *Guernica,* and I will return to this in Chapter 10, in which I will discuss the use of harmonics in transits.

I have also looked at the chart for the inauguration of the Third Reich, when Hitler was sworn in as the Chancellor of Germany. This

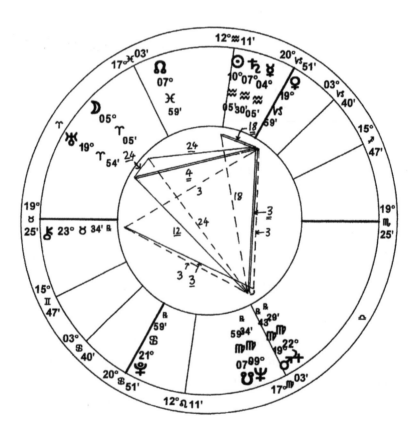

8.2 "The Nazi Chart": Threeness Aspects

chart (Figure 8.2) is sometimes referred to as "the Nazi chart", since it marked the start of the Nazi era.[5]

As I have said, *the chart for an event very often reflects the mindset of the person or people who caused the event to happen.* In the case of the "Nazi chart", the main person who caused the event to happen was Hitler himself (together with his supporters and followers), and what strikes me most about this chart is Hitler's intense pleasure at becoming Chancellor.

The dominant cluster of aspects in the chart is the T-square of (VE*-2-PL*)-*4*/4-UR: Venus on the Midheaven showing achievement of the goal of being loved and admired, opposite Pluto on the IC showing the immense determination and ruthlessness which brought this about, and square to Uranus showing that this was achieved by startling and original methods. But the chart also contains a very strong cluster of Threeness, which is shown in Figure 8.2:

(VE*-*3*-MA)-*4*/12-UR)-24/24/24-MO
  -*18*/18-SO
  -3/1-JU)-3/3/3-CH*

Here the very close Venus-Mars trine (with Venus on the Midheaven and Mars conjunct Jupiter on the 6th house cusp – rejoicing in one's ability to find love through forceful and expansive action) is linked by Threeness aspects to both Sun and Moon, so that it pervades the whole chart. Also it is linked to Chiron on the Ascendant, showing that Hitler at that moment believed that he could "heal the nation" by achieving power.

Thus I feel that the "Nazi chart" says nothing about the evils of Nazism. All it shows is the jubilation of Hitler and his supporters on achieving, at that moment, the goal towards which they had been striving.

We can also look at the chart for the 9/11 attack on the Twin Towers in New York. I have chosen the chart for 8.48 a.m., the moment when the first plane struck the northern tower. The strongest cluster in this chart is a cluster of Sevenness. I have included the asteroids in

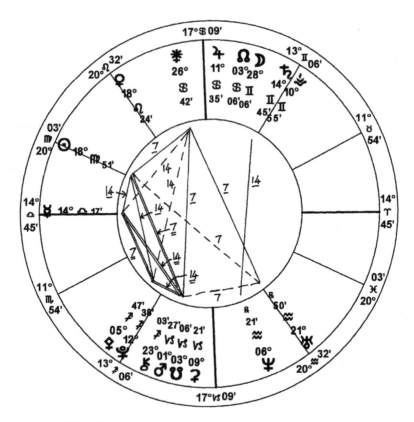

8.3 Twin Towers attack (with asteroids): Sevenness Aspects

this chart (Figure 8.3), in order to show how the asteroids Pallas (PA) and Juno (JN) are involved in this Sevenness. Thus, the cluster can be described as follows:

(((SO-Z-MA)-Z-JN)-7/7/Z-UR)-14/14/**14**/**14**/14/14/(14)/(14)-(ME*-Z-PA)

In order to understand this cluster, we need to see the attack *from the viewpoint of the hijackers,* who were the people who caused the attack. It was the inspiration of Sevenness that enabled them to carry out their plan. The four planets most tightly involved in the Sevenness are Sun, Mercury, Mars and Pallas. Mercury is on the Ascendant: this was the moment when their plan, which had been secret, was revealed to the world. ME*-**14**-MA shows how the plan was executed by inspirational action. The links to the Sun show their deep personal involvement: they were about to become martyrs. And then we have Pallas Athene, who was the Warrior Queen. I believe that the involvement of Pallas in the Sevenness shows how the hijackers were inspired by the idea of *jihad*, the holy war against the infidel.

The involvement of Juno is less easy to explain. Juno is described by Demetra George as the "significator of relationships": part of her role is to preserve fidelity in marriage and punish infidelity.[6] But note that the word "infidelity" is related to the word "infidel" which we used in the last paragraph! Maybe Juno increases the commitment to *jihad*, by causing the hijackers to feel that the infidel Americans have broken all the rules governing relationships in their own culture.

Thus, we can again see how the Twin Towers chart describes the mindset of the "perpetrators", but it does *not* describe the terrible destruction and suffering that they inflicted on thousands of innocent victims; and there is no indication of the immense effects that the events of 9/11 have had on the history of the United States and of the whole world.

From all these cases we can see how the chart for an event delineates the thoughts and feelings of the people who caused the event, but does not (usually) describe the *results* of the event. (However, there are exceptions to this. The "Guernica News" chart describes Picasso's mindset when he heard the news, but this mindset did of course affect the painting which he went on to create, and so the chart can to some extent be seen as a commentary on the painting.)

However, I am aware that rail crashes, terrorist attacks, and the creation of works of art are not typical of the subjects usually studied by mundane astrology. The book *Mundane Astrology* by Michael Baigent, Nicholas Campion and Charles Harvey has as its subtitle *An Introduction to the Astrology of Nations and Groups,* and most of the charts presented in the book are the charts for the foundation of nations and the charts for major events in the history of those nations.[7] For example, the "Nazi chart" (which I have taken from this book) is presented in the context of other charts including: the chart for the foundation of the German Empire; Hitler's birth chart; the chart for Hitler's order to invade Poland; the chart for the first shot fired in World War II; and the chart for the final surrender of the German forces (which marked the end of the Nazi regime). In comparing these charts, the aim of Baigent and his co-authors is not to analyse each chart in detail as a separate entity, but rather to indicate how particular points and areas within the zodiacal circle recur repeatedly through all the charts, and are therefore especially important for the German nation. While I recognize the value of this kind of analysis, it is not (at present) clear to me how the study of harmonic aspects could contribute to it.

In at least one case, however, Baigent and his co-authors do take a particular chart and look at its implications for the character of the country that it represents. This is the chart for the foundation of the U.S.A., which is taken to be the time of the approval by Congress of the Declaration of Independence (July 4, 1776, 05.10 p.m., Philadelphia, although it has to be said that this timing is disputed). They say, for instance, that SO-4-SA in this chart (with Saturn in the 10th house) "suggests the great value placed upon the self-made man who, by hard work and keen ambition, achieves greatness", but that it also suggests that "a basic self-doubt, a feeling of inadequacy, runs through the nation, leading to overcompensation, to acting louder, bigger, greater than any competition".[8] So can the study of harmonic aspects shed further light on this analysis?

I have presented this chart in Figure 8.4, and I have again included the four major asteroids. This shows that the chart contains a very strong cluster of Thirteenness, involving Sun, Neptune, Pluto, Chiron, and the asteroids Ceres (CE) and Juno (JN). The cluster can be set out as follows:

((SO-_13_-CH)-_13_/13-PL)-_26_/_26_/_26_/_26_/_26_/_2_/(26)/_26_/_26_-((NE-_13_-CE)-13-JN

The four planets with the closest Thirteenness links are Sun, Neptune, Chiron and Ceres. Thirteenness (especially if the Sun is involved) is about *taking risks in order to find one's true identity.* Thus,

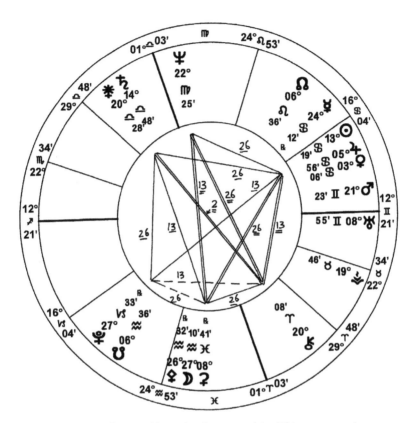

8.4 USA Foundation Chart (with asteroids): Thirteenness Aspects

this cluster implies a restless and risk-taking search for identity ("who are we really?"), conducted in an idealistic and imaginative manner (Neptune), and with the goals of healing (Chiron) and nurturing (Ceres). The further involvement of Pluto and Juno suggests that the search will be carried out with great determination, ruthlessly overcoming setbacks, and also that, despite the adventurousness implied by the Thirteenness, it will contain a commitment to the maintenance of family values.

I feel that this well describes an aspect of the distinctive character of the United States as a nation. (It carries echoes of the words on the Statue of Liberty: "Give me your tired, your poor, your huddled masses yearning to breathe free".) Therefore, on the basis of this one chart, I would say that it *may* be possible to discover something about the character of a nation by studying the harmonic aspects in its foundation chart.

On the other hand (since this chart refers to the approval by Congress of the Declaration of Independence), it could be that the chart should be regarded as the chart of the Declaration of Independence itself, rather than of the U.S.A. as a nation, and that the Thirteenness in the chart is simply an expression of the hopes and aspirations expressed in the Declaration. In this case, if we see a correspondence between the chart and the American psyche, this would be the result of the dissemination of the Declaration of Independence, rather than the direct result of the chart.

In any case, it would be unwise to build a theory on the basis of a single chart. Further research is needed.

Chapter 9
Harmonics in Synastry

Since harmonics are so valuable in the study of individual birth charts, they are potentially also valuable in synastry, which is the astrology of relationships between individuals. However, I have done very little work in this field, and so I will only be suggesting techniques which are potentially useful and which others may choose to use and develop.

I would like to take one example as a basis for exploration. This is the example of Prince Charles, who at the time of writing is Prince of Wales and the heir to the British throne, and his relationship with his two wives: Diana, Princess of Wales, whom he married in 1981 and divorced in 1996, and who died in 1997, and Camilla, Duchess of Cornwall, whom he married in 2005. I will not attempt to re-tell the story of Charles's relationship with these two women (a story which with most readers are probably already familiar), and in particular I will not try to assign blame for the break-up of Charles's marriage to Diana. Rather, I will simply be looking at whether the charts help us to understand the essential nature of the Charles-Diana and Charles-Camilla relationships, and whether the study of harmonic aspects contributes to this understanding.

It seems now to be generally agreed that Charles and Diana were hopelessly incompatible from the start. ("How awful incompatibility is", Charles wrote to one of his friends.[1]) Neither of them was to blame for this incompatibility, although it can be argued that Charles should not have allowed himself, at the age of 32, to be pressurized into marrying a woman 13 years younger than himself, with whom he was not in love. (He wept on the night before the wedding, realizing he had made a mistake.[2]) With Camilla, on the other hand, Charles seems to have enjoyed a remarkably loving, trusting and trouble-free

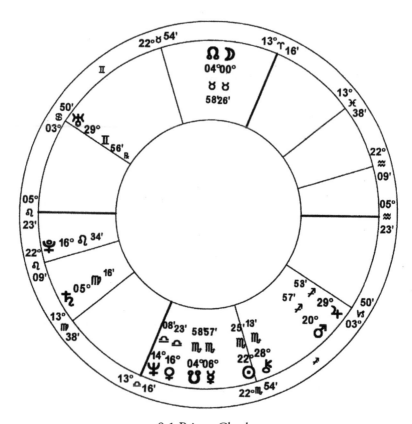

9.1 Prince Charles

relationship; there was (and still is) a deep compatibility between them.

The natal charts of Charles (November 14, 1948, 09.14 p.m., London, England), Diana (July 1, 1961, 07.45 p.m., Sandringham, England) and Camilla (July 17, 1947, 07.10 a.m., London, England) are shown in Figures 9.1, 9.2 and 9.3.

One way of looking at the synastry between Charles and Diana, and between Charles and Camilla, is to a compile a table of the harmonic aspects between all of their planets, and I have done this in the "Harmonic Synastry" tables shown on pages 206 and 209. I have compiled the tables by using the Harmonic Aspect Conversion Table (HACT) which is in Appendix II of this book. The procedure is as follows:

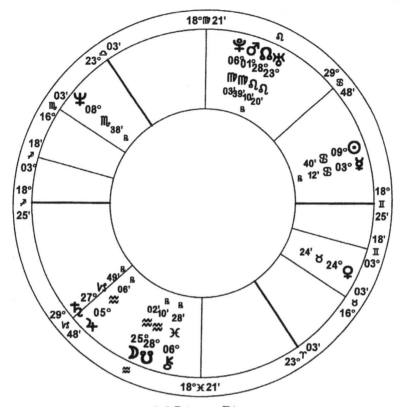

9.2 Princess Diana

If you have the Kepler or Sirius software which is provided by www.
AstroSoftware.com., then, having cast the two natal charts, you
can click on "Synastry" and then click on "Harmonic Aspect Grid
Compare", and you will find a list of the angular distances between
all the pairs of planets (not including Chiron or the asteroids) in the
two charts. For instance, for Prince Charles and Princess Diana, the
angular distance between his Sun and her Sun, Moon, Mercury and
Venus is given as follows:

His SO	Her SO	132°46'
His SO	Her MO	92°37'
His SO	Her ME	139°13'
His SO	Her VE	178°01'

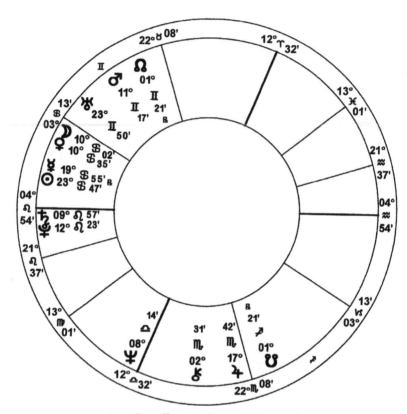

9.3 Camilla, Duchess of Cornwall

When we consult the Harmonic Aspect Conversion Table, we see that:

- 132°46' is within the range 132°45'-132°52', indicating a close "19" aspect.
- 92°37' is within the range 92°31'-92°41', indicating a wide "4" aspect and a wide "31" aspect.
- 139°13' is within the range 139°09'-139°16', indicating a wide "13" aspect and a close "31" aspect.
- 178°01' is within the range 177°00'-178°59', indicating a close "2" aspect.

However, in the Harmonic Synastry Tables below, I have included only "close" aspects (which I have shown in ordinary type) and "very close" aspects (shown in bold type and underlined); "wide" aspects have been omitted. This is because I believe that **in Synastry, the appropriate orbs to use are only half of those used for aspects in the natal chart: i.e. a maximum of 6° (instead of 12°) for the conjunction, and, for other harmonics, 6° divided by the number of the harmonic.** Thus, for the aspects listed above, I have entered the following in the Harmonic Synastry Table:

His SO	Her SO	19
His SO	Her MO	blank (as there are no "close" or "very close" aspects)
His SO	Her ME	31 (as the "13" aspect is "wide")
His SO	Her VE	2

As the list of synastry aspects in the Kepler/Sirius software does not include Chiron, I have had to manually calculate the angular distances between Chiron in each chart and the planets in the other chart. However, you may have a software package which contains a list of synastry aspects including Chiron.

I have included the Ascendant and Midheaven, but here I have shown only conjunctions and oppositions (orb 6° "close", 2° "very close"), squares (3°, 1°), and trines and sextiles (2°, 0°40'). (The orb for the conjunction is the same as that for the opposition, since a planet opposite the Ascendant is conjunct the Descendant; the same with trines and sextiles.) I feel that these basic aspects to the Angles are important, but that higher harmonics are best excluded, because any slight inaccuracy in the birth time will cause the harmonic aspects to the Angles to be severely inaccurate.

I have not included the Nodes (for the reasons explained in Chapter 2), but other astrologers experimenting with this technique are welcome to include them if they wish.

Also I have not included the four major asteroids. Ideally they should have been included, since at least three of these asteroids (Ceres, Juno and Vesta) are especially concerned with relationships, but their inclusion would have greatly increased the labour of compiling the tables.

I will start with the Charles-Camilla relationship, since I believe that the Charles-Camilla synastry reveals several indications of very close compatibility. The subsequent analysis of the Charles-Diana relationship will be partly concerned with the *absence* of these indications.

Prince Charles/Camilla, Duchess of Cornwall: Harmonic Synastry Table

	Camilla												
Charles	SO	MO	ME	VE	MA	JU	SA	UR	NE	PL	CH	AS	MC
SO	3	19		30	1	7	17		**18**	**18**			
MO	13	31	9			31	29	**27**	16		2		
ME	7						29	27	25		1	4	
VE		15	**25**	15	23	**23**		**16**		**26**			2
MA	22		**31**	9	19	11	**11**	2	5	**14**			
JU	30		**9**	**17**	**29**	17	**18**	29	22		25		
SA	**26**	**13**	8		**30**	5	14	5	11	16			
UR	15		**18**				**9**		**11**				
NE	9	23		27		32	28	13	1		15		**2**
PL	16	10	**27**	**10**	**11**	4			**7**	1	19		
CH	26	13	14		28		10	**7**	**17**	**14**			
AS							1				4	**1**	
MC				4	6				2	3			**1**

This table contains a great deal of very complex information about how each of the planets in Charles's chart interacts with each of the planets in Camilla's. (It is complex because people *are* complex.) Clearly we cannot analyse it in every detail, and we can only – in a very subjective way – pick on those particular aspects that seem to say something important about the relationship.

First, I would like to point to the figure "**1**" that occurs twice in the bottom-right corner of the table: Ascendant conjunct Ascendant, Midheaven conjunct Midheaven. Charles's Ascendant degree is almost exactly the same as Camilla's, and (because they were both born on the same latitude) their Midheaven degrees are also the same. And (because Camilla is only 16 months older than Charles) this means that they both have the outermost planets in the same houses: Pluto in the 1st house, Uranus in the 11th, and Neptune close to the I.C.

We are not all looking for partners who are the same as ourselves, but I feel that for Charles, who had been brought up to believe that as the heir to the throne he was "special" and different from everyone else, it must have been an enormous relief to find someone with whom he had so much in common. In particular, I believe that for Charles, Neptune on the I.C. signifies his idealistic feelings about his own royal heritage; but Camilla also has Neptune on the I.C. and yet is not carrying the same royal "baggage", and so she will have helped Charles to free Neptune of its royal associations and to express it more spontaneously.

Turning to the main body of the Table, I believe that the most important cluster of aspects – and one which is absolutely crucial to the success of the Charles-Camilla relationship – is the cluster of Nineness aspects linking Charles's Jupiter/Uranus to Camilla's Mercury/Saturn. This is shown in the Table as follows:

	Her ME	Her SA
His JU	9	18
His UR	18	9

Charles's chart contains an almost exact JU-UR opposition (JU-_2_-UR). As I wrote in *The Spirit of Numbers* (page 233):

> "Twoness links between Jupiter and Uranus appear to be common in the royal family. Charles's father Philip also has JU-_2_-UR, and his brother Edward has JU-_8_-UR. I feel that Jupiter (like Saturn but in a different way) is an indicator of royalty. Royalty brings duties and obligations, but it also brings immense wealth and fame and the opportunity to live life on a grand scale: but this opportunity to be flamboyantly royal can easily conflict with the Uranian desire to be true to oneself, to be original and experimental and unpredictable. I feel that Charles is constantly trying to find the right balance between these two directions. On the one hand he wants to make the

most of his opportunity to live opulently as a royal prince, but on the other hand he wants to break all the rules and just be himself."

Camilla, for her part, has an almost exact ME-*18*-SA, with Saturn rising and Mercury in the 12th house in Cancer, and this shows the immense *pleasure* (18 = 3 x 3 x 2) that she gets from communicating in a controlled and disciplined, yet also sensitive, way. The harmonic links show that this ME-*18*-SA ties in *exactly* with Charles's JU-*2*-UR, enabling her to infect him with her pleasure, and enabling him to overcome the tension of JU-*2*-UR and to think and talk about his difficulties in a light-hearted and sensible way. This must have been of huge importance to Charles.

Other indications of compatibility between Charles and Camilla include:

- His Sun trine to her Sun.

- The "**18**" links connecting his Sun to her Pluto and Chiron. In fact, if we were to include the asteroid Ceres (which signifies caring and nurturing) in the Table, we would see that Charles's Sun is also -*9*- Camilla's Ceres. This is the result of another cluster in Camilla's chart – (CH-*2*-CE)-*9*/18-PL – which shows that Camilla is strongly motivated towards *healing through nurturing* and greatly enjoys going about this in a thoroughgoing Plutonian way. The Nineness links to Charles's chart make him the ideal recipient of this caring, and show that this again brings him great pleasure. (I feel that Charles has a great need to be lovingly cared for. He got very little of this from his mother the Queen, and he also did not get it from Diana.)

- Charles's Saturn is -*26*- Camilla's Sun and -*13*- Camilla's Moon. Charles's Saturn is, in my view, very much concerned with his sense of his duties and responsibilities as a royal prince and a future king. In her own chart, Camilla has SO-26-MO, with both Sun and Moon in Cancer in the 12th house, which shows how Camilla is very much concerned with the *search for her own identity* (Thirteenness), and that she will tend to pursue this search through selfless involvement in the lives of others. The Thirteenness links between her Sun/Moon and Charles's Saturn show Camilla becoming willingly involved in the duties and responsibilities of royalty, and feeling that she can find her own identity by doing so.

This analysis has covered only a tiny part of the huge wealth of information provided in the Harmonic Synastry Table, but I believe that it has identified some of the factors that have helped to make the Charles-Camilla partnership so successful.

We can now turn to the Harmonic Synastry Table for Charles and Diana.

Prince Charles/Princess Diana: Harmonic Synastry Table

Charles \ Diana	SO	MO	ME	VE	MA	JU	SA	UR	NE	PL	CH	AS	MC
SO	19		31	2		5	**11**	4	**26**		7		
MO	26	10	23	**15**	3				29		**20**		
ME		**10**	32	31	11				**1**	6	**3**		
VE	26	**14**	7		**8**		32		16	9	**18**		
MA	29	28	15	7	23				**17**	24	19	1	
JU	19	13		5	3		13		**7**	19	27		
SA	13	17	**29**	**25**	1	**12**		**30**	17	**1**	2		
UR		1	10	29	5	26	**27**	**14**			**19**		
NE	19	**11**	25	18	17	13	7	7		19			
PL		**21**	25		**24**		29		22		**9**	3	
CH	**13**	29	5		25	27	6	19			**11**		
AS					**2**								
MC													

We can note, first of all, that Charles's Mercury is closely conjunct Diana's Neptune (in Scorpio), and that both his Mercury and her Neptune have many close harmonic links with planets in the other chart: his Mercury is -*10*- her Moon, -*32*- her Mercury, -*31*- her Venus, -*11*- her Mars, and -*3*- her Chiron, and her Neptune is -*26*- his Sun, -*17*- his Mars, -*7*- his Jupiter and -*14*- his Uranus. This makes me feel that the Mercury-Neptune link is absolutely central to the Charles-Diana relationship. It is what will make the relationship or break it.

Charles's Mercury is in his 4th house, along with several other planets; it shows that his way of thinking and communicating is very much bound in with his awareness of his royal heritage. But Diana's Neptune is in the 10th house, and shows her idealistic desire to be of service in the world. It is that which caused her to hold the hands of AIDS patients, and to campaign for the abolition of landmines. It is that which gained her the love of so many people, who could see that she wanted to help them. And it is also that which caused her to feel constrained and boxed in by the "stuffiness" of the royal duties which she took on when she married Charles.

Because his Mercury is conjunct her Neptune, Charles resonates strongly with this. In his thinking mind, he knows that she is right. And, with his Sun -**26**- her Neptune, he has a strong desire to find his own identity by following her vision (and this desire is amplified by the -**26**- link between his Moon and her Sun). Also, with his Mars -**17**- her Neptune, he wants to *campaign* for the causes that she stands for. But he cannot do it; it is too difficult and stressful for him. The Sevenness links between her Neptune and his Jupiter/Uranus will tend to exacerbate, rather than heal, the Jupiter/Uranus dilemma with which he is struggling. He wants to talk to her about it; but the stressful -**32**- link between his Mercury and her Mercury makes it hard for them to talk to each other.

There are many other harmonic links that I could mention, but I will confine myself to the strong Twoness link (-**8**-) between Diana's Mars and Charles's Venus. A Twoness link between *his* Mars and *her* Venus might indicate sexual attraction, but a link between *her* Mars and *his* Venus is more likely to cause trouble, especially when his Venus is in the 4th house conjunct Neptune and her Mars is in the 8th conjunct Pluto. (Charles "genuinely believed that he had, as a member of his staff put it, 'turned himself out' for her, but her needs were inexhaustible".[1])

Somewhat to my surprise, my overall impression from studying Charles's and Diana's harmonic synastry is that there were strong bonds of attraction between them. They were not indifferent to each other (as they might be if they had few harmonic links); they aroused strong emotions in each other, emotions which were mainly negative but which might, in other circumstances, have been more positive. In different circumstances (and, in particular, if she had not been 13 years younger than him), they might have had a fruitful relationship. She was a stronger character than he was, and she could have helped him to find new purpose in his life.

But probably they could not have had a lasting and stable marriage, because there is not enough Threeness (and Nineness) in their harmonic links. I feel that Threeness is essential for a lasting relationship, because it contains the qualities of pleasure, harmony, and relaxation. No wonder that Charles feels happier with Camilla, with whom he has many Threeness links, and with whom he can simply relax and not feel that he is being continually tested.

* * * * *

There is, however, another (and simpler) method of studying harmonic aspects in synastry, and this is by looking at the harmonic aspects in the Composite Chart. When we have cast the Composite Chart, we can use the "Table of Harmonics 1-32" (or we can cast the harmonic charts for the Composite Chart), and we can compile a List of Significant Harmonic Aspects in the same way as for a natal chart or a mundane chart.

The Composite Charts for Charles/Camilla and for Charles/Diana are shown in Figures 9.4 and 9.5, and their harmonic aspects are very interesting and surprising. The Charles/Camilla chart contains an exceptionally strong pattern of Fiveness, which can be described as follows:

(SO-_**10**_-MO)-_**20**_-NE
(MA-_**25**_-UR)-25-SO
ME-25-PL
JU-_**20**_-UR
JU-_**25**_-NE

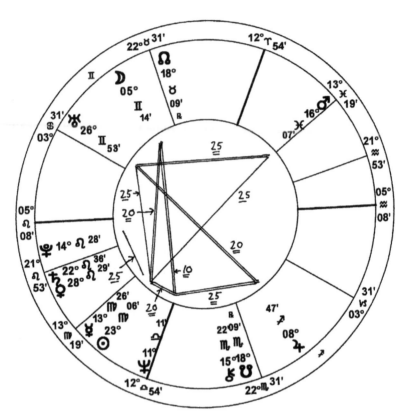

9.4 Charles/Camilla Composite Chart: Fiveness Aspects

Similarly, the Charles/Diana chart contains an exceptionally strong pattern of Threeness, making it perhaps the strongest Threeness chart that I have ever seen. The Threeness links are as follows:

((MA-*1*-NE)-9-SO)-9/9/9/9/*3*/*3*-(JU-*1*-CH)
    -18/*6*/18/*6*/6/18-(SA-9-PL)
    -9/9/9-VE
(JU-*1*-CH)-*6*-SA
MO-*3*-UR

These patterns are remarkable because they are quite different from those shown in the Harmonic Synastry Tables that we have already discussed. Thus, in the Charles/Camilla Synastry Tables, Fiveness is not very prominent; and in the Charles/Diana Synastry Tables there

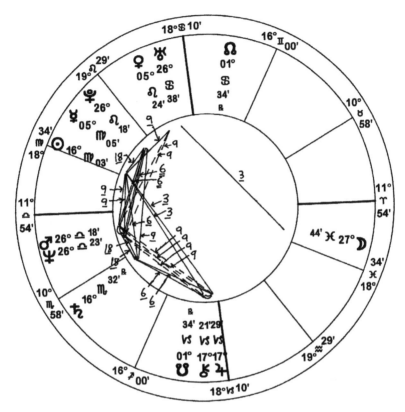

9.5 Charles/Diana Composite Chart: Threeness Aspects

is (as we have said) a marked absence of Threeness. So how can we explain this difference?

It seems to me that, whereas the Synastry Tables describe the way in which these two people relate to each other on a day-to-day basis, the Composite Chart is a chart of *the relationship* as a separate entity – almost as if it took on a life of its own, independently of the people who comprise it.

Thus, starting with Charles and Camilla: Fiveness is about consciously re-shaping the world to suit one's needs. Charles and Camilla do not relate to each other in a Fiveness way; they relate more in a relaxed and easy-going way which has more the quality of Threeness. Nevertheless, their relationship (as seen by the outside world) has taken on the quality of Fiveness, in that it has been deliberately built up. For many years Camilla was "the most hated woman in Britain" because of her role as the "other woman" in the Charles-Diana story; but now this hatred has evaporated, and Camilla is seen simply as Charles's loyal wife and is able to appear in public and fulfil her royal duties without arousing any hostility. This is a remarkable Fiveness achievement.

Charles and Diana, on the other hand, did not relate to each other in a relaxed Threeness way: their interaction was constantly full of stress and tension. Nevertheless, the memory of their relationship has brought joy and happiness to very many people, and these are the benefits of Threeness. Diana is seen as having brought fresh air and lightness into the story of the royal family, which previously had been lacking in the qualities of Threeness. Moreover, Charles and Diana had two sons, William and Harry, who continue to bring this Threeness quality into the royal family. In 2018 Harry married Meghan Markle, a mixed-race non-British divorcee, purely because he loves her: this would have been impossible in the days before Diana.

It could be objected that this Threeness quality is seen by the public as belonging to Diana personally, rather than to her relationship with Charles. But we need to remember that marriage to Charles was the making of Diana. If she had not married him, and had remained as an ordinary member of a minor aristocratic family, we would never have heard of her. The marriage enabled her to become "the people's Princess", and that is how she is remembered.

Thus, it seems that we can learn about how people interact with each other by studying the harmonic aspects between the planets in their individual birth charts; but, if we wish to understand the quality of their relationship as an entity in itself (and especially, the *legacy* of the relationship, the effects which it has had on the outside world), we need to study the harmonic aspects in the Composite Chart.

We can look at two more cases of Composite Charts to see how this works out in practice. First, we can mention the relationship between

John F. Kennedy and Jacqueline Kennedy. This is a relationship which (even though it too ended in tragedy) can be seen as having had a similar "legacy" in America to that of the Charles/Diana relationship in Britain: it brought into the White House a Threeness quality of ease and pleasure which had previously been absent. If we look at the Composite Chart for John and Jackie, we see that it contains a cluster of (SO-*1*-MO)-*9*-NE, with MO-*9*-NE completely exact and the other aspects also very close to exactitude, and with Neptune close to the Midheaven. Although there are only three planets involved, this is an extremely strong Threeness pattern.

Secondly, I would like to look in more detail at a quite different Composite Chart: that for the relationship between Karl Marx and Friedrich Engels, who together in 1848 wrote the *Communist Manifesto*. This is the document that contains the famous rallying cry which (loosely translated from the German) reads:

> "Workers of the world, unite! You have nothing to lose but your chains, and a world to win".

Marx and Engels wrote hundreds of letters to each other over many years, and it seems that their friendship and collaboration was invaluable to both of them. Marx was the theoretician, who on his own wrote *Das Kapital* in which he expounded his theory of capitalism and its tendency towards self-destruction, and the need to replace it with a communist system in which private property would be abolished. But Engels, being a successful businessman in Manchester, had more practical knowledge of how capitalism actually worked, and also was able to give Marx a great deal of financial help. Engels was also the author of *The Condition of the Working Class in England*, which is said to be a very moving account of working-class poverty. But they needed to come together to create the *Communist Manifesto*, in which Marx's theoretical genius and Engels's practical understanding are brought together to create a rousing call to action.

Here are two more quotes from the *Communist Manifesto:*

> "The theory of communism may be summed up in a single sentence: Abolition of private property."

> "Then the world will be for the common people, and the seeds of happiness will reach the deepest springs. Ah! Come! People of every land, how can you not be roused."

In *TSON* (pp.174-5) I pointed out that Marx's natal chart contains a very strong Twenty-threeness cluster involving ME, MA, JU, SA and CH. Twenty-threeness is about inventiveness and story-telling, and I suggested that Marx in his writings was essentially *telling a story* about the future of mankind. The downtrodden workers will cast off their chains and become masters of the universe. Like most Twenty-threeness stories, this contains an element of fantasy, and it is clear that, although Communism (or a version of it) has now been put into practice and has been dominant in a large part of the world for more than half a century, it has not brought universal happiness in the way that Marx had hoped.

If we now look at the Composite Chart for Marx and Engels (Figure 9.6), we see that it contains a cluster of Twenty-threeness which is even stronger than the one in Marx's natal chart. The chart contains an *exact* conjunction of Saturn, Pluto and Chiron, appropriately in the 11th house which is the house of society (such exact conjunctions of three planets are extremely rare), and all these planets are linked by close Twenty-threeness aspects to Sun (near the Midheaven) and Mars (in the 5th house of creativity), with Sun also very closely -*23*- Mars.

This would seem to be an accurate description of the "story" that is being told in the *Communist Manifesto.* The story is about revolution, through the overthrow of the system: Sue Tompkins says about Saturn/Pluto, "The dark face of authority sometimes has to be demolished in order for something new to be born".[3] But in this case the revolution causes *healing,* because Saturn and Pluto are exactly conjunct Chiron. And this is to be achieved through dynamic action

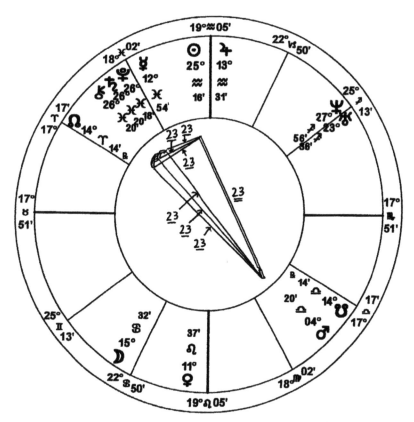

9.6 Karl Marx/Friedrich Engels Composite Chart:
Twenty-threeness Aspects

(SO-__23__-MA): the hero (who in this case is the workers collectively, who have come together to form a united force) riding into action to destroy the hated enemy.

This call to action (which inspired the Russian Revolution, and so changed the course of history) is the legacy of the Marx-Engels collaboration, and is clearly shown in their Composite Chart. In order to understand the actual relationship between Marx and Engels as individuals, we would have to study the harmonic aspects between the planets in their respective natal charts. But the Composite Chart shows the effect that their collaboration has had on the outside world.

For Composite Charts, the principle which I set out in Chapter 3 – "The chart shows only potential" – is even more important than it is for natal charts. We can create a Composite Chart for any two individuals, even if they never met, and doing so can offer a fascinating insight into what might have been. But clearly, even couples who have actually formed a relationship often fail to live up to the full potential of their Composite Chart.

Although in this chapter we have looked at only a very few examples, I hope that these comments will inspire other astrologers to look at other cases and to develop the theory and practice of harmonic synastry, which would seem to be a very promising field.

Chapter 10
Harmonics in Transits and Progressions

For many astrologers, transits are the most important part of astrology because of their value in prediction. And clearly, harmonics are potentially very important in the study of transits, since transits are about *aspects* between transiting planets and planets in the natal (or mundane) chart. We may, for instance, note that transiting Saturn is conjunct, or opposite, or square, or trine, to natal Sun. But it is just as possible for the Saturn-Sun relationship to have the qualities of Five, or Seven, or any other harmonic number. And the same applies to other predictive techniques, such as secondary and tertiary progressions, and solar and lunar returns.

John Addey in *Harmonics in Astrology* has a chapter entitled "Harmonics in Progressions, Transits and Other Directional Measures".[1] The essential point which he makes in this chapter is the following:

> "The different principles and forces at work in life are constantly moving between polarities of positive and negative, full and empty, tension and release, and that is why I believe the notion of progressed aspects which suddenly pop up from time to time and then are done with, is basically a false one; as a progressed planet A moves around the circle forming an ever-changing relationship to planet B, we are always dealing with a regular flux between positive and negative poles of experience".[2]

Thus, Addey is saying that Planet A and Planet B have an "ever-changing relationship", due to the constant appearance and disappearance of harmonic aspects which connect them. And I would suggest that this is not just a matter of flux between positive and negative; it also offers the possibility of new developments. Thus, for instance, a person might have a natal Sun-Saturn square, showing that the basic relationship between Sun and Saturn was one of effort and difficulty; but, if transiting Saturn formed a Sevenness aspect with natal Sun, this would offer the possibility of expressing Sun-Saturn in new and creative ways, and so maybe overcoming and resolving some of the Sun-Saturn tension that was present in the natal chart.

The problem, however, is that (to the best of my knowledge) there is no software available which would enable the astrologer easily to track the incidence of these harmonic aspects between all of the pairs of planets. Thus, we can say that the use of harmonics in predictive astrology is potentially hugely important, but that at the present time it remains almost entirely undeveloped.

In the present chapter I will confine myself to a few examples, which show how certain events have been affected by the harmonic transits in the natal charts of the people involved. I will not be making any predictions; rather, I will be looking at past events in the lives of famous people, and at the harmonic angles between the transiting planets at the time of those events and the planets in the person's birth chart.

We can start by looking at the chart for the time (April 29, 1937, 10.00 a.m., Paris) when Pablo Picasso received news of the bombing of Guernica, and was inspired to start work on his *Guernica* painting. I presented this chart in Chapter 8 (Figure 8.1), and showed that it contains an extremely strong pattern of Sevenness. In Figure 10.1 I am presenting this same chart on the outer wheel, and on the inner wheel is Picasso's natal chart (October 25, 1881, 11.15 p.m., Malaga, Spain). The "Guernica news" chart thus becomes a map of the transits affecting Picasso's natal chart at the time that he received news of the bombing.

In calculating the harmonic aspects between the transiting planets and the natal planets, I have followed the same procedure that I used for synastry in Chapter 9. Thus, you can cast both the natal chart and the transiting chart, and then (if you are using the Kepler/Sirius software) click on "Synastry", then click on "Aspect Grid Compare", and you will find a list of the angular distances between (in this case) all the natal planets and all the transiting planets. You can then use the Harmonic Aspect Conversion Table (Appendix II of this book) to convert these angular distances into harmonic aspects.

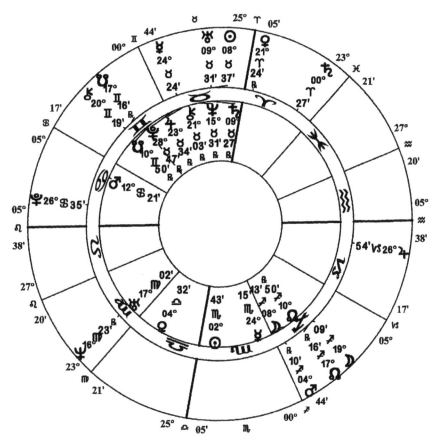

10.1 Inner wheel: Pablo Picasso
Outer wheel: Guernica news reaches Picasso

In the Harmonic Transits Table (p.222) I have shown the harmonic aspects between the transiting outer planets (MA, JU, SA, NE and PL) and all the natal planets (but excluding Chiron, as Chiron is not included in the Kepler/Sirius "Aspect Grid Compare" table: however, you may have other software which enables Chiron to be included). However, as in Chapter 9, I have shown only those aspects which are listed in the Harmonic Aspect Conversion Table as "close" or "very close". This is because **in my opinion, for transits as well as for synastry, the appropriate orbs to use are only half of those used for aspects within the natal chart: that is to say, a maximum of 6°**

(instead of 12°) for conjunctions, and, for other harmonics, 6° divided by the number of the harmonic.

Thus (to take three examples of aspects from the Harmonic Transits Table (H.T.T.) for Picasso and the "Guernica news" chart:

-   The angular distance from transiting Mars to natal Sun is 31°28'. Appendix II shows that this is within the range 31°24'-31°34', and signifies a "close" "23" aspect. This can be entered into the H.T.T. as "23".
-   The angular distance from transiting Saturn to natal Sun is 147°44', which is within the range 147°33'-147°49', signifying "wide" "17" and "22" aspects. This can be left blank in the H.T.T., as there are no "close" or "very close" aspects involved.
-   The angular distance from transiting Pluto to natal Sun is 96°08', which is within the range 95°52'-96°08', signifying a "very close" "15" aspect. This can be entered into the H.T.T. as "**15**".

Harmonic Transits Table: Pablo Picasso/Guernica news

	Transiting					
	MA	JU	SA	UR	NE	PL
Natal						
SO	23	30		27	31	**15**
MO	1		16	17	**22**	
ME		**23**	20		16	
VE	**6**	**16**		5	20	
MA			7	23		25
JU	**17**		27	26		
SA		**7**		**1**	**17**	**14**
UR	**14**		13		**1**	
NE	**29**	10	**8**	1	3	5
PL		3		19	10	25

This table shows that:

- At the time that he received the Guernica news, *Picasso's natal Saturn (which is in the 10th house) is very closely conjunct transiting Uranus,*

*and also very closely -7- transiting Jupiter (in his 6th house) and -**14**-
transiting Pluto (in his 12th house).* This shows that Picasso was picking
up the very strong Sevenness pattern of (JU-**2**-PL)-**7**/**14**-UR which
(as we showed in the Chapter 8) is present in the Guernica chart;
but it is his Saturn that is affected by this Sevenness. Picasso has five
planets in the 10th house (JU, NE, PL and CH as well as SA), which
could be one reason why his work shows such a diversity of styles;
but, at this particular time, he felt inspired to produce a work that
was Saturnian in nature but was also expressive of the widespread and
unprecedented devastation (JU, UR, PL) produced by the Guernica
bombs.

- Also, *Picasso's natal Uranus (in his 2nd house) is very closely conjunct
transiting Neptune and -**14**- transiting Mars (in his 5th house).* This
shows Picasso responding to MA-14-NE which was also present in
the Guernica chart, and showing that he feels inspired to produce a
work that, in addition to its Saturnian qualities, has also the Uranian
qualities of originality and "shockingness".

- *There are also two very close Seventeenness aspects: transiting Mars -**17**-
natal Jupiter, and transiting Neptune -**17**- Saturn.* Seventeenness is
about campaigning for a better world. News of the Guernica bombing
placed Picasso on the warpath: he wanted to campaign for peace.

- *Also there are two very strong Twoness aspects: transiting Jupiter -**16**-
natal Venus, and transiting Saturn -**8**- natal Neptune.* These aspects
show how deeply Picasso was *hurt* by hearing the Guernica news. His
natal Venus is in his 3rd house and relates perhaps to his love of the
beauty of his native country and its people, who had been so brutally
attacked.

Thus, all these aspects (and others) show in great detail how Picasso
was affected by the Guernica news. Without studying the harmonic
aspects, we would not have known any of this.

Next, we will look at the transits affecting Princess Diana's birth chart at the time of her fatal car crash. I will start by re-telling the story. Diana and her new boyfriend Dodi al Fayed were spending the night of August 30 in Paris, on the way back to England from a Mediterranean cruise. They went first to the Ritz Hotel (owned by Dodi's father), but shortly after midnight they set out towards Dodi's private apartment, in a limousine driven by Henri Paul, an employee of the Ritz Hotel, who is said to have been over the alcohol limit. No one was wearing seatbelts. Paul drove the car extremely fast in an attempt to shake off the *paparazzi*, the press photographers who were chasing Diana. In a tunnel, he swerved to avoid a Fiat Uno, and crashed the car into a pillar. Paul and Dodi were killed instantly.

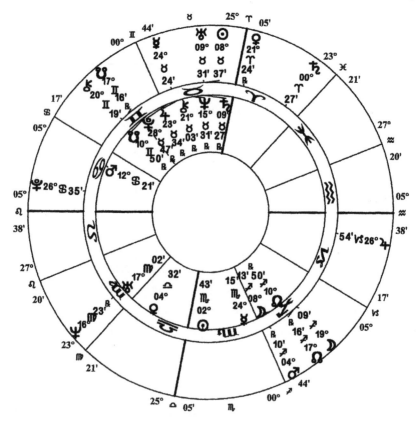

10.2 Inner wheel: Princess Diana
Outer wheel: Diana's fatal car crash

Diana suffered severe injuries and was rushed to hospital, where she died at 4.00 a.m.

Figure 10.2 shows Diana's birth chart on the inner wheel, and the transiting planets at the time of the crash (August 31, 1997, 00.23 a.m., Paris) on the outer wheel. I have compiled a Harmonic Transits table for this event, in the same way as for Picasso-Guernica.

Harmonic Transits Table: Princess Diana/Fatal car crash

		Transiting				
	MA	JU	SA	UR	NE	PL
Natal						
SO	3		_9_	Z	_20_	5
MO	_31_				13	
ME	17	13				12
VE	_13_	_18_	31			_21_
MA	21	31	_30_	7		4
JU	_17_		_29_	1		29
SA	14	22	_22_		_1_	13
UR	_14_		_32_	20	Z	
NE	_1_			_29_		15
PL	28	_25_	24		28	

This table shows, once again, an extremely strong pattern of Sevenness. If we extract the conjunctions and the Sevenness aspects from the rest of the table, we have the following:

		Transiting		
	MA	UR	NE	PL
Natal				
SO		Z		
VE				_21_
MA	21	7		
JU		_1_		
SA	14		_1_	
UR	_14_		Z	
NE	_1_			
PL	28		28	

There are two separate Sevenness clusters here. First, we can note that transiting Uranus is very closely conjunct natal Jupiter and is also very closely -7- natal Sun (and more widely -7- natal Mars). This shows that Uranus is activating the cluster of (SO-7-JU)-7-MA which is present in Diana's birth chart, showing that Diana, throughout her life, was *inspired* (Sevenness) by the idea of *self-expression* (Sun) through *forceful* (Mars) and *expansive* (Jupiter) action. At the time of the crash, transiting Uranus is pushing her towards expressing this in a particularly striking and reckless way. Maybe (because Dodi and Paul were under the spell of Diana's personality) this recklessness had an effect on those around her, causing them to tempt fate by driving too fast, not wear seatbelts...

And secondly, we see that there is a complex Sevenness cluster involving transiting Mars and Neptune and natal Saturn, Uranus and Pluto. This involves the coming-together of two Sevenness patterns, one in the natal chart and one in the transiting chart. First, in her natal chart Diana has (SA-7-UR)-28/28-PL: the effects of this cluster involving only the outer planets are difficult to describe, but I would suggest that it indicates a kind of fatalism, or a deep commitment to the Sevenness principle of magic and irrationality as opposed to the Fiveness principle of rationality and order. And then, the chart for the time of the crash has MA-*14*-NE, creating a strong tendency towards wild and irrational action. The coming-together of these two Sevenness patterns (through transits especially affecting Diana's natal Uranus) creates an explosive situation, in which something "crazy" and unexpected was bound to occur.

I will pass over most of the other aspects in the Harmonic Transits Table, since I believe them to be of lesser importance, but I would like to mention the remarkable fact that transiting Saturn is almost exactly -9- Diana's natal Sun. Nineness is about joy, peace and harmony. If we believe in an afterlife (I am myself agnostic about this), then we can see that this aspect is saying: Rest in peace, Diana. You have had a turbulent and stressful life. Now, with the death of the body, you can find the peace that you have always longed for.

These examples show that, in some cases, a study of harmonic transits can give a clear indication of the type of event – or, at least, the state of mind – that may befall the person at the time that the transits occur. However, I have to acknowledge that the situation is not always so clear-cut.

For instance, another case that I have looked at is the case of the Dunblane massacre. At 9.35 a.m. on March 13, 1996, Thomas Hamilton, a 43-year-old with no previous history of criminal behaviour or mental instability, walked into a primary school in Dunblane, Scotland, and shot dead 16 young children and their teacher, before turning the gun on himself. I have calculated the harmonic transits affecting Hamilton's birth chart at this time, but the resulting Harmonic Transits Table, although it contains some

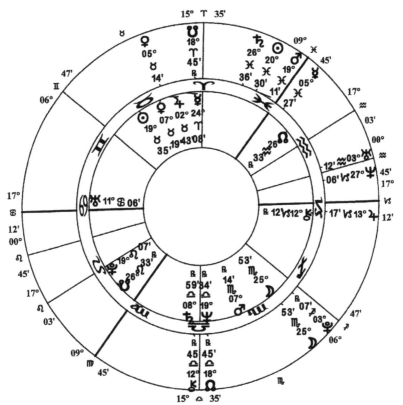

10.3 Inner wheel: Thomas Hamilton
Outer wheel: Lunar Return, March 10, 1996

relevant aspects, offers no explanation of how Hamilton was able to carry out such an extreme action at this particular time.

One possible reason is that March 13 may have been merely the date on which Hamilton put into practice an action which he had been planning for some time. It is therefore worthwhile to look at his last Lunar Return before the massacre, since the transits at the time of the Lunar Return will affect his actions over the whole of the following month.

Figure 10.3 shows Hamilton's natal chart (May 10, 1952, 08.50 a.m., Glasgow, Scotland) on the inner wheel, and on the outer wheel his Lunar Return for 07.19 p.m. March 10, 1996, Dunblane, Scotland, three days before the massacre. The Harmonic Transits Table for the time of the Lunar Return is as follows:

Thomas Hamilton/Lunar Return, March 10, 1996

	Transiting					
	MA	JU	SA	UR	NE	PL
Natal						
SO	6	20			**_16_**	13
MO			3	16		
ME	31	**_25_**	**_13_**		29	23
VE	**_15_**	19	9	23	18	**_7_**
MA	**_30_**		**_31_**	21	**_9_**	14
JU		23	**_10_**	**_4_**	15	12
SA	**_9_**		15		**_10_**	20
UR	29	2	**_31_**	16	11	
NE	12			7		
PL	**_12_**	**_5_**		11		

In his natal chart Hamilton has an almost exact MA-_31_-UR, which is emphasized by the closeness of Uranus to the Ascendant. He also has a very close SO-_31_-SA. These aspects make him prone to the influence of Thirty-oneness, which, as we saw in Chapter 5, is about surrendering to the demands of the _id_, and is prominent in the charts of the Marquis de Sade and of several sadistic serial murderers. MA-*31*-UR would seem to be especially prone to sudden and violent action of a Thirty-oneness nature, and SO-*31*-SA may indicate suicidal tendencies. But, because these are isolated aspects (not part of a cluster), Hamilton may be able to keep control over them for most of the time. However, the Harmonic Transits Table shows that, at the time of the Lunar Return in March 1996, there are *almost exact* -**31**- aspects connecting transiting Saturn to natal Mars and Uranus. These transiting aspects appear to have caused Hamilton to act out both MA-*31*-UR and SO-*31*-SA in an extremely violent way.

We can also look at Hamilton's last Solar Return, which occurred ten months before the massacre, at 02.13 p.m. on May 10, 1995 (calculated for Dunblane, Scotland). Here is the Harmonic Transits table for the time of the Solar Return:

Thomas Hamilton/Solar Return, May 10, 1995

	Transiting					
	MA	JU	SA	UR	NE	PL
Natal						
SO	23	**23**	25			
MO		21			6	1
ME	3	**11**			4	5
VE		**5**	**8**	**26**		16
MA		**10**	**8**	**13**	**23**	1
JU		13	9			
SA	8	28	11		27	7
UR	17			9		**13**
NE	13	27		25	**15**	**9***
PL	1	19	27	**29**	23	

Here, what is emphasized is the number of transiting planets affecting Hamilton's natal VE-*2*-MA. This VE-*2*-MA must have caused huge difficulties in relationships for Hamilton throughout his life; he was a loner, unable to make friends. The Solar Return shows Venus and Mars with Twoness links to transiting Saturn and

Pluto, Fiveness links to transiting Jupiter, and Thirteenness links to transiting Uranus. All this must have greatly increased the pain of his loneliness, and his determination to take some kind of drastic action to overcome it. For ten months he struggled with this without success, until in March 1996 the explosion of Thirty-oneness arising from the Lunar Return caused him to end his life, taking the lives of seventeen other people with him.

Since the Solar and Lunar Returns are so important in the case of Thomas Hamilton, I have also looked at the Solar and Lunar Returns preceding Princess Diana's death: the Solar Return on July 1, 1997, and the Lunar Return on August 18. But these Returns contain no very striking clusters of aspects, and add little or nothing to one's understanding of the events surrounding her death. Thus, it seems that in the cases of Picasso and Diana the important charts are the charts for the time of the actual event, whereas in Hamilton's case the Solar and Lunar Returns are more revealing. Presumably this is because with Picasso and Diana we are dealing with the person's response to unexpected events occurring on a particular day, whereas with Hamilton we are looking at an action planned by the person himself over a period of time.

The cases that we have looked at show that the study of harmonic transits can yield very valuable information. But of course we have not been making predictions: we have only been using harmonic transits to gain a deeper understanding of past events. So how could the study of harmonic transits be made into a tool for astrological prediction?

I acknowledge that, in attempting to use harmonic transits for prediction, one would encounter severe difficulties. This is because harmonic aspects change so fast that it would be necessary to compile a Harmonic Transits table for *each individual day.* (And even this might not be enough. Thus, if an astrologer had cast a Harmonic Transits table for Princess Diana for each day of August 1997, they would presumably have made the calculations for noon, and so would have missed the table for midnight on August 30-31, which is when the fatal crash occurred.)

In spite of this last point, I think that an astrologer who looked at Diana's harmonic transits for each day of August 1997 would have seen that something was going to come to a head on August 30-31, and might have been able to predict that Diana would be in danger at that time, and to advise her to be cautious and avoid taking unnecessary risks. But the compilation of Harmonic Transits tables is, at present, a laborious task; and, even if computer software is created (as I hope it will be) to allow these tables to be produced in an instant, I think that most astrologers would balk at the prospect of having to produce a separate table for *each day* of the period under investigation.

It is possible, however, that a computer program could be developed which would show the "rolling positions" of the transiting planets. For instance, we can look at the harmonic aspects formed by transiting Jupiter to Diana's natal Sun during the month of August 1997. On August 1, Jupiter had a -28- aspect to Diana's Sun, but this aspect moved out of orb on August 2. On August 11 a -5- aspect was formed: this aspect became very close (-**5**-) on August 17, reached exactitude on August 20, became less close (-5-) on August 24, and then moved out of orb on August 30. If we had a program that would chart these moving aspects for all the interplanetary pairs, the need for a separate Harmonic Transits table for each day would be obviated.

The use of the Solar and Lunar Returns is simpler and raises fewer problems. The harmonic aspects in a Solar or Lunar Return chart can be studied as easily as in a natal chart, and I think that (until further software is developed) this is the easiest way for an astrologer to use harmonic aspects in predictive work. When we looked at Amy Winehouse's chart in Chapter 6, we saw that the Solar Return chart for her 27th birthday yielded valuable information. Also her Lunar Return for July 13, 2011 (ten days before her death from alcohol poisoning) contains some very close Sevenness aspects (SO-*14*-ME, VE-*14*-MA, JU-*7*-SA) as well as ME-*13*-NE and VE-*31*-PL, and this might have enabled an astrologer to warn Amy about the danger of rash and self-harming action at this time.

In interpreting harmonic transits, I believe that the crucial point is to look for cases where the person has a cluster of harmonic aspects in the natal chart, and where all the planets in the cluster are simultaneously aspected by one or more transiting planets. Thus, in the Picasso case we saw that he has a natal cluster of (JU-2-PL)-7/14-UR, and that transiting Saturn formed Sevenness aspects to all of these planets. In the Diana case we saw that she has (SA-7-UR)-28/28-PL, and that these planets were linked by Sevenness aspects to transiting Mars and Uranus. In the Hamilton case we saw that he has an almost exact MA-31-UR, and that transiting Saturn formed almost exact Thirty-oneness links with both Mars and Uranus. Thus, the effect of these transits is to activate and amplify a tendency which was already present in the birth chart, and cause it to be acted out in the manner suggested by the transiting planet.

We have been talking entirely about transits, but the same techniques could equally well be applied to secondary and tertiary progressions, since progressed planets form harmonic aspects to natal planets in the same way that transiting planets do. We can note that, using the Kepler/Sirius software, it is possible (by clicking on "Harmonic Aspect Grid Compare") to obtain a full list of harmonic aspects between a progressed chart and a natal chart; also (by clicking on "Table of Harmonics 1-32") one can obtain a Table of Harmonic Aspects for a progressed chart, showing the harmonic aspects which progressed planets form with one another. However, I leave it to others to investigate this.

The use of harmonic analysis in predictive astrology is, I believe, a huge subject which has yet to be developed, and which has the potential to revolutionize the whole way in which astrologers do predictions. The present chapter is only a tiny, and very tentative, first step in that direction.

* * * * *

As a postscript to this chapter, I would like to mention the technique of "Age Harmonics". This was first proposed by John Addey, who says:

> "Now there is a possibility that the harmonic charts in succession may apply to each year of life, i.e. the 2nd harmonic chart to the second year of life, the 3rd to the third year, the 40th to the fortieth year and so on".[3]

This proposal has been taken up and used by a number of astrologers, one of whom is Alice Portman, who describes the technique in detail in her online article.[4]

We should note, however, that Addey proposes that the 2nd harmonic chart relates to the second year of life, i.e. to the year that starts on the first birthday, whereas Portman and others now propose that the 2nd harmonic relates to the year that starts on the *second* birthday, which is the *third* year of life. Portman says:

> "Each year of life emphasizes and unfolds one of the harmonics and their multiples. The period between 0-1 opens and develops harmonic fractions. The period between 1-2 opens and develops the first harmonic, the conjunction. The period between 2-3 opens and develops the 2nd harmonic, the opposition".

Which of these two proposals is more correct? I would like to investigate this by taking a example from my own life.

The year between my 43rd and 44th birthdays was perhaps the most transformative year of my whole life. It was during this year that I separated from my first wife, as a result of the complete breakdown of our marriage. Also, during this year I met, and started to live with, my second wife, to whom, 38 years later, I am still happily married. And also, this year saw the death of my mother (she was drowned at sea). Thus, my relationship with all of the three most important women in my life (my mother, my first wife, and my second wife) was transformed during this one year.

The question is: Which of the harmonic charts, the 43rd (which would fit Portman's theory) or the 44th (which would fit Addey's theory) is more indicative of these changes?

The 44th harmonic chart shows a very close Moon-Venus opposition (MO-_2_-VE) which is close to the Asc-Desc axis. It also contains a number of very appropriate harmonic aspects: notably, SO-_13_-VE, suggesting a willingness to strike out and be adventurous in my love life; SO-_15_-MA, suggesting an ability to be actively constructive in creating new relationships; and a cluster of (SO-_17_-SA)-_17_-MO, showing a "campaigning" desire to break free from Saturnian restrictions. All of these aspects are compatible with the transformation of my relationships with women. In contrast, the 43rd harmonic chart contains no such aspects, and I can see nothing in it which corresponds to the events of my 44th year.

Based on this case and on a few other cases that I have looked at, I would suggest that, if we are to use the technique of "Age Harmonics", we should follow John Addey's proposal, in which (for instance) the 20th harmonic corresponds to the 20th year of life, which is the year between the 19th and 20th birthdays.

Chapter 11
Harmonics in the Zodiacal and Diurnal Circles

We have been looking entirely at harmonics in the *aspectual* circles: that is, the circles that move from the conjunction between two planets, through the opposition, and back to the conjunction again. But readers of *Harmonics in Astrology* may be surprised to discover that only a small part of the book is devoted to the aspectual circles, and that Addey devotes more space to harmonics in the Zodiacal circle (the circle which shows the positions which the planets, or "wanderers," occupy in relation to the fixed stars, and which in traditional astrology is denoted by the twelve signs of the Zodiac) and in the diurnal circle (the circle which shows the positions occupied by the planets in relation to the Earth's horizon, and which is denoted by the twelve "houses".)

And yet the advances that have been made in harmonic astrology since Addey's time have been entirely (or almost entirely) concerned with the harmonics of the aspectual circles. When it comes to the harmonics of the Zodiacal and diurnal circles, it remains true that almost nothing is known, and there are no tools enabling the astrologer to use these harmonics in interpretation.

What are the reasons for this? There are many possible reasons, but I think that perhaps the most important reason is one that has not (so far as I know) been previously commented on. This is that, when we look at harmonics of the Zodiacal and diurnal circles, we are looking at *waves* rather than *signals*.

Let us go back to the definition of the word "harmonic" that we quoted in Chapter 1.

> "A harmonic is a signal or wave whose frequency is an integral (whole-number) multiple of the frequency of some reference signal or wave."

11.1 A 5th Harmonic
"Signal" Pattern

11.2 A 5th Harmonic
"Wave" Pattern

So there are two kinds of harmonics: signals and waves. The difference between the two can be illustrated by diagrams. Thus, Figure 11.1 shows a 5th harmonic *signal* pattern. At five equidistant points around the circle, a signal occurs which has the quality of the number Five. The closer one comes to the point of exactitude, the stronger the signal is. But in the intervals between the signals, the circle is regular, without peaks or troughs. We can say that in these intervals there is an *absence* of the quality of the number Five.

Figure 11.2, on the other hand, shows a 5th harmonic *wave* pattern. At five equidistant points around the circle, the wave forms a peak, and at five intermediate points it forms a trough. But the wave flattens out around the peak and around the trough, so one can no longer speak of a "point of exactitude". We can only say that, if there are qualities that are manifested in the "peak" areas, they are likely to be the *opposite* of the qualities that are manifested in the "trough" areas.

In the aspectual circles, a harmonic has the qualities of a signal. When Planet A is quintile to Planet B, there is a signal which has the quality of Fiveness. In the intervals between these signals, there is an absence of this quality. But in the zodiacal and diurnal circles, a harmonic has the qualities of a wave. This is because we are no longer talking about a relationship between two entities (Planet A and Planet B). We are talking about the position of a single planet within a circle.

Thus, in traditional astrology it is believed that there are twelve signs, which alternate between "positive" or "Yang" signs (Aries, Gemini, etc) and "negative" or "Yin" signs (Taurus, Cancer, etc). This implies a 6th harmonic wave, which moves between "positivity" and "negativity" six times around the circle. But there is no suggestion that there is a single point (or rather, six points) where the quality of "positivity" or "negativity" reaches a peak of intensity. Moreover, we cannot, in this context, speak about the presence or absence of the quality of Sixness. Sixness does not "belong" either to the positive or to the negative signs. We can only say that Sixness is the quality of the wave itself.

All this makes it very much more difficult to do research into the incidence and interpretation of harmonic patterns in the zodiacal and diurnal circles than in the aspectual circles. In the aspectual circles we know that, if there is a quality of Fiveness, it will manifest at the points where two planets are quintile to each other. Therefore, we can identify the charts in which there are the most (and the closest) quintiles, and from this discover much about the nature of Fiveness. But in the zodiacal and diurnal circles we have no such knowledge. Fiveness will be whatever occurs in five equidistant areas around the circle. But which areas will those be? We do not know. So there is no way in which we can identify the charts that are likely to display the strongest Fiveness.

Thus, as I have said, very little is known (at least in Western astrology) about the harmonics of the zodiacal and diurnal circles. But it is still worthwhile to summarize the work that has been done in these areas.

I will start with the zodiacal circle, because the harmonics of the zodiacal circle have an important role in ancient vedic astrology. I am not an expert on this, and readers who wish to know more should refer to specialized textbooks such as *The Essentials of Vedic Astrology* by Komilla Sutton.[1] Vedic astrology uses a number of "varga charts": "varga" means a part or division, and a varga chart is essentially the same as a harmonic chart, since it entails the division of the zodiac by a particular number. Thus, in the navamsha (or navamsa) (9th harmonic) chart, the zodiac is divided by 9 and so has a length of 40 degrees. Thus, a planet at 0°00' Aries in the natal chart would be conjunct in the navamsha chart with a planet at 10°00' Taurus, and they would both be placed at 0° Aries in the navamsha chart.

The vargas that are most frequently used correspond to the 2nd, 3rd, 4th, 5th, 7th and 9th harmonic charts. Each of these charts has its own significance: for instance, the saptamsha (7th harmonic) chart is traditionally about children and grandchildren, but Sutton suggests that it might cover other forms of creativity.[2] But the navamsha (9th harmonic) chart is the most important varga, and is an essential component of vedic astrology. John Addey says, "One of the primary meanings of the Navamsa chart is that it describes the marriage partner".[3] But Komilla Sutton says:

> "The navamsha chart reflects how the resources of the inner self cope with the ups and downs of everyday life and the spiritual challenges encountered by the outer self, and whether there will be a conflict between the two. It also shows parts of your personality which you may be reaching towards in your life, but which may still be causing you some stress at present because progress is slow".[4]

Essentially, the navamsha chart simply places the planets within signs in the 40-degree zodiac, and interprets them according to the signs in which they are placed. Thus, in terms of harmonics, vedic astrology is saying that there is a 9th harmonic wave which causes certain characteristics to appear and re-appear at 40-degree intervals around the 360-degree zodiac. But the problem for the Western astrologer is that it is very difficult (perhaps impossible) to integrate these insights into one's own practice. Vedic astrology is a complete system of astrology, as complex as Western astrology but very different, and (as far as I am aware) no attempt has yet been made to integrate the two into a unified system. (An additional problem is that vedic astrology uses the Sidereal Zodiac, not the Tropical Zodiac; also it does not use the outer planets, Uranus, Neptune, Pluto and Chiron.)

Thus, for the purpose of this book (which is to help Western astrologers to integrate harmonics into their existing practice), vedic astrology brings us no closer to understanding the harmonics of the zodiacal circle within our own system of astrology. It is important for us to recognize that vedic astrology is saying that these harmonics exist, but we have to look for new ways of interpreting them within our own system.

In Western astrology, there have been several attempts to identify harmonic patterns in the zodiacal circle. John Addey looked at the position of the Sun in the charts of 7302 British doctors, and found evidence of several harmonic waves, especially in the 6th and 12th harmonics.[5] (But this study was later replicated by a study of 6877 doctors in the U.S.A., which entirely failed to support Addey's findings.) He also studied the Sun's position in the charts of 1974 clergymen, and found evidence of a 7th harmonic wave. A number of other similar studies are reported on in *Harmonics in Astrology*.

From our point of view, however, the problem is that, even if we accept the validity of Addey's findings, they fall a long way short of being guidelines for interpretation. Thus, if we accept his findings about clergymen, we can say that there are seven equidistant areas around the ecliptic where, if you have the Sun in those areas, you are more likely to become a clergyman than if you have the Sun elsewhere (though Addey does not make it clear which areas these are). But that is all that we can say. We do not know what is the *quality* about the 7th harmonic that causes people with Sun in some areas to be drawn towards a priestly career, and (presumably) causes people with Sun in other areas to have an aversion to such a career. We do not know whether the effect is heightened by having the Moon or other planets in the same areas. For us, as working astrologers, the findings of Addey and others about harmonics in the zodiacal circle do not help us in interpreting the chart.

The same is true of harmonics in the diurnal circle. Here the starting point has to be the work of Michel Gauquelin, who (assisted by his wife Françoise) studied the charts of many thousands of people eminent in various professions whose time of birth had been officially recorded, and looked at the positions of various planets in the diurnal circle. He discovered that eminent sportspeople and soldiers were statistically more likely to have Mars in certain sectors of the diurnal circle (corresponding roughly to the 12th, 9th, 6th and 3rd houses) than in other sectors; similarly, eminent actors were likely to have Jupiter in these sectors, and eminent doctors and scientists were likely to have Saturn in these sectors.

Gauquelin did not use the word "harmonics", but John Addey claimed that what Gauquelin had discovered was a 4th harmonic wave, with peaks in the 12th, 9th, 6th and 3rd houses and troughs at the intermediate points. He also pointed out that, especially in the case of sportspeople and Mars, there is also a (less strong) 3rd harmonic wave, peaking roughly in the 12th, 8th and 4th houses. The incidence of Mars is strongest in the 12th house because this is where the two waves reinforce each other rather than acting against each other.

Some people question the validity of Gauquelin's findings, but I believe that he did make some genuine discoveries. But these discoveries are, once again, of very little use in interpretation. We can say to a client who has Mars (but not Jupiter or Saturn) in the "Gauquelin sectors" that he or she is more likely to achieve eminence as a sportsperson or a soldier than as an actor, doctor or scientist, but there is very little that we can say beyond that.

Thus, very little is known about the harmonics of the zodiacal and diurnal circles - and yet there is evidence that these harmonic waves do exist, and are worthy of further research.

My belief is that this research would best be done, not by Gauquelin-type studies which attempt to show a statistical correlation between astrological factors and a single variable such as profession, but rather by replicating, for the zodiacal and diurnal circles, the kind of research that I (and others) have done for the aspectual circles. Essentially this means *identifying those charts that are strongest in a particular factor, and then assessing what qualities these charts have in common.* This is what David Cochrane calls "qualitative research".[6] It does not prove anything scientifically, and yet this is how astrological discoveries are made.

For instance, if we were researching the 7th harmonic in the zodiacal circle, we could study the charts of several hundred famous people, and identify those charts which had the greatest number of planets in the "Aries" section (or, better still, in the first half of the "Aries" section) of the 7th harmonic chart. Having made this list, we would study the biographies of these people in order to assess what qualities they had in common. We would then repeat this exercise for all the other "signs" (or "half-signs") around the 7th harmonic zodiac. This would of course be a massive exercise, but it is likely that it would yield a massive amount of information about 7th harmonic waves in the zodiacal circle. And this information would cover not only the 7th harmonic, but also its sub-harmonics. For instance, if it was found that people with many planets in 7th harmonic "Aries" had similar qualities to those with planets in 7th harmonic "Leo" and "Sagittarius", this would be evidence of a 21st harmonic wave.

If we were researching the 7th harmonic in the diurnal circle, we would follow the same procedure, but we would be studying the 7th harmonic "houses" rather than the signs. Thus, we would identify those charts which had the greatest number of planets in the 7th harmonic 1st house (or in the first half of the 1st house), and then repeat this for all the other houses or half-houses. We should note that in a harmonic chart the houses are all of equal length, even if they are derived from a radical chart based on Placidus or some other house system. But we should also note that these harmonic "houses" are counted from the Ascendant, without reference to the Midheaven. We might therefore think it worthwhile to repeat the whole exercise using houses counted from the Midheaven (with the Midheaven, wherever it occurs in the harmonic chart, being seen as the cusp of the 10th house). This again would be a huge task, but again it would be likely to yield a huge amount of information about 7th harmonic waves in the diurnal circle. (Here, however, a word of caution needs to be added. The Angles of the chart move so fast over time that even a slight error in the birth time would lead to major errors in the higher harmonics. Maybe we could look for 7th harmonic waves in the diurnal circle, but ignore (for instance) 28th harmonic waves as these would be too error-prone.)

These exercises could be repeated for other harmonics, such as (for instance) the 5th, 9th and 11th harmonics, using information from the 5th, 9th and 11th harmonic charts. Thus, there is an enormous amount of research to be done, but the benefits for astrological interpretation would be equally massive. I personally think that this is the greatest research challenge facing astrology at the present time.

Until this research has been done, we can say that we cannot use the harmonics of the zodiacal and diurnal circles in interpretation. But I would like to suggest one method by which we *could* do so, by utilizing the knowledge that we already have about the zodiacal signs and the diurnal houses, and adjusting this knowledge so that it accords with harmonic theory. We could do this by adopting the model of "overlapping signs and houses", which I described in *Harmonic Charts*, and which I still believe to be valid.[7]

Overlapping Signs and Houses

Readers of this book will by now be aware that in traditional astrology, when we look at aspects between planets, we are already using a harmonic model of signals. The opposition is the aspect of the 2nd harmonic, the trine is the aspect of the 3rd harmonic, and so on. If the Sun is at 0° Leo and the Moon is at 0° Sagittarius, they are linked to each other in the 3rd harmonic.

But in the traditional view of the zodiacal and diurnal circles, we are *not* using a harmonic model. We are using, instead, a "boxes" model, which divides the zodiac into twelve "signs" and the diurnal circle into twelve "houses". These signs and houses are seen as having sharp boundaries (or "cusps"). So long as the Moon is in Scorpio, it retains the qualities of Scorpio, which do not change as it moves through the sign. But when it enters Sagittarius, it suddenly loses these Scorpionic qualities and acquires instead the qualities of Sagittarius. It has entered a different "box".

These two models (the harmonic model and the "boxes" model) are hard to reconcile with each other. Suppose the Sun is at 0° Leo and the Moon is at 29° Scorpio. Using the harmonic model, we say that the Moon is still trine to the Sun, because it is only one degree away from an exact 3rd harmonic aspect. But how can this be, when the Moon has not yet entered the Sagittarius "box" and so has not yet acquired the Sagittarian qualities which would cause it to be in harmony with the Sun in Leo?

My proposal is that we should retain our traditional beliefs about the qualities of the signs and houses (which are, after all, our most fundamental tools, without which we would be bereft of all of our skill as astrologers), but that we should move from a "boxes" model in which the signs and houses are separated by sharp boundaries, and adopt instead a "harmonics" ("waves") model in which the signs and houses merge into one another and overlap with one another, with the transition from Scorpionic to Sagittarian qualities being gradual rather than sudden. In such a model, a planet close to (but on either side of) the Scorpio/Sagittarius boundary would retain some of the qualities of Scorpio while also acquiring some of the qualities of Sagittarius.

My suggestion is that this can be achieved by postulating that, *as we proceed through a sign from 0° to 30°, the qualities of that sign become gradually more internalized.* We can illustrate this by taking any of the twelve signs, but, as Aries is counted as the first sign of the Zodiac, I will take Aries.

If we look at the qualities that are traditionally associated with Aries, we can see that these qualities can be expressed either *externally* or *internally.* A person who expresses Aries *externally* will be one whose surface behaviour is dynamic, assertive, quick-tempered, enthusiastic, impetuous. In contrast, a person who expresses Aries *internally* will be one who has within himself a deep self-belief, self-confidence, ambitiousness, and competitiveness. The suggestion is that, as we move through Aries from 0° to 30°, the way in which Aries is expressed will gradually change from surface assertiveness to inner self-confidence.

And then we can suggest that in the first few degrees of Aries – and also in the last few degrees of Pisces – the surface aggressiveness will arise out of a deep-seated Piscean emotionality and sensitivity. This will be a person who is inwardly Pisces and outwardly Aries. And furthermore, we can suggest that in the last few degrees of Aries – and also in the first few degrees of Taurus – the deep inner self-confidence will give rise to surface behaviour which is calm, sensible, reliable, stubborn, and essentially Taurean. This will be a person who is inwardly Aries and outwardly Taurus. In the central part of Aries, between these two extremes, we will have a person who is "pure Aries", expressing Aries qualities both in his external behaviour and in his inner beliefs and attitudes.

The same pattern would apply to other signs around the Zodiac. Thus, for instance, the last degrees of Taurus and the first degrees of Gemini would denote a person who had a deep inner sense of his own groundedness and stability, enabling him on the surface to develop a *persona* that was rational, talkative and inquisitive.

If we accept this proposal, we have done away with the sharp boundaries between the signs, and we have abandoned the "boxes" model and adopted instead a model of harmonic waves. In fact, four harmonic waves would be present: a 3rd harmonic wave (occurring three times around the circle) in which the movement was from Fire to Earth to Air to Water and back to Fire; a 4th harmonic wave, with a movement from Cardinal to Fixed to Mutable and back to Cardinal; a 6th harmonic wave, moving between Fire/Air (masculine, yang) and Earth/Water (feminine, yin); and a 12th harmonic wave, in which the movement was between the "pure" expression of a sign (peaking at 15° of each sign) and the mingling of two signs (peaking at 0° of each sign).

We can see that, if we use this model, the problem of the Sun at 0° Leo being trine to the Moon at 29° Scorpio would be solved, since both Sun and Moon would show a fiery external *persona* arising out of a deep inner emotionality, and so they would be in harmony with each other.

In practice, I would feel that, for the greater part of each sign, the traditional interpretations could be maintained without any modification. Thus, for the area between 5° Aries and 25° Aries, we would be free to interpret Aries as we have always done. But, for the areas within 5 degrees of the sign cusps (e.g. from 25° Pisces to 5° Aries, and from 25° Aries to 5° Taurus) it would be desirable to take into account the mingling of two signs.

All this is only a suggestion, as I have not done any research with the aim of demonstrating the truth of this theory. But it does fit in with my instinctive understanding of how the signs are connected to one another. It fits in also with my subjective impression that (for instance) people with planets in the first half of Aries display the qualities of Aries in a more *externalized* way than do people with planets in the second half of Aries.

As an example, we can take the poet Charles Baudelaire (Figure 11.3). I have already mentioned Baudelaire in Chapter 4, where I pointed out that he has a massive conjunction of six planets, with Mercury and Pluto in the last three degrees of Pisces and Mars, Chiron, Venus and Jupiter in the first ten degrees of Aries (including Mars almost exactly on the Pisces/Aries cusp). I said that he displayed "a dynamic and fiery Aries manner, arising out a deep Piscean emotionality". This is, I think, a good example of *externalized* Aries combined with *internalized* Pisces. I do not think one can meaningfully say that Baudelaire's ME and PL are pure Pisces and his MA and CH are pure Aries. All these planets are in conjunction, and they all display the qualities of Pisces and Aries combined.

Another example of a chart containing a conjunction straddling the boundary between two signs is the natal chart of the great mathematician Alan Turing, which is shown in Figure 11.4. Turing has a conjunction of (VE-*1*-PL)-*1*-SO)-1-ME, with Venus and

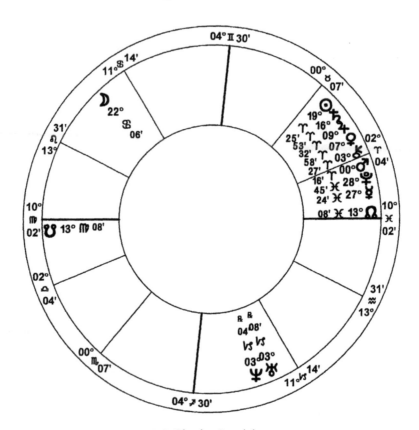

11.3 Charles Baudelaire

Pluto in the last degrees of Gemini and Sun and Mercury in the first degrees of Cancer. Turing has been described as "prickly and proud, yet self-effacing," and also as "shy but outspoken, nervous yet lacking deference".[8] I feel that this well describes *externalized* Cancer arising out of *internalized* Gemini: that is, behaviour which on the surface was Cancerian (emotional yet outspoken, "cardinal Water") but which arose out of a deep inner inquisitiveness about the world which is typical of Gemini.

We can note also that Turing has the Ascendant in the early degrees of Gemini, but it is conjunct Saturn in the last degrees of Taurus. Turing has been called "the father of modern computing," and clearly his Ascendant enabled him to display the intellectual curiosity of Gemini externally as well as internally, and yet I believe that this

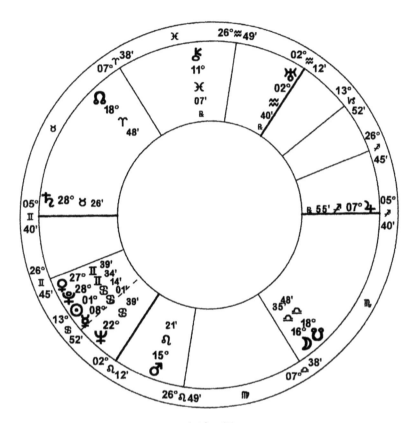

11.4 Alan Turing

curiosity arose out of a deep inner groundedness which is signified by Saturn in late Taurus. So here we have externalized Gemini arising out of internalized Taurus.

This proposal would also help to solve some astrological conundrums. In Chapter 3 I mentioned the case of two fraternal twins who have very different personalities even though they have almost the same birth chart. But one of them has Leo 3° rising and the other has Leo 12° rising, and the one with Leo 3° rising displays the characteristics of Leo in a much more *externalized* way than her twin.

We can turn now from the signs to the houses. At first sight it is more difficult to apply a "harmonic wave" model to the houses in the diurnal circle, because (unless we are using the Equal House system) the houses are of unequal length, and it is an essential principle of harmonic theory that the waves should be of equal length. It is possible that, in reality, there are two systems of harmonic waves operating within the diurnal circle: one based on the Ascendant/ Descendant axis (the "Self/Other" axis), and the other based on the I.C./Midheaven axis (the "past/future" axis).

However, in practice I feel that it is unnecessary to worry about these complexities. The houses are concerned, not with personality traits, but with areas of interest, and so the internal/external question does not arise. All we need to do is to acknowledge that the areas of interest denoted by the houses merge gradually into each other, rather than being separated by sharp boundaries at the house cusps. Thus, for instance, if we say that the first house is about the presentation of oneself, and that the second house is about money and possessions, then we can say that, around the area of the second-house cusp, there is an equal interest in *both* these areas; and perhaps we can suggest that these two areas tend to merge into one in the person's mind. (For instance, I believe that the 7th and 8th houses merged together in the mind of Baudelaire, whose multiple conjunction straddles the 8th house cusp). Thus, we have in effect adopted a "harmonic waves" model for the diurnal circle, as also for the zodiacal circle.

By adopting this model, we would be abandoning the "boxes" model. We would be saying that there are no sharp boundaries up there in the sky, and that everything is based on waves that gradually rise and fall and on signals that come and go, in a regular, rhythmical manner. We would be moving closer to John Addey's vision, in which "the harmonics, that is the rhythms and sub-rhythms of cosmic periods, can be demonstrated to provide the basis of all astrological doctrine".[9]

Chapter 12
The Future of Harmonic Astrology

At the time that John Addey's book *Harmonics in Astrology* was published in 1976, it was widely thought that it would herald a revolution in astrological practice, and that, in Addey's own words, astrology would be "reborn". It has to be admitted that this has not happened. Harmonic astrology is still very definitely not part of the "mainstream", and I have not found a single reference to harmonics in recent editions of the British *Astrological Journal.*

There are a number of reasons for this. Firstly, the development of harmonic astrology was held back by the untimely deaths of John Addey in 1982 and Charles Harvey in 2000; also, I did not help the process by my own 20-year absence from astrology which started in the late 1980s. Harmonic astrology has suffered from its failure to attract prominent advocates who would have taught it and promoted it with sufficient vigour.

And also, it has perhaps suffered because it has seemed too difficult and obscure. *Harmonics in Astrology* is very far from being a "how to do it" manual, and it may have alienated readers by the difficulty of its concepts and its emphasis on the need for further research. Most astrologers do not have the time or the inclination to do extensive research. They are in astrology in order to *practise* astrology, and, if a new approach is not presented in a way that can be immediately put into practice, they will not adopt it.

My own 1983 book *Harmonic Charts* was an attempt at a "how to do it" manual, but I feel now that (for the reasons which I explained in Chapter 1 of the present book) the "harmonic charts" technique was itself alienating for many astrologers. When trying to interpret a chart by the use of many harmonic charts, I became overwhelmed by the quantity of paper that I was using and the need to cross-reference between all these different charts.

Thus, harmonic astrology, although it is more than 40 years old, is in effect still in its infancy. However, I believe that things are now beginning to change. Since I came back to astrology I have been working very much on my own and have been out of touch with the astrological community, so there may well be developments of which I am unaware. But I would like to mention the work of David Cochrane, who teaches vibrational astrology at the Avalon School of Astrology in Florida.[1] Vibrational astrology has been described as "a complete system of astrology", using harmonics, midpoints, and also the work of Theodor Landscheidt which was concerned with cosmic cycles.[2] Cochrane has carried out his own research into the meaning of all the harmonics up to the 32nd, using research methods similar to my own, and his findings are described in his online book *The First 32 Harmonics, a Qualitative Research Study*.[3] His conclusions about the qualities attached to particular harmonics are in some cases different from mine (especially in the case of the 7th harmonic and its sub-harmonics), but he and I are in correspondence and are attempting to move towards a consensus about the qualities of these harmonics.

Thus, harmonic astrology, even if it is in its infancy, is now alive and well, and I am hoping that this book will enable astrologers to put it into practice. I believe that it is now possible for astrologers, using the methods described in this book, to practise harmonic astrology with some confidence that it will yield fascinating new insights which would not otherwise have been available. I have certainly found this to be true myself, and I hope that others will agree with me.

However, if harmonic astrology is to develop into its full maturity, a number of things need to happen. Firstly, there needs to be more research. Secondly, new software needs to be developed. And, thirdly and most importantly, there needs to be dialogue between practitioners of harmonic astrology, so that they can pool their experiences and learn from one another. I will deal with each of these issues in turn.

Firstly, research. There are a number of areas where further research would bring great benefits.

(1) Further research into the meaning of the harmonics up to 32 (in the aspectual circle). The meanings which I, and also Cochrane, have assigned to these harmonics are provisional and incomplete, and need to be elaborated and refined by further investigation, and by the publication of case studies illustrating particular examples. Especially, there needs to be research into the incidence of these harmonics in mundane (as opposed to natal) charts.

(2) Research into the meaning of the harmonics of numbers (and especially prime numbers) above 32. At the end of Chapter 5, I suggested a method by which this research could be done, taking one harmonic at a time.

(3) Research into the use of harmonics in synastry, and also in transits and progressions. These areas, which I discussed in Chapters 9 and 10, are virtually virgin fields, and the potential for research is vast.

(4) Research into the harmonics of the zodiacal and diurnal circles. I discussed this in Chapter 11, where I said: "There is an enormous amount of research to be done, but the benefits for astrological interpretation would be equally massive. I personally think that this is the greatest research challenge facing astrology at the present time."

(5) Finally (as I said in Chapter 19 of *TSON*) there is a need for research into the effects of *celestial latitude* and *parallax*. The zodiacal positions of the planets, as given in the Ephemeris, are not their actual positions in the sky; rather, they are the positions of their *nearest points on the ecliptic*. This is the effect of celestial latitude, which is the planet's angular distance from the ecliptic. And also, the Moon's position as given in the Ephemeris is its position in relation to the centre of the Earth, rather than to the point on the Earth's surface where the birth or other event took place: this is the effect of parallax. It is possible (with the aid of computer software) to correct the planets' positions for celestial latitude and parallax, so that their positions in the chart become their actual positions in relation to the place of birth; but this would have the effect of altering the harmonic aspects, especially for the Moon (because of parallax) and Pluto (because Pluto can have a

very high celestial latitude). There is a need for research to discover whether correction for celestial latitude and parallax leads to a better (or a worse) fit between the harmonic aspects and the birth (or other event) that they describe.

Secondly, the need for new software. I am not a software expert, so I will simply say that there is a need for software to be developed which would facilitate the identification of harmonic aspects, especially in relation to synastry and transits.

And thirdly, the need for dialogue, which I believe to be the most important issue.

I am now in my eighties. If I was 40 years younger, I would attempt to set up and direct courses in harmonic astrology, whether by means of face-to-face workshops or by means of online correspondence courses. I recognize that astrologers may need help in applying the methods described in this book: help with the mechanics of calculation, and help also with the interpretation of charts.

I would also attempt to facilitate means by which practitioners of harmonic astrology could communicate both with me and with each other, sharing their experiences, their insights and their difficulties, learning from one another, and furthering the development of harmonic astrology by this pooling of the wisdom of those who practise it. Maybe there could be a site on social media set up for this purpose. Maybe there could be a journal or newsletter devoted to the sharing of information about harmonic astrology.

At my age, however, I do not feel able to commit myself to these activities. Nevertheless, I would like to invite readers of this book to email me at pigleystair@yahoo.co.uk to tell me about their experiences in using harmonic astrology, and especially if they need help and advice in putting into practice the methods described in the book. I will undertake (health permitting) to reply, without charge, to all such emails; however, if the correspondence developed into a more formal and continuing teacher-pupil relationship, I might ask for payment.

Also I would welcome any help that readers can give me in setting up a forum (maybe through Facebook or other social media) for the sharing of information about harmonic astrology. I would gladly participate in such a forum, although I would prefer not to be in charge of it myself. My hope would be that such a forum would survive and thrive even when I am no longer able to take part in it.

Let us not forget that the quest on which we are engaged is of cosmic importance. In investigating the rhythmic patterns in the relationships between heavenly bodies, and the ways in which these patterns affect our lives here on Earth, we are, as John Addey said, "contemplating the great verities of man's estate and his relationship to the Cosmos and to God", and we are "glimpsing more clearly the mysteries and beauties of the Divine Order and Harmony".[4] We are investigating the *music of the spheres*. Let us rejoice that we have the opportunity to do this.

Appendix I
Chart Data

This list includes birth data for all the people mentioned in the book (apart from book authors, and a few others for whom birth times are not available); also data for all the mundane events mentioned.

Natal charts

John Addey: June 15, 1920, 08.15 a.m., Barnsley, England. RR: A.

Spiro Agnew: November 9, 1918, 09.00, Forest Hill, MD, USA. RR: AA.

Lita Albuquerque: January 3, 1946, 05.15 a.m., Santa Monica, CA, USA. RR: A.

Amma: September 27, 1953, 09.10 a.m., Parayakadavu, India (9N10. 76E31). RR: B.

Hans Christian Andersen: April 2, 1805, 01.00 a.m., Odense, Denmark. RR: AA.

Fred Astaire: May 10, 1899, 09.16 p.m., Omaha, NE, USA. RR: AA.

Aurobindo: August 15, 1872, 05.00 a.m., Calcutta, India. RR: B.

Bahá-u-lláh: November 12, 1817, 06.40 a.m., Tehran, Iran. RR: B.

Alice Bailey: June 16, 1880, 07.32 a.m., Manchester, England. RR: C (but I believe the birth time was provided by Bailey herself: see TSON p.314).

Honoré de Balzac: May 20, 1799, 11.00 a.m., Tours, France. RR: AA.

Jürgen Bartsch: November 6, 1946, 10.50 a.m., Essen-Rittenscheid, Germany. RR: AA.

Charles Baudelaire: April 9, 1821, 03.00 p.m., Paris, France. RR: AA.

Hector Berlioz: December 11, 1803, 05.00 p.m., La-Côte-Saint-André, France. RR: AA.

Robert Black: April 21, 1947, 08.35 p.m., Falkirk, Scotland. RR: AA.

Tony Blair: May 6, 1953, 06.10 a.m., Edinburgh, Scotland. RR: AA.

Ian Brady: January 2, 1938, 12.40 p.m., Glasgow, Scotland. RR: AA.

Bobby Brown: February 5, 1969, 05.21 a.m., Boston, MA, USA. RR: AA.

Frank Buchman: June 4, 1878, 04.00 a.m., Pennsburg, PA, USA. RR: A.

Carol Burnett: April 26, 1933, 04.00 a.m., San Antonio, TX, USA. RR: AA.

George W. Bush: July 6, 1946, 07.26 a.m., New Haven, CT, USA. RR: AA.

Lord Byron: January 22, 1788, 02.00 p.m., London, England. RR: AA.

Sophie Calle: October 9, 1953, 03.15 p.m., Paris, France. RR: AA.

Camilla Duchess of Cornwall: July 17, 1947, 07.10 a.m., London, England. RR: B.

Elias Canetti: July 27, 1905, 01.00 a.m., Ruse, Bulgaria. RR: AA.

Truman Capote: September 30, 1924, 03.00 p.m., New Orleans, LA, USA. RR: B.

Prince Charles: November 14, 1948, 09.14 p.m., London, England. RR: A.

Bruce Chatwin: May 13, 1940, 08.30 p.m., Dronfield (near Sheffield), England. RR: B.

Winston Churchill: November 30, 1874, 01.30 a.m., Woodstock, England. RR: A.

Kurt Cobain: February 20, 1967, 07.20 p.m., Aberdeen, WA, USA. RR: AA.

Leonard Cohen: September 21, 1934, 06.45 a.m., Montreal, Canada. RR: AA.

Toni Collette: November 1, 1972, 11.14 a.m., Sydney, Australia. RR: A.

Patricia Columbo: June 21, 1956, 11.52 a.m. (standard time), Chicago, IL, USA. RR: B.

Roberta Cowell: April 8, 1918, 02.00 a.m., Croydon, England. RR: A.

Jeffrey Dahmer: May 21, 1960, 04.34 p.m., Milwaukee, WI, USA. RR: AA.

Salvador Dali: May 11, 1904, 08.45 a.m., Figueras, Spain. RR: AA.

John Daly: April 28, 1966, 01.30 a.m., Carmichael, CA, USA. RR: AA.

Princess Diana: July 1, 1961, 07.45 p.m., Sandringham, England. RR: A.

Otto Dietrich: August 31, 1897, 10.45 p.m., Essen (N.R-Westph.), Germany. RR: AA.

Iain Duncan Smith: April 9, 1954, 09.02 p.m., Edinburgh, Scotland. RR: AA.

Marie Duplessis: January 15, 1824, 08.00 p.m., Nonant-le-Pin, France. RR: AA.

Marc Dutroux: November 6, 1956, 07.35 a.m., Ixelles, Belgium. RR: AA.

Amelia Earhart: July 24, 1897, 11.30 p.m., Atchison, KS, USA. RR: A.

Ralph Lee Earnhardt: February 23, 1928, 11.30 p.m., Concord, NC, USA. RR: AA.

Reinhold Ebertin: February 16, 1901, 04.45 a.m., Görlitz, Germany. RR: A.

Ira Einhorn: May 15, 1940, 03.33 p.m., Philadelphia, PA, USA. RR: A.

Tracey Emin: July 3, 1963, 06.50 a.m., Thornton Heath (London), England. RR: AA.

Friedrich Engels: November 28, 1820, 09.00 p.m., Barmen, Germany. RR: AA.

Rainer Werner Fassbinder: May 31, 1945, 01.55 a.m., Bad Wörishofen, Germany. RR: AA.

Dodi al Fayed: April 15, 1955, 06.45, Alexandria, Egypt. RR: C (but known to have Taurus rising).

Roger Federer: August 8, 1981, 08.40 a.m., Basel, Switzerland. RR: A.

Jane Fonda: December 21, 1937, 09.14 a.m., Manhattan, NY, USA. RR: AA.

Gerald Ford: July 14, 1913, 12.43 a.m., Omaha, NE, USA. RR: AA.

Steve Fossett: April 22, 1944. 01.58 a.m., Jackson, TN, USA. RR: AA.

A.J. Foyt: January 16, 1935, 01.25 a.m., Houston, TX, USA. RR: AA.

Sigmund Freud: May 6, 1856, 06.30 p.m., Freiburg, Austria (now Pribor, Czech Republic). RR: A.

John Wayne Gacy: March 17, 1942, 12.29 a.m., Chicago, IL, USA. RR: AA.

Indira Gandhi: November 19, 1917, 23.11, Allahabad, India. RR: A.

Mohandas Gandhi: October 2, 1869, 07.11 a.m., Porbandar, India. RR: C (rectified from approximate time).

Paul Gauguin: June 7, 1848, 10.00 a.m., Paris, France. RR: AA.

Françoise Gauquelin: June 19, 1929, 04.00 a.m., Neuchâtel, Switzerland. RR: A.

Michel Gauquelin: November 13, 1928, 10.15 p.m., Paris, France. RR: AA.

Jennifer Gibbons: April 11, 1963, 08.20 a.m., Aden, Yemen. RR: B.

June Gibbons: April 11, 1963, 08.10 a.m., Aden, Yemen. RR: B.

Allen Ginsberg: June 2, 1926, 02.00 a.m., Newark, NJ, USA. RR: A.

Graham Greene: October 2, 1904, 10.20 a.m., Berkhamsted, England. RR: A.

David Hamblin: August 8, 1935, 09.50 p.m., Manchester, England. RR: AA.

Thomas Hamilton: May 10, 1952, 08.50 a.m., Glasgow, Scotland. RR: AA.

Rolf Harris: March 30, 1930, 03.15 a.m., Perth, Australia. RR: A.

Prince Harry: September 15, 1984, 04.20 p.m., London England. RR: A.

Charles Harvey: June 22, 1940, 09.16 a.m., Little Bookham, England. RR: A.

Jimi Hendrix: November 27, 1942, 10.15, Seattle, WA, USA. RR: AA

O. Henry: September 11, 1862, 09.00 p.m., Greensboro, NC, USA. RR: AA.

Hermann Hesse: July 2, 1877, 06.30 p.m., Calw, Germany. RR: AA.

James Hillman: April 12, 1926, 09.08 a.m., Atlantic City, NJ, USA. RR: C (see note *at end of Appendix I).

Adolf Hitler: April 20, 1889, 06.30 p.m., Braunau, Austria. RR: AA.

Gerard Manley Hopkins: July 28, 1844, 04.15 a.m., Stratford (London), England. RR: B.

Whitney Houston: August 9, 1963, 08.55 p.m., Newark, NJ, USA. RR: AA.

L. Ron Hubbard: March 13, 1911, 02.01 a.m., Tilden, NE, USA. RR: A.

Fanny Imlay: May 14, 1794, 14.00, Le Havre, France. RR: B

Augustus John: January 4, 1878, 05.30 a.m., Tenby, Wales. RR: B.

Janis Joplin: January 19, 1943, 09.45 a.m., Port Arthur, TX, USA. RR: AA.

Carl Gustav Jung: July 26, 1875, 07.32 p.m., Kesswil, Switzerland. RR: A.

Frida Kahlo: July 6, 1907, 08.30 a.m., Coyoacán, Mexico. RR: AA.

John F. Kennedy: May 29, 1917, 03.00 p.m., Brookline, MA, USA. RR: A.

Reginald Kray: October 24, 1933, 08.00 p.m., London, England. RR: AA.

Ronald Kray: October 24, 1933, 08.10 p.m., London, England. RR: AA.

R.D. Laing: October 7, 1927, 05.15 p.m., Glasgow, Scotland. RR: AA.

Hedy Lamarr: November 9, 1914, 07.30 p.m., Vienna, Austria. RR: A.

Jerry Lewis: March 16, 1926, 12.15 p.m., Newark, NJ, USA. RR: AA.

Federico Garcia Lorca: June 5, 1898, 00.00 midnight, Fuente Vaqueros,
    Spain. RR: AA.

Humphrey Lyttelton: May 23, 1921, 07.00 a.m., Windsor, England. RR: A.

René Magritte: November 21, 1898, 07.30 a.m., Lessines, Belgium. RR: AA.

Marcel Marceau: March 22, 1923, 08.00 a.m., Strasbourg, France. RR: AA.

Marie Antoinette: November 2, 1755, 07.30 p.m., Vienna, Austria. RR: A.

Meghan Markle: August 4, 1981, 04.46, Canoga Park, CA, USA. RR: AA.

Karl Marx: May 5, 1818, 02.00 a.m., Trier, Germany. RR: AA.

Jean Miguères: May 11, 1940, 11.00 p.m., Algiers, Algeria. RR: AA.

Jessica Mitford: September 11, 1917, 04.30, Gloucester, England. RR: A

Nancy Mitford: November 28, 1904, 18.00, London, England. RR: B.

Diana Mosley: June 17, 1910, 02.00 p.m., London, England. RR: B.

Iris Murdoch: July 15, 1919, 08.00 a.m., Dublin, Ireland. RR: A.

Richard Nixon: January 9, 1913, 21.35, Yorba Linda, CA, USA. RR: AA

Madalyn Murray O'Hair: April 13, 1919, 09.00 a.m., Pittsburgh, PA,
    USA. RR: AA.

Laurence Olivier: May 22, 1907, 05.00 a.m., Dorking, England. RR: AA.

Jacqueline Kennedy Onassis: July 28, 1929, 02.30 p.m., Southampton, NY,
    USA. RR:A.

Dorothy Parker: August 22, 1893, 09.50 p.m., West End (Gloucester), NJ,
    USA. RR: B.

Henri Paul: July 3, 1956, 01.00, Lorient, France. RR: AA.

Cynthia Payne: December 24, 1932, 09.00 p.m., Bognor Regis, England.
    RR: A.

Gregory Peck: April 5, 1916, 08.00 a.m., La Jolla (San Diego), CA, USA.
    RR: AA.

Eva Peron: May 7, 1919, 05.14 a.m. (LMT = 05.00 a.m. Cordoba time),
    Los Toldos (Buenos Aires), Argentina. RR: DD.

Pablo Picasso: October 25, 1881, 11.15 p.m., Malaga, Spain. RR: AA.

Eva Pierrakos: March 30, 1915, 11.45 a.m., Vienna, Austria. RR: A.

Sylvia Plath: October 27, 1932, 02.10 p.m., Boston, MA, USA. RR: A.

Richard Pryor: December 1, 1940, 01.02 p.m., Peoria, IL, USA. RR: AA.

Vanessa Redgrave: January 30, 1937, 06.00 p.m., Blackheath, England.
    RR: B.

Pat Rodegast: March 17, 1926, 01.00 p.m., Stamford, CT, USA. RR: A.

Romain Rolland: January 29, 1866, 02.00 a.m., Clemecy, France. RR: AA.

Bertrand Russell: May 18, 1872, 05.45 p.m., Trelleck, Wales. RR: B.

Marquis de Sade: June 2, 1740, 05.00 p.m., Paris, France. RR: AA.

Antoine de Saint-Exupéry: June 29, 1900, 09.15 a.m., Lyon, France. RR: AA.

Peter Sellers: September 8, 1925, 06.00 a.m., Portsmouth, England. RR: A.

Mary Shelley: August 30, 1797, 11.20 p.m., London, England. RR: AA.

Percy Bysshe Shelley: August 4, 1792, 10.00 p.m., Horsham, England.
    RR: A.

Jean Sibelius: December 8, 1865, 12.30 a.m., Hameenlinna, Finland. RR: B.

Edith Sitwell: September 7, 1887, 01.30 p.m., Scarborough, England. RR: A.

Charles Sobhraj: April 6, 1944, 10.00 p.m., Saigon, Vietnam. RR: B.

Charles Starkweather: November 24, 1938, 08.10 p.m., Lincoln, NE,
    USA. RR: AA.

Pierre Teilhard de Chardin: May 1, 1881, 07.00 a.m. Orcières, France.
    RR: AA.

Alfred Lord Tennyson: August 6, 1809, 00.05 a.m., Somersby, England
    (53N23.0E12). RR: A.

Nikola Tesla: July 10, 1856, 00.00 midnight, Smiljan, Croatia. RR: B.

Saint Thérèse de Lisieux: January 2, 1873, 11.30 p.m., Alençon, France.
    RR: AA.

Dylan Thomas: October 27, 1914, 11.00 p.m., Swansea, Wales. RR: A.

Donald Trump: June 14, 1946, 10.54 a.m., Queens, NY, USA. RR: AA.

Alan Turing: June 23, 1912, 02.15 a.m., London, England. RR: A.

George Van Tassel: March 12, 1910, 08.30 a.m., Jefferson, OH, USA. RR: AA.

Alain Vareille: May 3, 1956, 07.45 a.m., Versailles, France. RR: AA.

Queen Victoria: May 24, 1819, 04.15, London, England. RR: AA

"Walk-in from Sirius": June 19, 1948, 02.00 a.m., Montreal, Canada. RR: A.

Andy Warhol: August 6, 1928, August 6, 1928, 06.30, Pittsburgh, PA,
    USA. RR: B

James D. Watson: April 6, 1928, 01.23 a.m., Chicago, IL, USA. RR: AA.

Prince William: June 21, 1982, 09.03 p.m., London, England. RR: AA.

Colin Wilson: June 26, 1931, 04.30 a.m., Leicester, England. RR: A.

Harold Wilson: March 11, 1916, 10.45 a.m., Huddersfield, England. RR: A.

Amy Winehouse: September 14, 1983, 10.25 p.m., Enfield (London), England. RR: A.

Malala Yousafzai: July 12, 1997, 08.30 a.m., Mingaora, Pakistan (34N47. 72E22). RR: C (but "her parents are sure that she was born between 8.00 and 9.00 a.m.").

Mundane charts

Princess Diana's fatal car crash: August 31, 1997, 00.23 a.m., Paris, France.

Dunblane massacre: March 13, 1996, 09.35 a.m., Dunblane, Scotland.

Second Battle of Fallujah: November 7, 2004, 07.00 p.m., Fallujah, Iraq (33N21.43E47).

Guernica bombing: April 26, 1937, 04.30 p.m., Guernica, Spain.

Guernica news reaches Picasso: April 29, 1937, 10.00 a.m., Paris, France.

"The Nazi Chart": January 30, 1933, 11.00 a.m., Berlin, Germany.

Nuneaton rail crash: June 6, 1975, 01.55 a.m., Nuneaton, England.

Paddington rail crash: October 5, 1999, 08.09 a.m., London, England.

Twin Towers attack: September 11, 2001, 08.45 a.m., New York, NY, USA.

Ufton Nervet rail crash: November 6, 2004, 06.12 p.m., Ufton Nervet (near Reading), England.

USA Foundation Chart: July 4, 1776, 05.10 p.m., Philadelphia, PA, USA.

* I have cast James Hillman's chart for 09.08 a.m., which is the time that he gave to Tony Joseph. (More recently, in 2005, he gave 09.13 a.m. to Liz Greene.) However, AstroDatabank says that in 2015 (four years after Hillman's death) "Rick Tarnas reported that Hillman had discovered a written note about his time of birth in his deceased mother's documents, in the 1990s, giving 10.20 as his time of birth".

Clearly we cannot know for sure which of these times is correct. I prefer the 09.08 chart to the 10.20 chart because I feel that Gemini rising, with Venus culminating in Pisces, fits Hillman's character better than Pluto rising in Cancer, with Uranus culminating in Pisces. But, for our purposes, the important thing is that the Seventeenness links are the same in both charts – except that in the 10.20 chart Hillman has an additional very close Seventeenness aspect in MO-17-SA. I am choosing not to interpret this aspect, because of the uncertainty about the birth time.

Appendix II:
Harmonic Aspect Conversion Table

0°00'-2°00'	*1*	13°37'-13°45'	26, 27
2°01'-6°00'	1	13°46'-13°47'	26, 27
6°01'-10°51'	1	13°48'-13°54'	26
10°52'-11°03'	1, 32	13°55'-13°56'	25, 26
11°04'-11°10'	1, 32	13°57'-14°05'	25, 26
11°11'-11°13'	1, *32*	14°06'-14°09'	25, 26
11°14'-11°19'	1, 31, *32*	14°10'-14°18'	25, 26
11°20'-11°24'	1, 31, 32	14°19'	25, 26
11°25'-11°26'	1, 31, 32	14°20'-14°29'	25
11°27'-11°32'	1, 31, 32	14°30'-14°38'	24, 25
11°33'-11°35'	1, *31*, 32	14°39'-14°44'	24, 25
11°36'-11°38'	1, 30, *31*, 32	14°45'-14°53'	24, 25
11°39'-11°41'	1, 30, *31*	14°54'	24
11°42'-11°47'	1, 30, 31	14°55'-15°05'	24
11°48'-11°49'	1, 30, 31	15°06'-15°07'	24
11°50'-11°55'	1, 30, 31	15°08'-15°15'	23, 24
11°56'-12°00'	1, *30*, 31	15°16'-15°22'	23, 24
12°01'-12°04'	29, *30*	15°23'-15°30'	23, 24
12°05'-12°12'	29, 30	15°31'-15°33'	23
12°13'-12°20'	29, 30	15°34'-15°44'	23
12°21'-12°24'	29, 30	15°45'-15°48'	23
12°25'-12°29'	28, 29	15°49'-15°55'	22, 23
12°30'-12°37'	28, 29	15°56'-16°05'	22, 23
12°38'-12°46'	28, 29	16°06'-16°10'	22, 23
12°47'-12°50'	28, 29	16°11'-16°16'	22
12°51'-12°52'	28	16°17'-16°27'	22
12°53'-12°55'	27, 28	16°28'-16°34'	22
12°56'-13°04'	27, 28	16°35'-16°38'	21, 22
13°05'-13°06'	27, 28	16°39'-16°51'	21, 22
13°07'-13°15'	27, 28	16°52'-16°55'	21, 22
13°16'-13°17'	27, 28	16°56'-17°02'	21
13°18'-13°22'	27	17°03'-17°15'	*21*
13°23'-13°24'	26, 27	17°16'-17°23'	21
13°25'-13°33'	26, 27	17°24'-17°26'	20, 21
13°34'-13°36'	26, 27	17°27'-17°41'	20, 21

17°42'-17°43'	<u>20</u>, 21	24°46'-24°48'	15, <u>29</u>
17°44'-17°53'	<u>20</u>	24°49'-24°51'	<u>29</u>
17°54'-18°06'	<u>***20***</u>	24°52'-24°54'	14, <u>29</u>
18°07'-18°18'	<u>20</u>	24°55'-25°02'	14, <u>29</u>
18°19'-18°36'	19, 20	25°03'-25°15'	14, 29
18°37'	19	25°16'	14
18°38'-18°50'	<u>19</u>	25°17'-25°33'	<u>14</u>
18°51'-19°03'	<u>***19***</u>	25°34'-25°52'	<u>***14***</u>
19°04'-19°16'	<u>19</u>	25°53'-26°09'	<u>14</u>
19°17'-19°19'	19	26°10'-26°12'	14
19°20'-19°35'	18, 19	26°13'-26°26'	14, 27
19°36'-19°39'	18	26°27'-26°34'	14, <u>27</u>
19°40'-19°52'	<u>18</u>	26°35'	<u>27</u>
19°53'-20°07'	<u>***18***</u>	26°36'-26°44'	<u>27</u>
20°08'-20°20'	<u>18</u>	26°45'-26°46'	<u>27</u>
20°21'-20°28'	18	26°47'-26°53'	13, <u>27</u>
20°29'-20°40'	17, 18	26°54'-27°07'	13, 27
20°41'-20°50'	17	27°08'-27°13'	13
20°51'-21°03'	<u>17</u>	27°14'-27°32'	<u>13</u>
21°04'-21°18'	<u>***17***</u>	27°33'-27°51'	<u>***13***</u>
21°19'-21°32'	<u>17</u>	27°52'-28°10'	<u>13</u>
21°33'-21°44'	17	28°11'-28°18'	13
21°45'-21°53'	16, 17	28°19'-28°33'	13, 25
21°54'-22°06'	16	28°34'-28°37'	13, <u>25</u>
22°07'-22°22'	<u>16</u>	28°38'-28°43'	<u>25</u>
22°23'-22°38'	<u>***16***</u>	28°44'-28°53'	<u>25</u>
22°39'-22°50'	<u>16</u>	28°54'-28°59'	<u>25</u>
22°51'-22°53'	<u>16</u>, 31	29°00'-29°02'	12, <u>25</u>
22°54'-23°01'	16, 31	29°03'-29°17'	12, 25
23°02'-23°10'	16, <u>31</u>	29°18'-29°29'	12
23°11'	16, <u>***31***</u>	29°30'-29°49'	<u>12</u>
23°12'-23°15'	15, 16, <u>***31***</u>	29°50'-30°10'	<u>***12***</u>
23°16'-23°18'	15, <u>***31***</u>	30°11'-30°30'	<u>12</u>
23°19'-23°26'	15, <u>31</u>	30°31'-30°46'	12
23°27'-23°35'	15, 31	30°47'-31°00'	12, 23
23°36'-23°37'	<u>15</u>, 31	31°01'	23
23°38'-23°51'	<u>15</u>	31°02'-31°12'	<u>23</u>
23°52'-24°08'	<u>***15***</u>	31°13'-31°23'	<u>***23***</u>
24°09'-24°24'	<u>15</u>	31°24'-31°34'	<u>23</u>
24°25'-24°37'	15, 29	31°35'-31°38'	23
24°38'-24°45'	15, <u>29</u>	31°39'-31°49'	11, 23

31°50'-32°10'	11	38°21'-38°29'	19, _28_
23°11'-32°32'	_11_	38°30'-38°32'	19, _28_
32°33'-32°55'	_11_	38°33'-38°38'	_28_
32°56'-33°17'	_11_	38°39'	_28_
33°18'-33°21'	11	38°40'-38°47'	9, _28_
33°22'-33°33'	11, 32	38°48'-39°00'	9, 28
33°34'-33°40'	11, _32_	39°01'-39°19'	9
33°41'-33°42'	11, _32_	39°20'-39°46'	_9_
33°43'-33°49'	11, 21, _32_	39°47'-40°13'	_9_
33°50'-33°56'	21, _32_	40°14'-40°40'	_9_
33°57'-33°59'	21, 32	40°41'-41°03'	9
34°00'-34°08'	_21_, 32	41°04'-41°17'	9, 26
34°09'-34°10'	_21_	41°18'-41°20'	9, _26_
34°11'-34°23'	_21_	41°21'-41°26'	_26_
34°24'-34°26'	_21_	41°27'-41°37'	_26_
34°27'-34°34'	_21_, 31	41°38'	_26_
34°35'-34°37'	21, 31	41°39'-41°46'	17, _26_
34°38'-34°45'	21, _31_	41°47'-41°59'	17, 26
34°46'-34°47'	21, _31_	42°00'	_17_, 26
34°48'-34°51'	10, 21, _31_	42°01'-42°13'	_17_
34°52'-34°53'	10, _31_	42°14'-42°28'	_17_
34°54'-35°02'	10, _31_	42°29'-42°42'	_17_
35°03'-35°13'	10, 31	42°43'-42°57'	17, 25
3514'-35°23'	10	42°58'-43°03'	17, _25_
35°24'-35°47'	_10_	43°04'-43°06'	_25_
35°48'-36°12'	_10_	43°07'-43°17'	_25_
36°13'-36°36'	_10_	43°18'-43°26'	_25_
36°37'-36°48'	10	43°27'-43°29'	25
36°49'-37°01'	10, 29	43°30'-43°41'	8, 25
37°02'-37°09'	10, _29_	43°42'-44°14'	8
37°10'-37°12'	10, _29_	44°15'-44°44'	_8_
37°13'-37°15'	_29_	44°45'-45°15'	_8_
37°16'-37°18'	19, _29_	45°16'-45°45'	_8_
37°19'-37°26'	19, _29_	45°46'-46°03'	8
37°27'-37°34'	19, 29	46°04'-46°14'	8, 31
37°35'-37°39'	_19_, 29	46°15'-46°22'	8, _31_
37°40'-37°47'	_19_	46°23'-46°25'	8, _31_
37°48'-38°00'	_19_	46°26'-46°30'	8, 23, _31_
38°01'-38°07'	_19_	46°31'	23, _31_
38°08'-38°13'	_19_, 28	46°32'-46°39'	23, _31_
38°14'-38°20'	19, 28	46°40'-46°42'	23, 31

46°43′-46°50′	23, 31	54°37′-54°54′	13
46°51′	23	54°55′-55°13′	13
46°52′-47°02′	23	55°14′-55°32′	*13*
47°03′-47°11′	23	55°33′-55°51′	13
47°12′-47°13′	15, 23	55°52′-56°03′	13, 32
47°14′-47°28′	15, 23	56°04′-56°10′	13, 32
47°29′-47°35′	15	56°11′-56°12′	13, 32
47°36′-47°51′	15	56°13′-56°18′	13, 19, 32
47°52′-48°08′	*15*	56°19′	19, 32
48°09′-48°24′	15	56°20′-56°26′	19, 32
48°25′-48°31′	15	56°27′-56°31′	19, 32
48°32′-48°48′	15, 22	56°32′-56°38′	19, 32
48°49′-48°59′	22	56°39′-56°44′	19
49°00′-49°10′	22	56°45′-56°57′	*19*
49°11′-49°13′	22	56°58′-57°06′	19
49°14′-49°21′	22, 29	57°07′-57°10′	19, 25
49°22′-49°26′	22, 29	57°11′-57°21′	19, 25
49°27′-49°34′	22, 29	57°22′-57°29′	19, 25
49°35′-49°38′	22, 29	57°30′	25
49°39′-49°42′	29	57°31′-57°40′	25
49°43′	7, 29	57°41′	25, 31
49°44′-49°51′	7, 29	57°42′-57°50′	25, 31
49°52′-50°04′	7, 29	57°51′-57°52′	25, 31
50°05′-50°35′	7	57°53′-57°59′	25, 31
50°36′-51°08′	7	58°00′-58°05′	6, 25, *31*
51°09′-51°43′	7	58°06′-58°08′	6, 31
51°44′-52°17′	7	58°09′-58°16′	6, 31
52°18′-52°51′	7	58°17′-58°27′	6, 31
52°52′-53°06′	7, 27	58°28′-58°59′	6
53°07′-53°09′	7, 27	59°00′-59°39′	6
53°10′-53°15′	27	59°40′-60°20′	*6*
53°16′-53°23′	27	60°21′-61°00′	6
53°24′	20, 27	61°01′-61°38′	6
53°25′-53°33′	20, 27	61°39′-61°51′	6, 29
53°34′-53°41′	20, 27	61°52′-61°59′	6, 29
53°42′-53°47′	20, 27	62°00′	6, 29
53°48′-53°53′	20	62°01′-62°05′	29
53°54′-54°06′	20	62°06′-62°08′	23, 29
54°07′-54°18′	20	62°09′-62°16′	23, 29
54°19′-54°27′	20	62°17′-62°20′	23, 29
54°28′-54°36′	13, 20	62°21′-62°29′	23, 29

62°30'-62°32'	23	69°18'-69°19'	26, 31
62°33'-62°42'	23	69°20'-69°28'	26, 31
62°43'-62°49'	23	69°29'-69°35'	26, 31
62°50'-62°53'	17, 23	69°36'	5, 26, 31
62°54'-63°08'	17, 23	69°37'-69°42'	5, 26, 31
63°09'-63°10'	17	69°43'-69°45'	5, 31
63°11'-63°24'	17	69°46'-69°53'	5, 31
63°25'-63°39'	17	69°54'-70°04'	5, 31
63°40'-63°50'	17	70°05'-70°47'	5
63°51'-63°53'	17, 28	70°48'-71°35'	5
63°54'-64°03'	17, 28	71°36'-72°24'	5
64°04'-64°12'	17, 28	72°25'-73°12'	5
64°13'-64°14'	17, 28	73°13'-74°03'	5
64°15'-64°21'	28	74°04'-74°16'	5, 29
64°22'-64°30'	11, 28	74°17'-74°24'	5, 29
64°31'-64°43'	11, 28	74°25'-74°29'	29
64°44'-64°53'	11	74°30'-74°34'	24, 29
64°54'-65°15'	11	74°35'-74°41'	24, 29
65°16'-65°38'	11	74°42'-74°44'	24, 29
65°39'-65°59'	11	74°45'-74°54'	24, 29
66°00'-66°12'	11	74°55'-75°05'	24
66°13'-66°26'	11, 27	75°06'-75°08'	24
66°27'-66°32'	11, 27	75°09'-75°15'	19, 24
66°33'-66°35'	27	75°16'-75°27'	19, 24
66°36'-66°44'	27	75°28'-75°30'	19, 24
66°45'-66°53'	16, 27	75°31'-75°40'	19
66°54'-67°06'	16, 27	75°41'-75°53'	19
67°07'	16, 27	75°54'-76°06'	19
67°08'-67°21'	16	76°07'-76°17'	19
67°22'-67°38'	16	76°18'-76°25'	14, 19
67°39'-67°53'	16	76°26'-76°42'	14
67°54'-67°59'	16	76°43'-76°59'	14
68°00'-68°15'	16, 21	77°00'-77°18'	14
68°16'	21	77°19'-77°35'	14
68°17'-68°27'	21	77°36'-77°44'	14
68°28'-68°40'	21	77°45'-77°59'	14, 23
68°41'-68°45'	21	78°00'	14, 23
68°46'-68°51'	21, 26	78°01'-78°10'	23
68°52'-68°59'	21, 26	78°11'-78°21'	23
69°00'-69°08'	21, 26	78°22'-78°32'	23, 32
69°09'-69°17'	26	78°33'	23, 32

78°34'-78°39'	23, _32_	85°09'-85°24'	17, 21
78°40'	9, 23, _32_	85°25'	21
78°41'-78°47'	9, 23, _32_	85°26'-85°36'	_21_
78°48'-78°49'	9, _32_	85°37'-85°49'	_**21**_
78°50'-78°56'	9, _32_	85°50'-85°54'	_21_
78°57'-79°08'	9, 32	85°55'-86°00'	_21_, 25
79°09'-79°19'	9	86°01'-86°09'	21, 25
79°20'-79°46'	_9_	86°10'-86°17'	21, _25_
79°47'-80°13'	_**9**_	86°18'	_25_
80°14'-80°40'	_**9**_	86°19'-86°28'	_25_
80°41'-80°53'	9	86°29'	_25_, 29
80°54'-81°04'	9, 31	86°30'-86°38'	_25_, 29
81°05'-81°12'	9, _31_	86°39'-86°41'	25, 29
81°13'-81°15'	9, _**31**_	86°42'-86°49'	25, _29_
81°16'-81°20'	9, 22, _**31**_	86°50'-86°53'	25, _**29**_
81°21'	22, _**31**_	86°54'-86°58'	_**29**_
81°22'-81°29'	22, _31_	86°59'	_29_
81°30'-8132'	22, 31	87°00'-87°06'	4, _29_
81°33'-81°40'	_22_, 31	87°07'-87°19'	4, 29
81°41'-81°43'	_**22**_	87°20'-88°29'	4
81°44'-81°54'	_**22**_	88°30'-89°29'	_4_
81°55'-82°05'	_22_	89°30'-90°30'	_**4**_
82°06'-82°09'	22	90°31'-91°30'	_4_
82°10'-82°22'	13, 22	91°31'-92°30'	4
82°23'-82°36'	13	92°31'-92°41'	4, 31
82°37'-82°55'	_13_	92°42'-92°49'	4, _31_
82°56'-83°14'	_**13**_	92°50'-92°52'	4, _**31**_
83°15'-83°33'	_13_	92°53'-92°58'	4, 27, _**31**_
83°34'-83°35'	13	92°59'-93°00'	4, 27, _31_
83°36'-83°47'	13, _30_	9301'-93°06'	27, _31_
83°48'-83°55'	13, _30_	93°07'-93°15'	_27_, 31
83°56'-83°59'	13, _**30**_	93°16'-93°17'	_27_, 31
84°00'	13, 17, _**30**_	93°18'-93°23'	_27_
84°01'-84°04'	17, _**30**_	93°24'	23, _**27**_
84°05'-84°12'	17, _30_	93°25'-93°33'	23, _27_
84°13'-84°20'	17, 30	93°34'-93°35'	23, 27
84°21'-84°24'	_17_, 30	93°36'-93°47'	_23_, 27
84°25'-84°34'	_17_	93°48'-93°49'	_23_
84°35'-84°49'	_**17**_	93°50'-94°00'	_**23**_
84°50'-85°03'	_17_	94°01'-94°05'	_23_
85°04'-85°08'	17	94°06'-94°11'	19, _23_

94°12'-94°24'	19, 23	100°54'-101°02'	_25_, 32
94°25'-94°26'	_19_, 23	101°03'	25, 32
94°27'-94°37'	_19_	101°04'-101°07'	25, _32_
94°38'-94°50'	_**19**_	101°08'-101°10'	7, 25, _32_
94°51'-95°03'	_19_	101°11'-101°17'	7, 25, _**32**_
95°04'-95°11'	19	101°18'-101°19'	7, _**32**_
95°12'-95°22'	15, 19	101°20'-101°26'	7, _32_
95°23'-95°35'	15	101°27'-101°38'	7, 32
95°36'-95°51'	_15_	101°39'-101°59'	7
95°52'-96°08'	_**15**_	102°00'-102°33'	_7_
96°09'-96°24'	_15_	102°34'-103°08'	_**7**_
96°25'-96°26'	15	103°09'-103°42'	_7_
96°27'-96°40'	15, 26	103°43'-104°07'	7
96°41'-96°48'	15, _26_	104°08'-104°18'	7, 31
96°49'	_26_	104°19'-104°26'	7, _31_
96°50'-97°00'	_**26**_	104°27'-104°29'	7, _**31**_
97°01'-97°05'	_26_	104°30'-104°34'	7, 24, _**31**_
97°06'-97°09'	11, _26_	104°35'	24, _**31**_
97°10'-97°23'	11, 26	104°36'-104°43'	24, _31_
97°24'-97°37'	11	104°44'	24, 31
97°38'-97°59'	_11_	104°45'-104°54'	_24_, 31
98°00'-98°22'	_**11**_	104°55'-105°05'	_**24**_
98°23'-98°44'	_11_	105°06'-105°08'	_24_
98°45'-98°53'	11	105°09'-105°15'	17, _24_
98°54'-99°06'	11, 29	105°16'-105°30'	17, 24
99°07'-99°14'	11, _29_	105°31'	17
99°15'-99°16'	11, _29_	105°32'-105°45'	_17_
99°17'-99°19'	_**29**_	105°46'-106°00'	_**17**_
99°20'-99°23'	18, _29_	106°01'-106°12'	_17_
99°24'-99°31'	18, _29_	106°13'-106°14'	_17_, 27
99°32'-99°39'	18, 29	106°15'-106°26'	17, 27
99°40'-99°44'	_18_, 29	106°27'-106°35'	17, _27_
99°45'-99°52'	_18_	106°36'-106°44'	_**27**_
99°53'-100°07'	_**18**_	106°45'-106°47'	_27_
100°08'-100°18'	_18_	106°48'-106°53'	10, _27_
100°19'-100°20'	_18_, 25	106°54'-107°07'	10, 27
100°21'-100°33'	18, 25	107°08'-107°23'	10
100°34'-100°40'	18, _25_	107°24'-107°47'	_10_
100°41'-100°42'	_25_	107°48'-108°12'	_**10**_
100°43'-100°51'	_25_	108°13'-108°36'	_10_
100°52'-100°53'	_25_, 32	108°37'-109°02'	10

109°03'-109°12'	10, 23	115°30'-115°38'	25, _28_
109°13'-109°17'	23	115°39'-115°41'	25, _28_
109°18'-109°28'	_23_	115°42'-115°43'	_28_
109°29'-109°39'	_**23**_	115°44'-115°47'	_28_, 31
109°40'-109°50'	_23_	115°48'-115°54'	_28_, 31
109°51'-110°05'	13, 23	115°55'-115°56'	_28_, _31_
110°06'-110°17'	13	115°57'-115°59'	28, _31_
110°18'-110°37'	_13_	116°00'-116°02'	3, 28, _31_
110°38'-110°55'	_**13**_	116°03'-116°09'	3, 28, _**31**_
110°56'-111°14'	_13_	116°10'-116°11'	3, _**31**_
111°15'-111°17'	13	116°12'-116°19'	3, _31_
111°18'-111°30'	13, 29	116°20'-116°30'	3, 31
111°31'-111°38'	13, _29_	116°31'-117°59'	3
111°39'-111°41'	13, _**29**_	118°00'-119°19'	_3_
111°42'-111°44'	_**29**_	119°20'-120°40'	_**3**_
111°45'-111°47'	16, _**29**_	120°41'-122°00'	_3_
111°48'-111°55'	16, _29_	122°01'-123°21'	3
111°56'-112°06'	16, 29	123°22'-123°33'	3, 32
112°07'-112°08'	_16_, 29	123°34'-123°40'	3, _32_
112°09'-112°21'	_16_	123°41'-123°42'	3, _**32**_
112°22'-112°38'	_**16**_	123°43'-123°49'	3, 29, _**32**_
112°39'-112°53'	_16_	123°50'-123°55'	3, 29, _32_
112°54'-113°02'	16	123°56'	3, _29_, _**32**_
113°03'-113°15'	16, 19	123°57'-124°00'	3, _29_, 32
113°16'-113°21'	19	124°01'-124°03'	_29_, 32
113°22'-113°34'	_19_	124°04'-124°08'	_**29**_, 32
113°35'-113°47'	_**19**_	124°09'-124°12'	26, _**29**_
113°48'-113°59'	_19_	124°13'-124°20'	26, _29_
114°00'	_19_, 22	124°21'-124°22'	26, 29
114°01'-114°16'	19, 22	124°23'-124°31'	_26_, 29
114°17'-114°19'	19, _22_	124°32'-124°33'	_**26**_, 29
114°20'-114°27'	_22_	124°34'-124°41'	_26_
114°28'-114°38'	_22_	124°42'	23, _**26**_
114°39'-114°42'	_22_	124°43'-124°51'	23, _26_
114°43'-114°49'	_22_, 25	124°52'-124°56'	23, 26
114°50'-114°57'	22, 25	124°57'-125°05'	_23_, 26
114°58'-115°06'	22, _25_	125°06'-125°07'	_23_
115°07'-115°16'	_25_	125°08'-125°18'	_**23**_
115°17'	_**25**_, 28	125°19'-125°23'	_23_
115°18'-115°26'	_25_, 28	125°24'-125°29'	20, _23_
115°27'-115°29'	25, 28	125°30'-125°42'	20, 23

125°43'-125°44'	_20_, 23	132°13'-132°18'	19, 30
125°45'-125°53'	_20_	132°19'-132°24'	_19_, 30
125°54'-126°06'	**_20_**	132°25'-132°31'	_19_
126°07'-126°18'	_20_	132°32'-132°44'	**_19_**
126°19'-126°21'	20	132°45'-132°52'	_19_
126°22'-126°36'	17, 20	132°53'-132°57'	_19_, 27
126°37'-126°43'	17	132°58'-133°06'	19, 27
126°44'-126°56'	_17_	133°07'-133°15'	19, _27_
126°57'-127°11'	**_17_**	133°16'	19, _27_
127°12'-127°21'	_17_	133°17'-133°24'	**_27_**
127°22'-127°25'	_17_, 31	133°25'-133°29'	_27_
127°26'-127°32'	17, 31	133°30'-133°33'	8, _27_
127°33'-127°40'	17, _31_	133°34'-133°47'	8, 27
127°41'-127°42'	17, **_31_**	133°48'-134°14'	8
127°43'-127°46'	14, 17, **_31_**	134°15'-134°44'	_8_
127°47'-127°49'	14, **_31_**	134°45'-135°15'	**_8_**
127°50'-127°57'	14, _31_	135°16'-135°45'	_8_
127°58'-128°07'	14, 31	135°46'-136°07'	8
128°08'	_14_, 31	136°08'-136°20'	8, 29
128°09'-128°24'	_14_	136°21'-136°28'	8, _29_
128°25'-128°43'	**_14_**	136°29'-136°30'	8, **_29_**
128°44'-129°00'	_14_	136°31'-136°34'	**_29_**
129°01'-129°06'	14	136°35'-136°37'	21, **_29_**
129°07'-129°21'	14, 25	136°38'-136°45'	21, _29_
129°22'-129°25'	14, _25_	136°46'-136°51'	21, 29
129°26'-129°30'	_25_	136°52'-136°58'	_21_, 29
129°31'-129°41'	**_25_**	136°59'-137°02'	_21_
129°42'-129°49'	_25_	137°03'-137°15'	**_21_**
129°50'	11, _25_	137°16'-137°26'	_21_
129°51'-130°05'	11, 25	137°27'-137°32'	21
130°06'-130°21'	11	137°33'-137°43'	13, 21
130°22'-130°43'	_11_	137°44'-137°59'	13
130°44'-131°06'	**_11_**	138°00'-138°18'	_13_
131°07'-131°28'	_11_	138°19'-138°37'	**_13_**
131°29'-131°35'	11	138°38'-138°56'	_13_
131°36'-131°47'	11, 30	138°57'	13
131°48'-131°55'	11, _30_	138°58'-139°08'	13, 31
131°56'-131°59'	11, **_30_**	139°09'-139°16'	13, _31_
132°00'	11, 19, **_30_**	139°17'-139°19'	13, **_31_**
132°01'-132°04'	19, **_30_**	139°20'-139°23'	13, 18, **_31_**
132°05'-132°12'	19, 30	139°24'-139°25'	18, **_31_**

139°26'-139°37'	18, <u>31</u>	147°33'-147°49'	17, 22
139°38'-139°39'	18, 31	147°50'-147°52'	17
139°40'-139°43'	<u>18</u>, 31	147°53'-148°06'	<u>17</u>
139°44'-139°52'	<u>18</u>	148°07'-148°21'	<u>17</u>
139°53'-140°07'	<u>*18*</u>	148°22'-148°32'	17
140°08'-140°20'	<u>18</u>	148°33'-148°35'	<u>17</u>, 29
140°21'-140°35'	18, 23	148°36'-148°45'	17, 29
140°36'-140°40'	18, <u>23</u>	148°46'-148°53'	17, <u>29</u>
140°41'-140°46'	<u>23</u>	148°54'-148°56'	17, <u>*29*</u>
140°47'-140°57'	<u>23</u>	148°57'-148°59'	<u>*29*</u>
140°58'-140°59'	<u>23</u>	149°00'-149°02'	12, <u>*29*</u>
141°00'-141°08'	<u>23</u>, 28	149°03'-149°10'	12, <u>29</u>
141°09'-141°12'	23, 28	149°11'-149°23'	12, 29
141°13'-141°21'	23, <u>28</u>	149°24'-149°29'	12
141°22'-141°23'	23, <u>*28*</u>	149°30'-149°49'	<u>12</u>
141°24'-141°30'	<u>*28*</u>	149°50'-150°10'	<u>*12*</u>
141°31'-141°35'	<u>28</u>	150°11'-150°30'	<u>12</u>
141°36'-141°39'	5, <u>28</u>	150°31'-150°34'	12
141°40'-141°52'	5, 28	150°35'-150°45'	12, 31
141°53'-142°47'	5	150°46'-150°53'	12, <u>31</u>
142°48'-143°35'	<u>5</u>	150°54'-150°56'	12, <u>*31*</u>
143°36'-144°24'	<u>5</u>	150°57'-151°00'	12, 19, <u>*31*</u>
144°25'-145°12'	<u>5</u>	151°01'-151°02'	19, <u>*31*</u>
145°13'-145°51'	5	151°03'-151°10'	19, <u>31</u>
145°52'-146°03'	5, 32	151°11'-151°15'	19, 31
146°04'-146°10'	5, <u>32</u>	151°16'-151°21'	<u>19</u>, 31
146°11'-146°12'	5, <u>32</u>	151°22'-151°28'	<u>19</u>
146°13'-146°19'	5, 27, <u>32</u>	151°29'-151°41'	<u>*19*</u>
146°20'-146°24'	5, 27, <u>32</u>	151°42'-151°49'	<u>19</u>
1462°5'-146°26'	27, <u>32</u>	151°50'-151°54'	<u>19</u>, 26
146°27'-146°35'	<u>27</u>, 32	151°55'-152°03'	19, 26
146°36'-146°38'	<u>27</u>, 32	152°04'-152°12'	19, <u>26</u>
146°39'-146°42'	<u>27</u>	152°13'	19, <u>26</u>
146°43'-146°44'	22, <u>27</u>	152°14'-152°23'	<u>26</u>
146°45'-146°53'	22, <u>27</u>	152°24'-152°32'	<u>26</u>
146°54'-146°59'	22, 27	152°33'	26
147°00'-147°07'	<u>22</u>, 27	152°34'-152°46'	7, 26
147°08'-147°10'	<u>22</u>	152°47'-153°26'	7
147°11'-147°21'	<u>22</u>	153°27'-153°59'	<u>7</u>
147°22'-147°31'	<u>22</u>	154°00'-154°34'	<u>7</u>
147°32'	17, <u>22</u>	154°35'-155°08'	<u>7</u>

155°09'-155°35'	7	162°12'-162°18'	20, 31
155°36'-155°55'	7, 30	162°19'-162°22'	20, 31
155°56'-155°59'	7, 30	162°23'-162°30'	20, 31
156°00'	7, 23, 30	162°31'-162°32'	20, 31
156°01'-156°04'	23, 30	162°33'-162°36'	11, 20, 31
156°05'-156°12'	23, 30	162°37'-162°39'	11, 31
156°13'-156°14'	23, 30	162°40'-162°47'	11, 31
156°15'-156°24'	23, 30	162°48'-162°58'	11, 31
156°25'	23	162°59'-163°04'	11
156°26'-156°36'	23	163°05'-163°26'	11
156°37'-156°44'	23	163°27'-163°49'	11
156°45'-156°47'	16, 23	163°50'-164°11'	11
156°48'-157°02'	16, 23	164°12'-164°29'	11
157°03'-157°06'	16	164°30'-164°43'	11, 24
157°07'-157°21'	16	164°44'	24
157°22'-157°38'	16	164°45'-164°54'	24
157°39'-157°53'	16	164°55'-165°05'	24
157°54'	16	165°06'-165°13'	24
157°55'-158°09'	16, 25	165°14'-165°15'	13, 24
158°10'-158°15'	16, 25	165°16'-165°30'	13, 24
158°16'-158°18'	25	165°31'-165°41'	13
158°19'-158°29'	25	165°42'-165°59'	13
158°30'-158°38'	25	166°00'-166°18'	13
158°39'	25	166°19'-166°37'	13
158°40'-158°53'	9, 25	166°38'-166°42'	13
158°54'-159°19'	9	166°43'-166°55'	13, 28
159°20'-159°46'	9	166°56'-167°04'	13, 28
159°47'-160°13'	9	167°05'-167°11'	28
160°14'-160°40'	9	167°12'-167°13'	15, 28
160°41'-160°57'	9	167°14'-167°22'	15, 28
160°58'-161°10'	9, 29	167°23'-167°35'	15, 28
161°11'-161°18'	9, 29	167°36'-167°51'	15
161°19'-161°20'	9, 29	167°52'-168°08'	15
161°21'-161°23'	29	168°09'-168°21'	15
161°24'-161°27'	20, 29	168°22'-168°24'	15, 32
161°28'-161°35'	20, 29	168°25'-168°33'	15, 32
161°36'-161°41'	20, 29	168°34'-168°40'	15, 32
161°42'-161°48'	20, 29	168°41'-168°42'	15, 32
161°49'-161°53'	20	168°43'-168°48'	15, 17, 32
161°54'-162°06'	20	168°49'	17, 32
162°07'-162°11'	20	168°50'-168°56'	17, 32

168°57′-169°03′	17, 32
169°04′-16°908′	<u>17</u>, 32
169°09′-169°17′	<u>17</u>
169°18′-169°32′	*<u>17</u>*
169°33′-169°46′	<u>17</u>
169°47′-169°53′	17
169°54′-170°07′	17, 19
170°08′-170°12′	19
170°13′-170°25′	<u>19</u>
170°26′-170°38′	*<u>19</u>*
170°39′-170°51′	19
170°52′-171°08′	19, 21
171°09′-171°10′	19, <u>21</u>
171°11′-171°21′	<u>21</u>
171°22′-171°32′	*<u>21</u>*
171°33′-171°38′	<u>21</u>
171°39′-171°43′	<u>21</u>, 23
171°44′-171°53′	21, 23
171°54′-172°00′	21, <u>23</u>
172°01′-172°04′	<u>23</u>
172°05′-172°15′	*<u>23</u>*
172°16′-172°18′	<u>23</u>
172°19′-172°26′	<u>23</u>, 25
172°27′-172°33′	23, 25
172°34′-172°41′	23, <u>25</u>
172°42′	<u>25</u>
172°43′-172°52′	*<u>25</u>*
172°53′	<u>25</u>, 27
172°54′-173°02′	<u>25</u>, 27
173°03′-173°06′	25, 27
173°07′-173°15′	25, <u>27</u>
173°16′-173°17′	25, *<u>27</u>*
173°18′-173°22′	*<u>27</u>*
173°23′-173°24′	<u>27</u>, 29
173°25′-173°33′	<u>27</u>, 29
173°34′-173°35′	27, 29
173°36′-173°43′	27, <u>29</u>
173°44′-173°47′	27, *<u>29</u>*
173°48′	*<u>29</u>*
173°49′-173°52′	<u>29</u>, 31
173°53′-173°59′	<u>29</u>, 31

174°00′	2, 29, 31
174°01′-174°07′	2, 29, <u>31</u>
174°08′-174°13′	2, 29, *<u>31</u>*
174°14′-174°16′	2, *<u>31</u>*
174°17′-174°24′	2, <u>31</u>
174°25′-174°35′	2, 31
174°36′-176°59′	2
177°00′-178°59′	<u>2</u>
179°00′-180°00′	<u>2</u>

Appendix III
Alicia Gaydos 1965 – 2018

Alicia emailed me on September 2, 2016, saying how much she had enjoyed reading my book *The Spirit of Numbers*. We immediately recognized each other as kindred spirits, and we started to write to each other several times a week, communicating about our personal histories, about astrology, and about the nature of the universe and of interpersonal relationships.

After about two months I told her that I was planning to write another book. She volunteered to help with this, and over the next 14 months she acted as my Muse. Without her help and support I would never have written the book.

I have never known anyone as multi-talented as Alicia. She was talented as a poet, an astrological writer, a painter, a sculptor, a photographer, a pianist, a singer, and (in her paid work) an interior designer. She also was an insatiable researcher into ancient history and mythology, Jungian psychology, philosophy, quantum theory, and anything which could teach her about how the cosmos works. She was also a first-class astrologer: a friend has told me that "her astrology readings were amazing, the best I've ever experienced".

However, Alicia was modest about her own abilities and achievements, and unwilling to thrust herself into the limelight. She had a tremendous gift of empathy: she was able to really *listen* to people, feel how it was for them, and so give them valuable help and support. I myself benefited hugely from this, and I am sure that many others have benefited also.

Alicia was unmarried and had no children. She had a long-term partner, Charles, whom she was hoping to marry, but he fell ill and she spent two painful years nursing him until he died after a series of heart attacks.

Alicia was born at 3.48 p.m. on July 5, 1965, in Elizabeth, NJ, USA. She died in a road accident at 5.54 p.m. on February 13, 2018, in Burlington NJ. She was an amazing person, and the world is a poorer place as a result of her passing.

References

Preface
1. David Hamblin, *The Spirit of Numbers: a New Exploration of Harmonic Astrology*, Bournemouth: The Wessex Astrologer, 2011.
2. John Addey, *Astrology Reborn*, Sutton, England: Faculty of Astrological Studies, 1971.
3. John Addey, *Harmonics in Astrology*, Romford, England: L.N. Fowler, 1976.
4. John Addey, *Harmonics in Astrology*, op.cit., p.13.
5. David Hamblin, *Harmonic Charts*, Wellingborough: Aquarian Press, 1983.
6. Garry Phillipson, *Astrology in the Year Zero*, London: Flare Publications, 2000.

Chapter 1: Introduction to Harmonic Astrology
1. David Hamblin, *The Spirit of Numbers*, op.cit.
2. www.whatis.techtarget.com/definition/harmonic
3. John Addey, *Harmonics in Astrology*, op.cit.
4. David Hamblin, *Harmonic Charts*, op.cit.
5. Michael Harding and Charles Harvey, *Working with Astrology*, London: Arcana, 1990.

Chapter 3: What does the Chart Show?
1. David Hamblin, *The Spirit of Numbers*, op.cit., pp.47-48.
2. Alice Miller, *For Your Own Good: The Roots of Violence in Child-Rearing*, London: Virago Press, 1987.
3. Stanislav Grof, *The Adventure of Self-Discovery*, Albany, NY: State University of New York Press, 1988.
4. Pierre Teilhard de Chardin, *The Divine Milieu*, New York: Harper & Row, 1960, pp.76-77.

Chapter 4: From One to Seven
1 Joe Landwehr, *Astrology and the Archetypal Power of Numbers: Part One, A Contemporary Reformulation of Pythagorean Number Theory*, Whittier,

North Carolina: Ancient Tower Press, 2010; *Part Two, Arithmology in the Birthchart,* Whittier, North Carolina: Ancient Tower Press, 2018.

2. Sue Tompkins, *Aspects in Astrology,* London: Rider, 1989, p.197.

3. Gareth S. Hill, *Masculine and Feminine: The Natural Flow of Opposites in the Psyche,* Boston & London, Shambhala, 1992.

4. Sue Tompkins, op.cit., p.49.

5. David Hamblin, *Harmonic Charts,* op.cit., p.119.

6. www.sylviaplath.de/plath/bio/html

7. Harding and Harvey, op.cit., pp.201-5 (this chapter is by Charles Harvey).

8. www.theguardian.com/politics/1995/may/25/obituaries

9. Harding and Harvey, op.cit., Chapter 13 (this chapter is by Michael Harding).

10. www.pathwork.org/eva-pierrakos

11. www.historylearningsite.co.uk/nazi-germany/nazi-leaders/otto-dietrich

12. www.express.co.uk/sport/golf/161442/Revealed-John-Daly-s-record-rap-sheet

Chapter 5: The Higher Prime Numbers

1. Colin Wilson, quoted by John Ezard, *Colin Wilson Obituary,* www.theguardian.com/books/2013/dec/09/colin-wilson

2. Colin Wilson, *The Outsider,* quoted by Ezard, op.cit.

3. Romain Rolland, as quoted in Norbert Guterman, *A Book of French Quotations* (1963), p.365.

4. Romain Rolland, *Jean-Christophe: Journey's End, The Burning Bush,* quoted in www.wikiquote.org/wiki/Romain_Rolland#Journey_Within_(1947)

5. A.J. Foyt, quoted in www.izquotes.com/author/a.-j.-foyt

6. Hermann Hesse, *Peter Camenzind* (1904).

7. Peter O'Toole, quoted by Peter Evans, *Peter Sellers, the Mask Behind the Mask,* revised edition, London: New English Library, 1980, p.171.

8. Germaine Greer, *Yes, Frankenstein really was written by Mary Shelley,* The Guardian, September 4th, 2007.

9. http://csac.buffalo.edu/mariabraun.pdf

10. www.theguardian.com/science/2011/dec/21/james-hillman

11. James Hillman, *Re-Visioning Psychology,* quoted in www.mythosandlogos.com/Hillman.html

12. Marion Meade, *Dorothy Parker: What Fresh Hell is This?,* New York: Penguin Books, 1987, p.177.

13. Santeri Levas, *Sibelius, a Personal Portrait,* London: J.M. Dent & Sons, 1972, p.47.

14. www.litaalbuquerque.com/bio

15. www.quotesondesign.com/lita-albuquerque

16. www.azquotes.com/author/34535-Toni_Collette

17. www.presidentialham.com/u-s-presidents/gerald-ford-with-ham

18. www.pbs.org/newshour/spc/character/essays/ford.html

19. www.theguardian.com/news/2003/jun/14/guardianobituaries.film

20. www.azquotes.com/author/11463-Gregory_Peck

21. Sue Tompkins, op.cit., p.125.

22. www.scandalouswoman.blogspot.com/2007/12/marie-duplessis-real-lady-of-camellias.html

23. www.biography.com/people/charles-sobhraj-236026

24. www.mensxp.com/special-features/today/26664-the-story-of-charles-sobhraj-a-lethal-criminal-who-escaped-tihar-jail-is-chilling-as-well-as-fascinating.html

25. www.britannica.com/biography/Honore-de-Balzac

26. www.english.illinois.edu/maps/poets/g_l/ginsberg/life.htm

27. As quoted in *Life* magazine, 4 January 1963.

28. As quoted in *The Observer*, 20 April 1950.

29. www.telegraph.co.uk/comment/personal-view/3595037/Diana-Mosley-unrepentantly-Nazi-and-effortlessly-charming.html

30. Sarah Ditum, www.newstatesman.com/2013/05/great-crapsy-why-iain-duncan-smith-isnt-all-he-seems

31. www.verywell.com/what-is-the-id-2795275

32. www.prairieghosts.com/gacy.html

33. Tim Allen, "Story 2: Astrology versus death row", in Geoffrey Dean (ed.), *Tests of Astrology*, Amsterdam: AinO Publications, 2016.

34. www.webalice.it/filibertomaida/orgasm.htm

35. www.jahsonic.com/SadeBio.html

36. Robert Pring-Mill in www.boppin.com/lorca

37 Eva Wiseman, 'A Woman Without Fear', *The Observer Magazine*, July 2, 2017.

38. David Cochrane, *The First 32 Harmonics, a Qualitative Research Study*, www.astrosoftware.com/harmonicfirst32.pdf

Chapter 6: Guidelines for Harmonic Analysis

1. Harding and Harvey, *Working with Astrology*, op.cit., p.19.

2. Harding and Harvey, op.cit.

3. www.avalonastrology.com

4. Reinhold Ebertin, *The Combination of Stellar Influences*, Tempe, AZ: American Federation of Astrologers, 2004 (first published in 1940).

5. Harding and Harvey, op.cit., p.21.
6. Ebertin, op.cit., p.84.
7. Ebertin, op.cit., p.205.
8. Ebertin, op.cit., p.87.
9. Ebertin, op.cit., p.164.

Chapter 7: Case Studies
1. A.N. Wilson, *Iris Murdoch as I Knew Her,* London: Hutchinson, 2003.
2. These quotations are taken from www.brainyquote.com, but I have been unable to locate their original source.
3. A.N. Wilson, op.cit., p.88.
4. See note 2 above.
5. Iris Murdoch, *The Sovereignty of Good,* Abingdon & New York: Routledge, 2001 (first published 1970) p.100.)
6. Peter J. Conradi, *Iris Murdoch, a Life,* London: HarperCollins, 2001, p.592.
7. Iris Murdoch, *Metaphysics as a Guide to Morals,* London: Chatto & Windus, 1992.
8. Avril Horner & Anne Rowe (eds), *Living on Paper: Letters from Iris Murdoch 1934-1995,* London: Vintage, 2015.
9. Iris Murdoch, *The Sovereignty of Good,* op.cit., p.101.
10. See note 2 above.
11. Horner & Rowe, op.cit., p.11.
12. Glenn Everett (1988), *Hopkins on 'Inscape' and 'Instress',* www.victorianweb.org/authors/hopkins/hopkins1.html
13. Gerard Manley Hopkins, *As Kingfishers Catch Fire.*
14. Norman White, *Hopkins, a Literary Biography,* Oxford: Clarendon Press, 1992, p.10.
15. Robert Bernard Martin, *Gerard Manley Hopkins, a Very Private Life,* London: Faber & Faber, 2011, p.48-9.
16. Glenn Everett (1988), *Gerard Manley Hopkins, a Brief Biography,* www.victorianweb.org/authors/hopkins/hopkins12.html
17. Martin, op.cit., p.302.
18. Martin, op.cit., p.387.
19. Martin, op.cit., p.413.
20. Martin, op.cit., p.66.
21. www.collinsdictionary.com/dictionary/english/surreal
22. Quotes from Magritte are taken from various websites, none of which state their original sources.

23. www.theguardian.com/artanddesign/2011/jun/19/rene-magritte-surrealist-favourites-tate

24. www.theguardian.com/artanddesign/jonathanjonesblog/2016/sep/22/rene-magritte-pompidou-centre-surrealism

25. www.jessicaadams.com/2016/08/27/the-meaning-of-ceres-in-astrology

26. See https://livingintheforest.com/2015/09/17/chiron-rising-empathy-connectedness-and-metamorphosis for an insightful account of the effects of Chiron rising.

27. www.theguardian.com/music/2012/feb/12/whitney-houston-obituary

28. From the soundtrack of the film *Whitney: Can I Be Me.*

29. All my information on Patricia Columbo is taken from www.murderpedia.org/female.C/c/columbo-patricia.htm

30. Clark Howard, *Love's Blood,* New York: Crown Publishers, 1993.

Chapter 8: Harmonics in Mundane Charts

1. www.thoughtco.com/iraq-war-second-battle-of-fallujah-2360957. "Operations began at 7.00 p.m. on November 7."

2. Roland Penrose, *Picasso, His Life and Work,* 3rd edition, London: Granada, 1981, p.301.

3. www.pbs.org/treasuresoftheworld/a_nav/guernica_nav/main_guerfrm.html

4. www.pablopicasso.org/guernica.jsp

5. Michael Baigent, Nicholas Campion and Charles Harvey, *Mundane Astrology,* 2nd edition, London: Aquarian Press, 1992, p.417.

6. Demetra George and Douglas Bloch, *Asteroid Goddesses,* Lake Worth, FL: Ibis Press, 2003, Chapter 10.

7. Baigent et al., op.cit.

8. Baigent et al., op.cit., p.246.

Chapter 9: Harmonics in Synastry

1. www.pressreader.com/uk/daily-mail/20171401/281500751093810

2. www.express.co.uk/news/royal/821191/Prince-Charles-Princess-Diana-wedding-mistake-book

3. Sue Tompkins, op.cit., p.246.

Chapter 10: Harmonics in Transits and Progressions

1. John Addey, *Harmonics in Astrology,* op.cit., Chapter 16.

2. John Addey, op.cit., p.157.

3. John Addey, op.cit., p.165.

4. www.aliceportman.com/age-harmonics

Chapter 11: Harmonics in the Diurnal and Zodiacal Circles

1. Komilla Sutton, *The Essentials of Vedic Astrology*, Bournemouth: The Wessex Astrologer, 1999. See especially pp.238-252, which deal with the vargas.
2. Komilla Sutton, op.cit., p.242.
3. John Addey, *Harmonics in Astrology*, op.cit., p.102.
4. Komilla Sutton, op.cit., pp.242-3.
5. John Addey, *Harmonics in Astrology*, op.cit., chapters 7 and 8.
6. David Cochrane, *The First 32 Harmonics*, op.cit.
7. David Hamblin, *Harmonic Charts*, op.cit., pp.272-4.
8. www.turing.org.uk/publications/lausannebio.html
9. John Addey, *Harmonics in Astrology*, op.cit., p.13.

Chapter 12: The Future of Harmonic Astrology

1. www.avalonastrology.com
2. https://landscheidt.wordpress.com
3. David Cochrane, *The First 32 Harmonics*, op.cit.
4. John Addey, *Harmonics in Astrology*, op.cit., p.236.

Index

Note that all birth data, and the times of mundane events, are in Appendix I (pp.255-260). In the Index, figures in italics refer to charts; upright figures refer to text.

Also from The Wessex Astrologer
www.wessexastrologer.com

Martin Davis
Astrolocality Astrology: A Guide to What it is and How to Use it
From Here to There: An Astrologer's Guide to Astromapping

Wanda Sellar
The Consultation Chart
An Introduction to Medical Astrology
An Introduction to Decumbiture

Geoffrey Cornelius
The Moment of Astrology

Darrelyn Gunzburg
Life After Grief: An Astrological Guide to Dealing with Grief
AstroGraphology: The Hidden Link between your Horoscope and your Handwriting

Paul F. Newman
Declination: The Steps of the Sun
Luna: The Book of the Moon

Deborah Houlding
The Houses: Temples of the Sky

Dorian Geiseler Greenbaum
Temperament: Astrology's Forgotten Key

Howard Sasportas
The Gods of Change

Patricia L. Walsh
Understanding Karmic Complexes

M. Kelly Hunter
Living Lilith: the Four Dimensions of the Cosmic Feminine

Barbara Dunn
Horary Astrology Re-Examined

Deva Green
Evolutionary Astrology

Jeff Green
Pluto Volume 1: The Evolutionary Journey of the Soul
Pluto Volume 2: The Evolutionary Journey of the Soul Through Relationships
Essays on Evolutionary Astrology (ed. by Deva Green)

Dolores Ashcroft-Nowicki and Stephanie V. Norris
The Door Unlocked: An Astrological Insight into Initiation

Greg Bogart
Astrology and Meditation: The Fearless Contemplation of Change

Henry Seltzer
The Tenth Planet: Revelations from the Astrological Eris

Ray Grasse
Under a Sacred Sky: Essays on the Practice and Philosophy of Astrology

About the Author

David Hamblin was born in 1935, and has a degree in Classics from Oxford University. For many years he was a Lecturer in the School of Management at Bath University, but he took early retirement in 1985 to work as a psychotherapist, having been trained at the Psychosynthesis and Education Trust and at the Bath Centre for Psychotherapy and Counselling. After taking up astrology in the 1960s, he became a Tutor for the Faculty of Astrological Studies and was also Chairman of the Astrological Association of Great Britain in the 1980s. His book *Harmonic Charts* (Aquarian Press) was published in 1983 and his book *The Spirit of Numbers* (The Wessex Astrologer) was published in 2011. Since his retirement as a psychotherapist in 2000, he has written several articles, and has also (his proudest achievement) walked the 630-mile South West Coast Path. He is married, with two daughters and two granddaughters. His email address is pigleystair@ yahoo.co.uk and his website is www.davidhamblin.net.

Lightning Source UK Ltd.
Milton Keynes UK
UKHW020236240120
357502UK00003B/323